Jewish Fundamentalism
Comparative Perspective

G000071052

New Perspectives on Jewish Studies

A Series of the Philip and Muriel Berman Center for Jewish Studies
Lehigh University, Bethlehem, Pennsylvania

General Editor: Laurence J. Silberstein

Jewish Fundamentalism in Comparative Perspective: Religion, Ideology, and the Crisis of Modernity
Edited by Laurence J. Silberstein

New Perspectives on Israeli History: The Early Years of the State
Edited by Laurence J. Silberstein

Jewish Fundamentalism in Comparative Perspective

Religion, Ideology, and the Crisis of Modernity

Edited by
Laurence J. Silberstein

NEW YORK UNIVERSITY PRESS
New York & London

Copyright © 1993 by New York University
All rights reserved
Manufactured in the United States

Library of Congress Cataloging-in-Publication Data

Jewish fundamentalism in comparative perspective : religion, ideology,
    and the crisis of modernity / edited by Laurence J. Silberstein.
        p.   cm. -- (New perspectives on Jewish studies)
    Includes bibliographical references and index.
    ISBN 0-8147-7966-2 (cloth) -- ISBN 0-8147-7967-0 (pbk.)
        1. Orthodox Judaism--Israel--Congresses. 2. Judaism and politics-
    -Congresses. 3. Jewish-Arab relations--Religious aspects-
    -Congresses. 4. Judaism--20th century--Congresses.
    5. Fundamentalism--Congresses. 6. Islamic fundamentalism-
    -Congresses. 7. Religion and politics--Congresses.
    I. Silberstein, Laurence J. (Laurence Jay), 1936- . II. Series.
    BM390.J48 1993   92-31615
    296'.09'04--dc20   CIP

New York University Press books are printed on acid-free paper,
and their binding materials are chosen for strength and durability.

This volume is dedicated to the memory of my parents, Rose and Moses B. Silberstein. While I have sorely missed their physical presence these many years, their love and wisdom remain with me always.

Contents

III. Religious Fundamentalism and Judaism: Selected Issues

Acknowledgments

The original impetus for this volume arose out of a conference on "Fundamentalism as a Political Force in the Middle East," sponsored by the Berman Center at Lehigh University in May 1989 and a seminar series on religious fundamentalism held at Lehigh during the 1988–89 academic year. I wish to express my appreciation to Elie Rekhess of Tel Aviv University, who initiated and organized the conference during his term as Berman Visiting Scholar at Lehigh. Earlier versions of chapters 5, 6, 7, and 11 were delivered at the conference, while earlier versions of chapters 2 and 4 were presented at the seminar.

As with the first volume in this series, Shirley Ratushny, Assistant to the Director of the Berman Center, was primarily responsible for the copyediting and technical preparation of the manuscript. We are both grateful to Erica Nastasi, the Secretary-Coordinator of the Center, for typing the manuscript and for her many contributions to its preparation. We are also appreciative of the assistance and counsel of Despina Papazoglou Gimbel of NYU Press. This volume, and the series of which it is a part, would not be possible without the continuing support and generosity of Philip and Muriel Berman.

We wish to thank the following publications and publishers for graciously granting us permission to reprint or cite material:

James Davison Hunter's chapter also appears as "Fundamentalism in its Global Contours" in *The Fundamentalism Phenomenon*, edited by Norman J. Cohen, copyright © 1990 by William B. Eerdmans Publishing Company, Grand Rapids, Michigan, used by permission of the publisher; Koppel Communications, Inc., for permission to quote excerpts from "The Koppel Report: The Billion Dollar Pie"; Hava Lazarus-Yafeh's essay was first published by *The Jerusalem Quarterly* (Summer 1988); the chapter by Ehud Sprinzak is an excerpt from his volume *The Ascendance of Israel's Radical Right,* by permission of Oxford University Press, copyright © 1991 by Oxford University Press, Inc.; "Jewish Zealots: Conservative versus Innovative" by Menachem Friedman is reprinted from *Religious Radicalism and Politics in the Middle East,* edited by Emmanuel Sivan and Menachem Friedman, by permission of State University of New York Press, copyright © 1990 State University of New York.

Part I

Religious Fundamentalism and Modernity:
Theoretical Issues

Chapter 1

Religion, Ideology, Modernity: Theoretical Issues in the Study of Jewish Fundamentalism

Laurence J. Silberstein

I. Fundamentalism: Conceptual Problems

The recent plethora of journalistic articles and scholarly studies on religious fundamentalism reflects a growing recognition of its significant social, cultural, and political force. The recent appearance of the first volume in a projected five-part series on religious fundamentalism across the globe is a further indication of the seriousness with which this phenomenon is regarded in the scholarly community. Sponsored by the American Academy of Social Sciences, this series is the result of a cooperative effort by an eminent group of international scholars.

A number of factors contributed to this awakening of interest. Undoubtedly, the attainment by Islamic fundamentalists of political hegemony in Iran has been an important factor in fostering this recognition. In addition, there is the growing role of religious fundamentalism in the Israeli-Arab conflict on both the Jewish and Arab sides. The increasing political role of Islam in several of the former Soviet republics is but another indication of the political power of fundamentalist groups. Finally, closer to home, the recent televangelical scandals made the American people more aware than ever of the growing economic and cultural power of fundamentalist groups.

It is not surprising, therefore, that Jewish fundamentalism, until recently a barely noticed phenomenon in Jewish life, has attracted increasing scholarly attention. Over the past few years, a number of works, in both Hebrew and English, have focussed on two groups identified by most scholars as representing fundamentalism in its Jewish

3

guise, the Haredim and Gush Emunim. Through these works, students have become more aware of the significance of fundamentalist groups in the shaping of modern Jewish discourse.

Any discussion of religious fundamentalism is immediately confronted by a methodological/conceptual issue. What and who are we talking about when we speak of fundamentalism? Are there common characteristics shared by all fundamentalist groups? Is fundamentalism, a term that originally emerged within the context of American Protestantism, limited to Christianity or is it equally applicable to other religions of Near Eastern origin such as Judaism and Islam? And finally, can one speak about fundamentalism among religions originating in the Far East?

As Max Weber warned at the beginning of the century, whenever we subsume under a term such as fundamentalism multiple actions, persons, events, ideas, and writings that occurred over a period of decades, we should recognize that we are dealing with a mental construct, or what Weber termed an ideal type. In seeking to distinguish a phenomenon such as fundamentalism, the scholar must, of necessity, select, highlight, and place in the foreground some data while excluding, minimizing, and placing in the background other data. Thus, as recent scholarly efforts acknowledge, we are ill advised to begin a discussion by attempting to arrive at a final, fixed definition of a term such as fundamentalism. Fundamentalism is, like all words ending in "ism," an ideal type or mental construct. Accordingly, many scholars have chosen to begin their inquiry by asking what characteristics we have in mind when we use a term like fundamentalism.

Another problem confronting scholars derives from the desire to apply the term fundamentalism cross-culturally. Thus, students of Islam and Judaism, drawing upon a term that originated within American Christianity, have used it to illuminate their own areas of study. Nevertheless, many scholars are reluctant, if not opposed, to apply the term to the non-Christian tradition. Indicative of this reluctance is the preference of many scholars, including some in this volume, to speak of religious extremists, religious radicals, and zealots, rather than fundamentalists.

In three of the most significant recent efforts to explore the nature of fundamentalist movements, the authors acknowledge the conceptual and methodological dilemma posed by concepts such as fundamentalism. Rejecting what they consider to be an essentialist approach that would seek to isolate essential characteristics inherent in all fundamentalist movements, these authors, referring to Wittgenstein, prefer to speak of "family resemblances" among the various groups identified as fundamentalist.[1]   At the same time, while acknowledging the contextual differences among various movements defined as fundamentalist, they nevertheless argue in favor of the scholarly benefits that such comparative study can yield.

In confronting the problem of applying the term fundamentalism cross-culturally, the editors of the ambitious, wide-ranging University of Chicago series "The Fundamentalism Project" have opted for the plural form, entitling their first volume *Fundamentalisms Observed*.[2]   In their effort to avoid an essentialistic definition, Martin Marty and Scott Appleby speak in terms of family resemblances rather than inherent characteristics.[3]   According to them, when we speak of fundamentalists, we speak of religious groups which: (1) arise in response to crises that they perceive as threatening to the identity of the group; (2) see themselves engaged in struggle against various "others" including secularizers, modernists, secular nationalists, and the established authorities of their own religious community whom they perceive to compromise with modernity and secularization; (3) tend to mythologize/demonize their "others"; (4) view historical events as part of a cosmic, often eschatological pattern; (5) reject historical consciousness; (6) establish rigid socio-cultural boundaries to protect themselves from contamination by outsiders; and (7) follow male, charismatic leaders whom they consider to be the authorized interpreters of traditional sacred texts.

Summing up their findings, Marty and Appleby describe fundamentalism as

> a tendency, a habit of mind found within religious communities and paradigmatically embodied in certain representative individuals and movements, which manifests itself as a strategy, or set of strategies, by which beleaguered believers attempt to preserve their distinctive identity as a people or group. . . . Feeling this identity to be at risk in the contemporary era, they fortify it by a selective retrieval of doctrines, beliefs, and practices from a sacred past. These retrieved fundamentals are refined, modified, and sanctioned in a spirit of shrewd pragmatism: they are to serve as a bulwark against the encroachment of outsiders who threaten to draw the believers into a syncretistic, areligious, or irreligious cultural milieu.[4]

Bruce Lawrence, the author of another recent study of fundamentalism, argues that the term fundamentalist can be applied to non-Christian groups "if the term draws attention to qualities among these groups that, when clustered together, make more sense of what they do, or claim to do, than other abstracting umbrella categories."[5] Lawrence finds that fundamentalism is best described as a religious ideology, indicative of the fact that it "connotes a fixed and unquestioned set of beliefs, views, and assumptions that constitute the general framework within which all other questions take place."[6] In addition, ideologies provide mandates for action and promote group solidarity.

Lawrence gives particular emphasis to the combative, oppositional, minority character of fundamentalist groups. To Lawrence, "the single, most consistent common denominator is opposition to all those individuals or institutions that advocate Enlightenment values and wave the banner of secularism or modernism."[7] Moreover, hatred and fear of modernism defines the "tone of fundamentalist rhetoric."[8]

Lawrence believes fundamentalist movements share a number of other characteristics in common: (1) they are comprised of "secondary-level male elites," led by charismatic figures; (2) they utilize a technical vocabulary or discourse, such as the Jewish *halakhah* (religious law) or Islamic *sharia* (judicial system); (3) they profess totalistic, unquestioning allegiance to sacred scripture; and (4) they relegate the authority to determine scriptural meaning to a select group of leaders.

In his opinion, the questions that determine whether or not a group should be labelled as fundamentalist include: Are they "minority advocates of scriptural idealism who are oppositional to the dominant ethos"? Do their leaders tend to be secondary-level male elites who are bound to one another by a religious ideology that relies on insider, technical language? Despite their own claims to "distant and near antecedents," are those considered to be fundamentalists "only to be found in the Technical age as tenacious opponents of modernist ideologies that challenge their scriptural ideals and spiritual loyalties"?[9]

A somewhat different approach is taken by Lionel Caplan, the editor of a recent anthology of comparative studies of fundamentalist movements. Agreeing with Marty, Appleby, and Lawrence concerning the futility of essentialistic definitions, Caplan, like Lawrence, suggests that we distinguish a fundamentalist movement "in terms of a significant 'other,' to which it is antithetical and with which it constantly engages."[10] Agreeing that fundamentalism is a distinctively modern phenomenon, he nevertheless warns against viewing fundamentalism and its significant conceptual "other," modernism, as binary opposites. Instead, he asserts, fundamentalism and modernism should be viewed in dialectical relationship to one another.[11]

Given the conceptual problems raised by scholars concerning the notion of fundamentalism, it is appropriate that the first section of this book be devoted to an exploration of theoretical issues. In the opening essay, James Davison Hunter argues that whatever else is shared in common by those whom we designate as fundamentalists, all forms of religious fundamentalism believe that history has gone awry or that it remains unfulfilled. Like most other scholars cited, Hunter believes that a crisis of identity resulting from the confrontation of religious groups with modernity provides the context for the emergence of many fundamentalist movements. Thus, fundamentalism provides a window on the strains and pressures experienced by religious communities in their encounter with modernity.[12]   Fundamentalists, according to Hunter, are engaged in a struggle for "control over the mechanisms of cultural reproduction."[13]

In her succinct overview of various approaches to fundamentalism, Hava Lazarus-Yafeh distinguishes ten characteristics that all movements identified as fundamentalistic seem to share. Like Caplan and Lawrence, Lazarus-Yafeh finds that fundamentalist movements, as oppositional communities, can be characterized by the common things they oppose, including modernity, secular Western values, and the established religious authorities within their own communities. Moreover, fundamentalists share a contempt for all outsiders or "others," including "others" within and "others" outside of their own historic community.

Infused with an apocalyptic mood, fundamentalists see themselves as living in a period of immanent redemption. Treating sacred Scripture as textbooks through which they can understand the present and predict the future, fundamentalists believe that they are able to circumvent hermeneutic processes and gain direct access to the meaning of Scripture. Privileging the authority of their own leaders, they willingly subordinate democratic values and processes to this authority.

While the articles by Ian Lustick and Alan Mittleman focus on specific dimensions of Jewish fundamentalism, their theoretical approaches merit consideration here as well. Both Lustick and Mittleman, albeit in different ways, shift the focus of the discussion of fundamentalism to the political dimension. For Lustick, fundamentalism refers to a particular kind of political style in which "political action, dedicated toward rapid and comprehensive transformation of society, is seen to express uncompromisable, cosmically ordained, and more or less directly received imperatives."[14]   Consequently, while excluding from the category of fundamentalism quietistic religious groups like the Haredim, the Jewish ultra-Orthodox groups discussed below by Friedman, Cromer, and Kirschenbaum, Lustick includes such political groups as cultural revolution Maoists.

Critically exploring a number of theories, including those of Hunter, Lazarus-Yafeh, and Lustick, Mittleman emphasizes two basic points. First, fundamentalism is a uniquely modern phenomenon and must be distinguished from all pre-modern religious movements. Second, the characteristics ascribed to fundamentalism must sufficiently distinguish it from religions in general.

According to Mittleman, to grasp the distinctiveness of fundamentalism as a modern phenomenon, we must shift the focus of our discussion from the realm of ideas to the socio-structural sphere. Thus, the distinguishing features of fundamentalism lie in "its social base, its way of legitimating social action, the social structural relationships out of which it develops, and its political focus."[15] Moreover, fundamentalism is best understood as "the modern form of transcendence-driven politics," a politics that emerges in reaction to secularization. According to Mittleman, although Lustick correctly focusses on the political dimension of fundamentalism, his definition is essentialistic and does not adequately distinguish fundamentalism as a modern phenomenon from pre-modern forms.

A distinctive and highly suggestive approach to fundamentalism is found in Susan Harding's chapter, "Contesting Rhetorics in the PTL Scandal." Drawing on contemporary theories of discourse, narrative, and representation, Harding focusses on the ways in which fundamentalism is discursively represented. According to her, the shift of focus from fundamentalism as an object to the discursive representation of fundamentalism frees us from the marginalizing/otherizing bias that dominates most discussions of the topic.[16] Attending to the discourses used to talk about fundamentalism by both fundamentalists and their critics, she analyzes the interests and ideologies reflected in these discourses.

Harding, an anthropologist, situates the battle over fundamentalism within the wider context of debates concerning cultural identity and modernity within American society. Critical of those who approach fundamentalism through the privileged voice of Enlightenment rationalism, Harding challenges the pose of neutrality affected by Ted Koppel. Far from being the voice of neutrality that he tries to be, Koppel, she argues, should be seen as representing but one of several competing discourses aspiring to cultural hegemony in contemporary America.

II. Fundamentalism, Discourse, Power

In applying to the discussion of fundamentalism contemporary theories of discourse, Harding opens up new analytic possibilities. As suggested by Richard Terdiman, the author of a recent work on the subject, discourses

> are complexes of signs and practices which organize social existence and social reproduction. In their structured, material persistence, discourses are what give differential substance to membership in a social group or class or formation, which mediate an internal sense of belonging, an outward sense of otherness.[17]

The inherent relationship of discourse to social practices has also been emphasized by Michel Foucault, who was instrumental in elevating the category of discourse to a central place in current scholarly discussion. Coining the term discursive practices, Foucault asserts:

> Discursive practices are not purely and simply ways of producing discourse, they are embodied in technical processes, in institutions, in patterns for general behavior, in forms for transmission and diffusion, and in pedagogical forms which, at once, impose and maintain them.[18]

Through discourse, we differentiate outsiders from insiders, we from them, self from other, and our community from other communities. Moreover, as Foucault has shown in a series of studies, discourses organize, legitimate, and sustain forms of social organization and processes of social reproduction; establish and police norms; and establish hierarchies of identity and difference, of subservience and authority, of taste and vulgarity. Viewed in this light, discourse is the starting point for understanding the ways in which identities are formed, conceptions of reality shaped and changed, human interactions interpreted, meanings established, institutions legitimated, and beliefs and knowledge formulated, disseminated, and perpetuated.

To Foucault, discourses generate, legitimate, support, and empower certain kinds of meanings, questions, debates, and conversations while suppressing, delegitimating, and disempowering others. Thus, "discourse is not simply that which expresses struggles or systems of domination, but that for which and by which, one struggles; it is the power which one is struggling to seize."[19]   Thus, as the objects of struggle for power, words are never benign. "The facts of domination, of control, are inscribed in the signs available for use by all members of a social formation."[20]

Caplan, one of the few scholars of fundamentalism to refer to Foucault, considers his concept "regime of truth" to be particularly useful. According to this concept, "truth" is to be understood not as an eternal, inherent characteristic of statements, but as a system of ordered procedures for the production, regulation, distribution, circulation, and operation of true statements: "Truth is linked in a circular relation with systems of power which produce and sustain it, and to effects of power which it induces and which extend it. A 'regime' of truth."[21]

Viewed in this light, truth is not found, but produced through processes of codification and prescriptions that determine rules and procedures as well as discursive methods by means of which "it is possible to articulate true or false propositions."[22]   As explained by Stuart Hall, a key figure in the field of cultural studies,

> discursive formations (or ideological formations that operate through discursive regularities) "formulate" their own objects of knowledge and their own subjects; they have their own repertoire of concepts, are driven by their own logics, operate their own enunciative modality, constitute their own way of acknowledging what is true and excluding what is false within their own regime of truth.[23]

Thus, when the concept "regime of truth" is applied to the study of fundamentalism, our attention shifts from ideas to the discursive processes, codes, rules, and prescriptions which order the life of the community, and by means of which the community generates and sustains a domain of objects/subjects about which it is possible to make true or false statements. Accordingly, our concern would no longer be the group's basic ideas or teachings, but rather the processes by means of which these teachings and ideas are generated, formulated into a domain of "truths," and inculcated into the consciousness of the followers so as to situate them in particular subject positions which generate their sense of identity.

Although Foucault eschewed the use of the concept of ideology, especially in its Marxist formulations, the concept is particularly useful for highlighting the struggles of fundamentalist movements for cultural, social, and political hegemony.[24]   Deconstructing such Marxist binary oppositions as base/superstructure, consciousness/material, ideology/-science, ideology/truth, class/ideology, contemporary social theorists, many of them influenced by Foucault, have approached ideology in terms of the discursive processes of signification and representation.[25] Seen in this light, ideologies (1) render socially constructed discourses, practices, and social formations "natural"; (2) position individuals and groups in particular identities; (3) constitute, legitimate, and perpetuate particular social and cultural forms; (4) define and delimit the parameters of the realm of common sense; and (5) construct the field and structures of our experience.[26]   Or, as formulated by contemporary theorists, ideologies tell us who we are, how we are to relate to the world around us, what is real and true, what is good/bad, what is possible/impossible.[27]

Stuart Hall, who accepts many of Foucault's ideas, argues that a revised concept of ideology helps to uncover the "relative power and distribution of different regimes of truth in the social formation at any one time—which have certain effects for the maintenance of power in the social order," what he calls the "ideological effect."[28]   To Hall, ideological practices "construct the necessity, the naturalness, the 'reality' of particular definitions and interpretations. . . . Ideology is the naturalization of a particular historical articulation."[29]

Hall conceives of ideology as "the frameworks of thinking and calculation about the world—the 'ideas' people use to figure out how the social world works, what their place is in it, and what they ought to do."[30]   Thus, ideologies provide us with the "bedrock of presuppositions by means of which we make sense of and organize everyday experiences." However, like Althusser, Hall argues that all ideologies are "materialized in practice." Thus, ideology is instantiated in and disseminated through a network of institutional and discursive apparatuses including schools, religious organizations, and family.

Hall's concept of cultural identity is also useful for highlighting the relationship of fundamentalism to the crisis of identity. To Hall, a pioneer in the field of cultural studies, culture refers not to a fixed, continuous system of symbols or ideas, but rather to a contested process.[31]   Accordingly, cultural identity, far from being stable and permanent, is contextual, relational, and contested:

> Cultural identity . . . is a matter of "becoming" as well as of "being." . . . It is not something which already exists transcending place, time, history, and culture. Cultural identities come from someplace,

have histories. But, like everything else which is historical, they undergo constant transformation. Far from being eternally fixed in some essentialized past, they are subject to the continuous play of history, culture, and power. Far from being grounded in a "mere" recovery of the past, which is waiting to be found, and which, when found, will secure our sense of ourselves into eternity, identities are the names we give to different ways we are positioned by, and position ourselves within, the narratives of past.[32]

Thus, in light of the ongoing struggle among groups to install their particular conception of cultural identity, "cultural poesis—and politics—is the constant reconstitution of selves and others through specific exclusions, conventions, and discursive practices."[33]

The concept of tradition, basic to any discussion of fundamentalism, has also been revised in a way that accentuates the role of power and power struggles. Rather than depict tradition as a body of inherited truths and practices, Chantal Mouffe defines it as "the set of language games [union of linguistic rules, objective situations and forms of life] that make up a given community" as well as "the set of discourses and practices that form us as subjects." To Mouffe, the struggle over "new usages for the key terms of a given tradition, and of their use in new language games that make new forms of life possible" is what we know as politics.[34] Seen in this light, the struggle of fundamentalists against traditional religious authorities and secular, modernizing forces over the true meaning of tradition is, in Mouffe's terms, a political struggle.

When these concepts of ideology, culture, identity, and tradition are applied to the study of fundamentalism, it is seen not as a fixed "object" or entity, but as a contested cultural formation or ideological configuration that includes both discourse, practices, techniques, and strategies. Consequently, in analyzing particular fundamentalist movements, our attention is drawn to the ways in which they (1) constitute, legitimate, and perpetuate particular social and cultural forms; (2) define and delimit the parameters of the realm of common sense; (3) construct the field and structures of our experience; (4) position individuals and groups in particular identities; and (5) render socially constructed discourses, practices, and individual and group identities "natural" or self-understood. Thus, we are led to approach fundamentalism in terms of the ongoing struggles over discourse, power, and identity within a given culture or society.

III. Jewish Fundamentalism and the Crisis of Jewish Identity

In light of the above discussion, the study of Jewish fundamentalism serves as an important vehicle for analyzing the essential ideological conflicts within the Jewish world, particularly in Israel. Whatever other characteristics they have in common, Jews whom we label as fundamentalists engage in and are fully committed to a struggle to generate, disseminate, and transmit a particular view of Judaism, Jewish history, and Jewish identity. Accordingly, Jewish fundamentalists are engaged in a struggle over the power to delimit discourse and establish the appropriate meaning and usage of key terms drawn from traditional Judaism. Jewish fundamentalists and their opponents are seeking to hegemonize conflicting conceptions of history, identity, society, culture, and tradition.

Insofar as Israel is the site of the most concentrated Jewish fundamentalist activity, most of the articles on Jewish fundamentalism focus on Israeli society and culture. Moreover, since Israel is the most conspicuous, concentrated site of the confrontation between Judaism and modernity, the ideological and cultural struggles within that society are indicative of the struggles over meaning, identity, and power within the Jewish world as a whole.

Secular Zionism is the most significant "other" for both groups of Jewish fundamentalists, Haredim and Gush Emunim. Besides comprising the underlying ideology upon which the State of Israel was founded, Zionism has been the most powerful ideological force shaping modern Jewish discourse as a whole. The Zionist interpretations of Judaism, Jewish identity, and Jewish history provide the basic myths, symbols, and rituals through which a significant proportion of Jews both form and give expression to their self-understanding as Jews and set the terms and the limits of the contemporary Jewish discourse.

Thus, Jewish fundamentalism is dialectically related to the dominant ideological streams within Zionism. In their effort to formulate, disseminate, and perpetuate alternative interpretations, fundamentalists cannot avoid coming into conflict with Zionism. Accordingly, Zionism serves as the significant "other" for the pro- and anti-Zionist fundamentalists alike.

From its inception in late nineteenth-century Europe, Zionism, as both a political program and a socio-cultural movement, provided new, frequently radical alternatives to the prevailing theological and ideological conceptions of Judaism, Jewish identity, and Jewish history. In the process, Zionism appropriated and recast many traditional religious terms in a secular ideological mold. Rebelling against the long-time hegemony of traditional religious authorities, Zionist writers struggled to win the Jewish people over to a new, secular nationalist way of understanding Jewish life and history. Moreover, Zionism sought to call into being a new type of Jew, or new Hebrew, who would represent a new kind of Jewish identity.

Like all ideologies, Zionism sought to establish a regime of truth in which certain statements, concepts, and claims are taken as natural or given, i.e., as true reflections of social, cultural, and historical reality. From the outset, however, Zionism has been the object of ongoing struggle and conflict. This heteroglossic condition has been succinctly captured in the following comment of Amos Oz:

> From the beginnings of modern Zionism, some one hundred years ago, it was a tense federation of varying, even contradictory visions, pursuing a continuous struggle, sometimes overt, sometimes repressed, over differing basic programs. . . . [35]

Although Zionism appeared to have achieved political, cultural, and social hegemony in the early years of the state, the ongoing struggles within Zionism concerning the interpretation of Judaism, Jewish history, and Jewish identity have characterized Israeli society as well.[36] Continuing the process that emerged with the rise of Zionism, Israeli society has been marked by ongoing debates over such issues as: Do Jews constitute a national-ethnic group or a religious community? What is the relationship between Zionism and Judaism? Between Israeli culture and traditional Jewish culture? Between Israeli identity and Jewish identity? Between the State of Israel and diaspora Jewry? Are Israeli society and culture continuous or discontinuous with the Jewish historical past formed in the diaspora? Is Israel a hegemonic Jewish state or a pluralistic, democratic, secular state?

The various ideological streams within Israel differ not so much over the significance of these issues, but rather over the appropriate discursive frameworks within which to situate these concepts. Moreover, while concepts such as Zion, exile, and redemption are shared by virtually all segments of Israeli society, there is widespread debate over the appropriate discursive framework within which to situate these terms.

According to Amos Oz, Israeli society, in the wake of the wars of 1967, 1973, and 1982, has been rife with conflict over "who we are, what we want to be, and what our source of authority should be."[37]

Moreover, as Oz observes, the basic conflicts within Israel are not only between differing conceptions of Jewish identity, but between "differing concepts of Judaism—some of them humanitarian, others tribal and primitive, and still others midway between."[38]   In Oz's view, the real dispute within Israel is not about territories, security, or borders, but "an argument about the nature of Judaism and the image of man."[39]

These disputes are clearly reflected in the debates between Jewish fundamentalists and their opponents.   As Friedman and Cromer show, both anti- and non-Zionist Haredim seek to replace the prevailing secular nationalist Zionist ideology with a transcendental, religious, anti-secular ideology.   In contrast, Gush Emunim, the form of Jewish fundamentalism described by Lustick and Sprinzak, seeks to replace the prevailing secular Zionist discourse with a new, religiously grounded, messianic Zionist discourse.   In each instance, the conflict revolves around competing notions of history, identity, truth, and socio-cultural reality.

The parallels and differences between fundamentalisms in relation to the struggles over national, social, and cultural identity in both the Jewish and Islamic worlds are clearly reflected in the essays by Elie Rekhess and James Piscatori on the one hand, and Menachem Friedman, Ian Lustick, Gerald Cromer, and Ehud Sprinzak on the other.   The essays by Rekhess and Piscatori provide the context for a comparison of Jewish and Islamic fundamentalism in the Middle East.   While Piscatori focusses on the complex process by means of which Islamic fundamentalism rose to become a significant political factor in the contemporary Middle East, Rekhess concentrates his attention on the West Bank and Gaza.

The view that fundamentalist movements emerge in a situation of social and political crises is clearly supported in the case of Islam.   For both Rekhess and Piscatori, the emergence of Islamic fundamentalism as a political force can only be understood against the background of Arab military defeats, particularly in the Arab-Israeli war of June 1967.   The political and cultural crisis that followed in the wake of the devastating Arab defeat created a situation of political instability and religious turmoil.   Loss of control of Jerusalem, the home of such holy Islamic sites as the Temple Mount, the Dome of the Rock, and the El Aksa mosque, generated a religious crisis within Islam.   This loss, coupled with the ensuing political vacuum, opened the way for the growth of fundamentalist movements.   This growth was fueled by the ongoing sense of shame, frustration, and victimization fostered by the continued occupation by Israel of an Arab population of 1.5 million in Jerusalem, the West Bank, and Gaza.

As Rekhess and Piscatori show, Islamic fundamentalists are engaged in an ongoing conflict over the definition of Islamic society and culture. Struggling against Western culture and secular nationalism on the one hand, and the traditional/established Islamic authorities on the other, Moslem fundamentalists aspire to hegemonize their own discourse, thus defining and delimiting the meaning and character of Islam on the one hand, and Arab societies and cultures throughout the Middle East on the other.

The career of Gush Emunim, discussed in the chapters by Lustick and Sprinzak, represents, in many ways, a mirror image of the career of Arab fundamentalism. Whereas the Arabs, as a result of the June 1967 war, experienced frustration and anomie, the Jews experienced elation. While the Arabs bewailed the loss of holy sites, Israelis rejoiced over the conquest of such religious sites as Jerusalem, the Temple mount, the Western Wall, and Hebron. Moreover, religious Zionists considered the Israeli victory to be a sign of divine deliverance and a portent of immanent redemption, while even some secular Israelis spoke of it in theological terms.

The elation and accompanying confusion resulting from the sudden and unexpected recovery of holy sites allowed long-submerged messianic feelings to surface among religious Zionists. Fired with messianic yearnings, yet frustrated by a government and a populace unwilling to take the radical action deemed necessary to hasten the redemption, Gush Emunim, like its Islamic counterparts, defied government authority, a defiance that was most radically expressed in terrorist activities that threatened the political stability of the Middle East.

As both Lustick and Sprinzak show, the debate over the territories occupied by Israel in the wake of the June 1967 war was a formative factor in the career of Gush Emunim. In contrast to those annexationists in Israel who justify the permanent acquisition of the West Bank and Gaza on the grounds of security, economy, demography, and Zionist ideology, the members of Gush Emunim view it as "a metaphysical question of transcendent importance."[40] Moreover, in Gush Emunim ideology, historical events such as the Holocaust, the June 1967 war, and the Yom Kippur war of 1973 are understood as part of the redemptive process of history. Framing the debate over the territories within a redemptive messianic vision of history, Gush

Emunim strives to replace a pragmatic, defense-oriented political discourse with a religious, eschatological one.

The analyses of Lustick and Sprinzak lend strong support to the idea that the struggle over Jewish fundamentalism is a struggle over the meaning of Judaism and Jewish history. As Lustick points out, Gush Emunim followers view their brand of fundamentalism as "the authentic representation of Judaism, of Jewish values, and even of what Zionism was always meant to be." In addition, whereas Zionism undertook to normalize Jewish life, Gush Emunim endeavors to perpetuate a metaphysical view of Jews as unique, divinely elected, and different. Furthermore, whereas mainstream Zionist thinking sought to incorporate the values of Western humanism, Gush Emunim views Judaism and Western humanism as antithetical.

Sprinzak provides a particularly valuable analysis of the processes by means of which Gush Emunim has succeeded in achieving cultural and political hegemony within the West Bank and Gaza. In his view, the movement owes its success to its "invisible realm," "a highly sophisticated political, economic and cultural network." Through a system of communal settlements, *yeshivot* (academies for talmudic study), schools, adult education programs, and short-term learning centers (*midrashot*), Gush Emunim effectively disseminates its ideology among the populace. Sprinzak uses the label "invisible" to indicate that most of the institutions are not overtly identified with Gush Emunim. In his view, this invisible realm, with its own district security and defense organization, was made possible through actions taken by the Israeli government.

Lustick's controversial claim that Gush Emunim alone represents authentic Jewish fundamentalism is rejected by Menachem Friedman and Gerald Cromer. To Friedman, Lustick's political definition of fundamentalism is too narrow and exclusionary. As he argues in "Jewish Zealots: Conservative versus Innovative" in this volume, it would be more accurate to speak of two forms of Jewish fundamentalism—the conservative form represented by the Haredim, the pietistic, ultra-Orthodox Jews, and the innovative, radical form represented by Gush Emunim. Both conservative and innovative fundamentalists are committed, according to Friedman, "to use whatever religious and political means are necessary to actualize these realities in the here and now."[41] In addition, both groups share a propensity for strict and stringent religiosity and tend to ground themselves in the same body of halakhic, midrashic, kabbalistic literary sources. Moreover, both groups operate with an eschatological view of history rooted in the dialectical tension of exile and redemption.

However, as Friedman points out, the groups diverge in their interpretations of redemptive history. The conservative fundamentalists emphasize the idealized Jewish society of the past, which they endeavor to replicate in the present. As non- or anti-Zionists, these fundamentalists oppose the secular Jewish state as an impediment to messianic redemption. Accordingly, the Israeli victory in the June 1967 war, which plays a fundamental role in the ideology of the radical fundamentalists, has little, if any, significance for the conservatives or Haredim. In contrast, the radical or innovative fundamentalists of Gush Emunim, embracing the state as a necessary stage on the path to redemption, seek to transform the victory in keeping with their radical vision of a messianic kingdom occupying the entire space of what they construe as the biblical borders of Israel.

While the strategies formulated by the Haredim and Gush Emunim clearly differ, the Haredim, as Cromer clearly demonstrates, also engage in a struggle for cultural, social, and political hegemony. Focussing on the various strategies employed by the haredi wing of Jewish fundamentalism in the ongoing battle with its "others" within Israeli society, Cromer's analysis provides an illuminating complement to Sprinzak's.

Cromer emphasizes the dialectical relationship between the strategies of withdrawal from and activist engagement with the surrounding secular society. Like Islamic fundamentalists and Gush Emunim, Haredim, according to Cromer, see themselves as "engaged in a holy war against the 'sons of secular darkness.'" Thus, his analysis calls into question the widespread image of haredi Jews as politically quietistic.

Like Friedman and Mittleman, Cromer sees haredi strategies as uniquely modern. Structuring his interpretation around the areas of education, parliamentary legislation, and extra-parliamentary protest, Cromer portrays the ways in which the strategies of withdrawal and conquest both diverge and interact. Of particular interest is his depiction of the ways in which the adoption of one strategy yields latent manifestations of the other. Thus, while providing helpful examples of the ways in which a fundamentalist movement seeks to establish boundaries protecting it from the surrounding secular society, his analysis of the dialectic of separation and militant engagement warns us against a one-sided interpretation.

Seeking to dispel the conventional conception of a homogeneous haredi society, Cromer depicts the ideological variations among Haredim. While some Haredim, like the Neturei Karta and the Edah Haredit, are anti-Zionist, many other Haredim adopt a more moderate, non-Zionist position of benign tolerance toward the state. Moreover, as Cromer shows, these two blocs employ different criteria in evaluating and criticizing the Jewish state.

IV. Dimensions of Jewish Fundamentalism

Whereas the essays in Part II of this volume discuss Jewish fundamentalism within the context of Israel and the Middle East, those in Part III explore specific dimensions of Jewish fundamentalism in general. Thus, whereas Lustick and Sprinzak provide important insights into the struggle between Jewish fundamentalists and secular Zionism, Kirschenbaum, Friedman, and Mittleman provide important insights into the factors separating Jewish fundamentalists from other traditional (Orthodox) Jews.

To Aaron Kirschenbaum, Orthodox Jews differ from ultra-Orthodox Jews (Haredim) in five basic areas: attitudes toward modernity, particularly Western culture; their interpretive approach to biblical and rabbinic sacred texts; the legitimacy of the secularized State of Israel and their relationship to secular Jews; the social role of women; and the degree of stringency in religious practice. In addition, he distinguishes between the infrastructure of Orthodox Jewry, including rabbinic leadership, the religious kibbutz movement, the National Religious Party, and pro-Zionist *yeshivot*, and that of the Haredim.

In contrast to modern Orthodox (Datiim), who seek to effect a synthesis between Jewish tradition and modernity, Haredim reject modern social mores, modern culture, and secular education. Similarly, while the Datiim, adhering to the interpretive methods of rabbinic Judaism, tolerate diverse interpretations of Scripture, the Haredim adopt a literalist approach to Scripture and to the messianic passages in rabbinic literature. However, both the Datiim and the Haredim reject the notion of a pluralistic Jewish society that would legitimize diverse interpretations of Judaism.

According to Kirschenbaum, the ultra-Orthodox community is comprised of three distinct groups. Besides the hasidic and anti- and non-hasidic ultra-Orthodox, Kirschenbaum identifies the Sephardim, a group that is increasingly playing a significant role in Israeli culture and politics. Whereas the first two groups derive from Eastern and Central European roots (Ashkenazim), the ethnic and cultural roots of the Sephardim are in North Africa, the Balkans, and Middle Eastern countries. Moreover, while the Sephardim are, for the most part, hawkish, the ashkenazic groups are divided on this issue.

Kirschenbaum takes issue with those who see the recent success of ultra-Orthodox political parties in Israeli elections as indicative of an upsurge of fundamentalism. In his view, these successes are better explained in terms of the general growth of orthodoxy since World War II. Thus, he sees the increased birth rates among the Orthodox, awakening of ethnic pride among sephardic Jews, a newly acquired self-confidence among Orthodox Jews, and the growing movement of born-again Jews (*baalei teshuvah*) as primary causes of the growing political strength of the religious parties.

In the chapter "The Market Model and Religious Radicalism," Menachem Friedman locates a major factor differentiating haredi Jews from pre-modern traditional Judaism in their approaches to *halakhah*. Friedman argues against those who see the haredi emphasis on the stringent application (*humrah*) of *halakhah* as characteristic of traditional Judaism in general. In pre-modern Judaism, efforts by elite groups to adopt a stringent interpretation of *halakhah* were opposed by communal authorities owing to social concerns. Only the erosion of traditional Judaism in the wake of secularization opened the way for the strict haredi attitude toward tradition to flourish.

Using the "market model" of modern society derived from the writings of the sociologist Peter Berger, Friedman argues that the propensity for strictness in legal interpretation is best understood in terms of the unique situation of religion in the modern, voluntaristic world.[42] In the marketing situation in which religious groups compete with one another for adherents, the Haredim employ their stringent approach to *halakhah* as a marketing tool. Whereas in the closed society of pre-modern Jewry, a strong communal rabbinic authority prevented the widespread adoption of a stringent approach to *halakhah*, the processes of secularization and pluralization significantly undermined that authority.

Alan Mittleman's chapter on Agudat Yisrael, discussed earlier in relation to its theory of fundamentalism, is the only one in the volume to focus on Judaism in the European setting. To Mittleman, fundamentalism is best understood in the context of the struggle of religious groups to combat the erosive social and ideological forces of secularization. Asserting religious truths to be the main legitimating force in society, fundamentalists challenge the secularized conception of group identity espoused by modern nationalism.

Mittleman's analysis of Jewish fundamentalism focusses on the orthodox Agudat Yisrael movement, founded in 1912 in the former German province of Silesia. To Mittleman, the movement's anti-secularist orientation, its view of religion as the main legitimating force in polity, and its embodiment in a lay organization motivated by transcendence-driven politics all qualify Agudat Yisrael as a fundamentalist movement. Mittleman detects two distinct political philosophies within the movement reflecting the diverse approaches of its Eastern and Western European constituencies. While Eastern Jews conceived of Agudat Yisrael as a way of achieving political effectiveness in a modern, secular nation state, Western European Jews viewed it as a way of countering the secularizing forces and achieving a theocratic society. Thus, whereas Easterners adopted a "defensive, mildly modernist, and pragmatic" approach to political activity, the Westerners' approach was "utopian, restorative, and in some respects messianic."

V. Concluding Remarks

In most studies of Judaism, the issue of power, if raised at all, tends to be disguised.[43] Academic discussions of Judaism usually ignore the fact that, like any culture, Judaism is characterized by an ongoing conflict over differing conceptions of history, identity, and truth. Similarly, within the non-academic Jewish community, the relationship of religious beliefs and practices, community institutions, and the exercise of power often passes unrecognized.

The militancy of Jewish fundamentalism makes it difficult, if not impossible, to overlook the issues of power in modern Jewish life. While seemingly a peripheral or marginal phenomenon, Jewish fundamentalists have succeeded in sharpening the divisions among Jews concerning the meaning of Judaism, the significance of Jewish history, and the nature of Jewish identity. Thus, as the chapters in this volume make clear, the study of Jewish fundamentalism tends to highlight the conflicting ideologies within contemporary Jewry.

Moreover, the influence of the ideological positions discussed in this volume is by no means limited to members of haredi communities or Gush Emunim. Through such apparatuses as schools, synagogues, interpretative procedures, youth movements, journals, newspapers, books, and broadcast media, the ideology of Jewish fundamentalism makes its way into the public discourse of the community. Thus, Jewish fundamentalism has succeeded in shaping the public discourse within the Jewish community, particularly in Israel, in ways that are not fully recognized. As Lustick and Sprinzak point out, the ideology of Gush Emunim finds strong support among a significant number of political leaders. By phrasing political, social, and cultural issues in terms of a transcendence-driven ideology, Jewish fundamentalists have challenged Jews of all persuasions to sharpen their own ideological position on these issues. The result is a heightened awareness of the fault lines within the Jewish community and a bringing to consciousness of ideological conflicts that might otherwise be overlooked.

NOTES

1. See Lionel Caplan, ed., *Studies in Religious Fundamentalism* (Albany: SUNY Press, 1987), 4; Bruce B. Lawrence, *Defenders of God: The Fundamentalist Revolt against the Modern Age* (San Francisco: Harper and Row, 1989), 24; and Martin E. Marty and R. Scott Appleby, eds., *Fundamentalisms Observed* (Chicago and London: University of Chicago Press, 1991), chap. 15.

2. While acknowledging the problematic of the term, Marty and Appleby conclude that, for better or for worse, it is here to stay, and offers a useful distinction from such terms as orthodoxy, traditionalism, conservatism:

   Having spent two of the five years set aside for research and study comparing "fundamentalism" to alternatives, we have come to two conclusions. No other coordinating term was found to be as intelligible or serviceable. And attempts of particular essayists to provide distinctive but in the end confusing accurate alternatives led to the conclusion that they were describing something similar to what are here called fundamentalisms. (Marty and Appleby, *Fundamentalisms Observed*, viii)

   Consequently, they suggest to their readers that "what we here call 'fundamentalism' refers to 'fundamentalist-like' movements" (Marty and Appleby, *Fundamentalisms Observed*, viii–ix).

3. Marty and Appleby, *Fundamentalisms Observed*, ix.

4. Ibid., 835.

5. Lawrence, *Defenders of God*, 95.

6. Ibid., 78. Lawrence sees ideologies as explicit, conscious, volitional, and rational, a very different view from the conception of ideology that I shall employ below which, following Althusser and Hall, emphasizes the implicit, unconscious, frequently non-volitional character of ideologies. Thus, while I accept the label of religious ideology as appropriate to fundamentalism and agree with his emphasis on the combative nature of

these movements, I find his conception to be lacking for reasons that will become clear below.

7. Ibid., 6.
8. Ibid., 5.
9. Ibid., 236.
10. Caplan, *Studies in Religious Fundamentalism*, 9.
11. Another approach to the problem is suggested by Jonathan Webber, one of the contributors to Caplan's volume. Rather than looking at movements said to be fundamentalist to see what common traits they share, Webber suggests that we focus on the ways in which those who label others as fundamentalists use the term. Moreover, he argues, our attention should focus on "the ideological structures that generate the reference to fundamentalism" among the groups that use the term, "and the particular circumstances that have given rise to their use of the category, whether it be seen as a 'response' to modernism or simply as a re-statement of traditional orthodox tenets which modernists classify as 'fundamentalist' so as to make their own position appear normative by contrast." To Webber, the advantage of this approach is that "it suggests locating its character elsewhere than within itself, and specifically draws attention to the force of external categorization in shaping its identity" (Caplan, *Studies in Religious Fundamentalism*, 97).
12. See James Davison Hunter in this volume.
13. Ibid., 33–34.
14. See Ian S. Lustick in this volume, 105–6.
15. See Alan L. Mittleman in this volume, 222–23.
16. See, on this point, Susan Harding, "Representing Fundamentalism: The Problem of the Repugnant Cultural Other," *Social Research* 58, 2 (Summer 1991): 373–93.
17. Richard Terdiman, *Discourse/Counter-Discourse* (Ithaca: Cornell University Press, 1985), 54.
18. Michel Foucault, *Language, Counter-Memory, Practice: Selected Essays and Interviews*, edited with an Introduction by Donald F. Bouchard (Ithaca: Cornell University Press, 1977), 200.
19. Michel Foucault, *L'ordre du discours* (Paris: Gallimard, 1971), 12, cited in Terdiman, *Discourse/Counter-Discourse*, 55.
20. Terdiman, *Discourse/Counter-Discourse*, 38.
21. Michel Foucault, *Power/Knowledge: Selected Interviews and Other Writings, 1972–1977*, ed. Colin Gordon (New York: Pantheon, 1980), 132.
22. Michel Foucault, "Questions of Method," in *The Foucault Effect: Studies in Governmentality*, ed. Graham Burchell, Colin Gordon, and Peter Miller (Chicago: University of Chicago Press, 1991), 79.
23. Stuart Hall, "Toad in Garden," in *Marxism and the Interpretation of Culture*, ed. Cary Nelson and Lawrence Grossberg (Urbana and Chicago: University of Illinois Press, 1988), 51.
24. Hegemony, as used here, refers to a form of social cohesion brought about

through "practices, techniques, and methods which infiltrate minds and bodies, cultural practices which cultivate behavior and beliefs, tastes, desires, and needs as seemingly naturally occurring qualities embodied in the psychic and physical reality (or 'truth') of the human subject" (Barry Smart, "The Politics of Truth and the Problem of Hegemony," in *Foucault: A Critical Reader*, ed. David Couzzens [Oxford and New York: Basil Blackwell, 1986], 160). Smart's conception of hegemony is, as he readily acknowledges, indebted to Foucault.

25. Among the theorists of ideology I have in mind are Louis Althusser, Goran Therborn, Stuart Hall, John Frow, Tony Bennet, Ernesto Laclau, Chantal Mouffe, John Thompson, and Terry Eagleton.

26. For a dynamic conception of experience, see Joan Scott, "The Evidence of Experience," *Critical Inquiry* 17 (Summer 1991): 773–97.

27. For this conception of ideology, see Goran Therborn, *The Ideology of Power and the Power of Ideology* (London: Verso, 1980).

28. Stuart Hall, "On Postmodernism and Articulation: An Interview with Stuart Hall," *Journal of Communication Inquiry* 10, 2 (Summer 1986): 49.

29. Lawrence Grossberg, "History, Politics, and Postmodernism: Stuart Hall and Cultural Studies," *Journal of Communication Inquiry* 10, 2 (Summer 1986): 67.

30. Stuart Hall, "Signification, Representation, Ideology: Althusser and the Post-Structuralist Debates," *Critical Studies in Mass Communication* 2, 2 (1985): 99.

31. For an illuminating discussion and historical overview of the concept of culture as a field of struggle, see Terdiman, *Discourse/Counter-Discourse*, 25–81.

32. Stuart Hall, "Cultural Identity and Diaspora," in *Identity, Community, Culture, Difference*, ed. Jonathan Rutherford (London: Lawrence & Wishart, 1990), 225. For further discussion of a process view of identity compatible with Hall's, see Theresa de Lauretis, "Feminist Studies/Critical Studies: Issues, Terms, and Contexts," in *Feminist Issues/Critical Studies*, ed. Theresa de Lauretis (Bloomington: Indiana University Press, 1986), 8–10; and Linda Alcoff, "Cultural Feminism versus Post-Structuralism: The Identity Crisis in Feminist Theory," *Signs: Journal of Women in Culture and Society* 13, 3 (1988): 405–36. Feminist theorists like Alcoff and de Lauretis speak of a "positional view of identity" in which identity is seen as the outcome of a constantly shifting context that includes economic conditions, cultural and political institutions, ideologies, and discursive frameworks. Identity, viewed in this way, is not

a given thing, but is, instead, a posit or construct, formalizable in a non arbitrary way through a matrix of habits, practices, and discourses. Further, it is an interpretation of our history within a particular discursive constellation, a history in which we are both subjects of and subjected to social construction. (Alcoff, "Cultural Feminism versus Post-Structuralism," 431)

33. James A. Clifford and George E. Marcus, eds., *Writing Culture: The Poetics and Politics of Ethnography* (Berkeley and London: University of California Press, 1986), 24. Clifford, like Hall, emphasizes the constructed, discursive character of culture in general:

> Cultures are not scientific "objects" (assuming such things exist, even in the natural sciences). Culture, and our views of "it," are produced historically, and are actively contested. There is not a whole picture that can be "filled in," since the perception and filling of a gap lead to the awareness of other gaps. . . . If culture is not an object to be described, neither is it a unified corpus of symbols and meanings that can be definitively interpreted. Culture is contested, temporal, and emergent. (Clifford and Marcus, *Writing Culture*, 18)

Mikhail Bakhtin also offers a dynamic, conflictual view of discourse and culture. According to Bakhtin, culture or society embodies conflicting ideological orientations. This results in part from the central role of language. Insofar as language, in Bakhtin's view, is the site of ongoing conflict, then society and culture are as well:

> At any given moment of its historical existence, language is heteroglot from top to bottom: it represents the co-existence of socio-ideological contradictions between the present and the past, between differing epochs of the past, between different socio-ideological groups in the present, between tendencies, schools, circles and so forth, all given a bodily form. These "languages" of heteroglossia intersect each other in a variety of new ways, forming new socially typifying "languages." (Mikhail Bakhtin, *The Dialogic Imagination* [Austin: University of Texas Press, 1981], 291)

Goran Therborn, focussing on the discursive character of ideologies and their role in shaping individual and group identities, has pointed out the combative nature of ideologies:

> Ideologies differ, compete and clash not only in what they say about the world we inherit, but also in telling us who we are, in the kind of subject they interpellate. (Therborn, *Ideology of Power*, 78)

34. Chantal Mouffe, "Radical Democracy: Modern or Postmodern?" in *Universal Abandon: The Politics of Postmodernism*, ed. Andrew Ross (Minneapolis: University of Minnesota Press, 1988), 40.
35. Amos Oz, *Slopes of Lebanon* (New York: Harcourt, Brace, Jovanovich, 1987), 70. To Oz, heteroglossia, a term derived from Bakhtin, is inherent in the very nature of culture:

> A living civilization is a drama of struggle between interpretations, outside influences, and emphases, an unrelenting struggle over what is the wheat and what is the chaff, rebellion for the sake of innovation, dismantling for the purpose of reassembling differently, and even putting things in storage to clear the stage for experiment and

new creativity. (Amos Oz, *In the Land of Israel* [New York: Random House, 1984], 137)

36. See, for example, Tom Segev, *1949—The First Israelis* (New York: The Free Press, 1986); Peter Y. Medding, ed., *Israel: State and Society, 1948–1988* (New York and Oxford: Oxford University Press, 1989), especially 3–168; and Laurence J. Silberstein, ed., *New Perspectives on Israeli History: The Early Years of the State* (New York and London: New York University Press, 1991). The argument that Zionism had, in fact, achieved hegemony which was only disrupted in the period beginning in 1967 is made by S. M. Eisenstadt in *The Transformation of Israeli Society* (Boulder: Westview, 1985).

37. Oz, *Slopes of Lebanon*, 75. Oz has graphically depicted the fault lines within Israeli culture and society in *In the Land of Israel*.

38. Oz, *Slopes of Lebanon*, 205.

39. Ibid., 236.

40. See Ian S. Lustick in this volume, 108.

41. See Menachem Friedman in this volume, 148.

42. In addition to the article cited by Friedman, Berger develops his argument regarding the market model in *The Sacred Canopy* (Garden City: Doubleday, 1967), chap. 6.

43. In his newly published ethnographic study of haredi society, *Defenders of The Faith: Inside Ultra-Orthodox Jewry* (New York: Schocken Books, 1992), Samuel Heilman describes the various social and cultural vehicles through which haredi discourse is disseminated. However, Heilman's ethnographic orientation tends to minimize the role of power and struggle in haredi Judaism. Thus, while referring to Clifford concerning the formative role of the ethnographer, Heilman stops short of embracing Clifford's view of culture as contested and power-ridden. The result is a somewhat benign picture of Haredim that significantly softens the agonistic dimension emphasized by Cromer.

Chapter 2

Fundamentalism:
An Introduction to a General Theory

James Davison Hunter

Scholars very often wince when journalists, popular pundits, and political ideologues invoke the term *fundamentalism* as descriptive of a wide variety of religio-political movements in different parts of the world. Religious historians and area specialists are particularly aggravated by the cavalier, even sometimes reckless, usage of the term. It is as though the word has evolved as just another synonym for religious dogmatism or ideologically rooted authoritarianism of whatever historical manifestation.

Their grievances cannot be easily discounted as mere academic pedantry. The roots of the concept *fundamentalism* derive from the specific historical experience of American Protestantism in the late nineteenth and early twentieth century. The term, then, is context-bound. To simply apply the term universally without regard for the national setting, the particular history of a religious faith, whether the religion is a dominant or a minority faith, and a host of other factors, would seem to make its broad usage impossible. Such movements around the world are, perhaps, better understood as different forms of religious radicalism or religious revitalization, but certainly not as fundamentalism. Or so it is argued.

In the final analysis these objections may carry the day. Certainly, for every generalization that can be made about so-called religious fundamentalism, one could probably find an exception. Given this probability, it might be folly to even try to derive a more or less unified conceptual understanding of the phenomena of fundamentalism. Nevertheless, important commonalities found in the experience of a wide variety of religions all over the world repeatedly press themselves upon our imaginations in such a way that it would seem imprudent to ignore them.   Minimally, it would be appropriate to tentatively explore the formal properties the various empirical cases typically called fundamentalist seem to share in common.   At the broadest level of generalization, then, the concept of fundamentalism may actually have a certain utility.

Fundamentalism and Orthodoxy: The Essential Difference

The great pretense of all "fundamentalists" of whatever stripe is their conviction that what they espouse and what they seek to promote is a basic unaltered orthodoxy. This, I would argue, is not at all the case. Orthodoxy as a cultural system represents what could be called a "consensus through time"—more specifically, a consensus based upon the ancient rules and precepts derived from divine revelation.   Its authority and its legitimacy derive from an unfaltering continuity with truth as originally revealed—truth in its primitive and purest expression (Hunter 1987).   Fundamentalism, it is fair to say, is something else. In a word, *fundamentalism is orthodoxy in confrontation with modernity.*

The argument can be framed in this way. Sociologically, all religious traditions confronting the modern world order—its rationality, its pluralism, its public/private dualism, its secularity—are faced with basically three options. One option is that the religious community, as bearers of the tradition, can withdraw from engagement. In this there is a principled refusal to deal with the outside world beyond what is absolutely necessary for survival. The community becomes, for all practical purposes, a closed and total world, caring for its own educational, medical, commercial, and spiritual needs.   The archetypal examples of this are found among the Amish, the old order Mennonite and Brethren communities, and some forms of Hasidic Judaism, such as the Satmar Hasidism.

A second option it can follow is simply to accommodate the traditions to the social and cultural forces of the modern world. Here the traditions come to conform increasingly to the cognitive and normative assumptions of contemporary secular society, be it materialism, scientism, humanism, or hedonism. The most obvious illustrations of this are found in those religious communities where the traditions are so liberalized and de-sacralized that the languages of traditional faith are translated into the languages of contemporary therapy, politics, or science.

A third option is that the religious community can resist modernity and the pressures that would dilute the purity of traditional religious expression. Fundamentalism, I would maintain, derives its identity principally from a posture of resistance to the modern world order. Of course, the sociological reality is that for traditions to engage with modernity there is generally a dialectical process at play which involves both accommodation (perhaps unwitting) and cultural resistance. Some accommodate more than others, while others resist more than others. Nevertheless, fundamentalist religion is defined principally by a defensive reaction against the "world-disaffirming" qualities inherent to the modern world. At root, there is no fundamentalism without modernity.

Fundamentalism: Making History Right Again

The argument that fundamentalism emerges out of the defensive interplay between orthodoxy and modernity can be crystallized through three simple propositions. Nearly everything else that distinguishes fundamentalism in its global contours derives from these. Namely, *what fundamentalisms share in common is the deep and worrisome sense that history has gone awry. What "went wrong" with history is modernity in its various guises. The calling of the fundamentalist, therefore, is to make history right again.*

Take, as an example, what may be the paradigmatic case of American Protestant fundamentalism. From the early colonial period, in New England, to the late nineteenth century, there was tremendous optimism that God was doing a wondrous work in this world through the heirs of the Reformation, particularly those who settled on American shores. America would be a "Christian commonwealth," a "righteous empire," a "redeemer nation" (to use Ernest Lee Tuveson's phrase). The blessings of revivalistic awakenings as well as the hardships of famine and war—first with the French and later with the British for independence, and even the Civil War in the mid-nineteenth century—were all viewed as part of a providential design. God's favor for America would continue as long as its people remained true to faith. Yet the pernicious effects of modernism—in the forms of higher criticism, evolution, the "Social Gospel," ecumenism, and the like—threatened not only the integrity of the true faith as they saw it, but also the very hope of the cause of Christianity in America. History was going awry, and it was up to the faithful followers of the gospel to make it right again.

It is only in the light of this purpose that one can really understand the emergence of dozens of Bible colleges and institutes, the founding of numerous fundamentalist periodicals, the establishment of the World Christian's Fundamentalist Association (in 1919), the wars within denominations (the Baptists and Presbyterians most notably) and denominational seminaries, and the fight between the creationists and evolutionists in the late nineteenth and early twentieth century. It is also only in this light that one can properly understand, nearly a century later, their efforts to reverse the legal status of abortion, to delegitimate progressive sexual and familial attitudes, to return the practice of prayer to public schools, to elect Christian politicians, and so on. Nothing less than the course of American history was and is at stake.

The story of Islamic fundamentalism bears a strong resemblance in its general contours but is different, of course, in the details (Smith 1957; Hodgson 1974; Voll 1982). Early Islamic history, of course, was marked by tremendous success. The community of believers expanded numerically, grew in geo-political dominance, and prospered in its cultural and religious accomplishments. In its first five centuries it established a new and vibrant civilization. It was as though Allah was confirming the truth of the Islamic vision within history itself. Even after the Mongol invasion in the thirteenth century and collapse of the growing Muslim dynasty, there was a revitalization and expansion of Arab civilization in its medieval period which allowed Muslims to reinterpret this crisis as occurring within the divine pattern of historical development. This has not been possible for Muslims in the face of Islam's second major crisis: the confrontation with the modern world order.

The confrontation with the modern world order came as early as the seventeenth and eighteenth century with the expansion of Western capitalism into the Middle East, Mongol India, and the Ottoman Empire. By the end of the eighteenth century, various Western powers had established direct economic, political, and military control over much of that region as a result of the area's deep economic, technological, and intellectual dependence on the West. What European hegemony meant, among other things, was the introduction of radical political and administrative reform and subjugation of Islamic culture and ideals to Western traditions of rationalism, secularism, and dualism.

Muslim society had indeed lost control over its collective destiny. History had indeed gone awry. Ever since, there has been a pervasive confusion over how to salvage that history—even fundamental doubt as to whether that history can be salvaged at all.

Yet this has not impeded the effort. From the earliest (proto-) fundamentalist reactions against the internal "deterioration" of Islam in the early eighteenth and nineteenth century (including the Wahhabi movement of Arabia, the Waliyuhl movement in India, the Sansusi movement in Libya, the Madhi movement in the Sudan, and Sarekat Islam in Indonesia, among others) to the twentieth-century movements (including al-Ikhwan al-Muslimun [the Muslim Brotherhood], Jund al-Rahman [Soldiers of God], Jamaat al-Muslimun [the Muslim Group], Shabab Mohamed [Muhammad's Youth], al-Takfir wa al-Hijra [Repentance and Holy Flight], and al-Jihad [Holy War]), all share in the common passion to recover the classical experience of Islam (a history without deviation) and the original meaning of the Islamic message (a faith without distortion).

In Hinduism the clearest case of fundamentalism is Rashtriya Swayamsevak Sangh (hereinafter referred to as RSS) or the National Pure Service Society. Once more the story is being retold (Mishra 1980; Malkani 1980; Anderson and Shridhar 1987; Gupte 1985; Heim 1986). According to the Hindu revivalists of the late nineteenth century (those from whom the RSS derived inspiration), Hindu society had degenerated because Hindus had not observed *dharma* (a code of conduct for various social categories, situations, and stages of life). Its degeneration had created conditions conducive to foreign domination (by the "British and Muslim villains") which itself intensified the pollution and degradation of classical Hindu culture. Because, according to orthodox Hindu doctrine, the good society can exist only when it is rooted on correct principles of *dharma*, India could not regenerate itself—indeed, antiquity could not be recovered—until the rules of *dharma* were again properly observed. In this conviction lay the central religious justification for all nationalistic and independence movements of the twentieth century. It was a particularly powerful justification for the RSS because of its fundamental passion to recover the purity of Hindu antiquity. In the cyclical reality defined by Hindu cosmology, "making history right again" meant returning to the pure forms of Hindu culture that had degenerated during foreign rule.

In Judaism, fundamentalism emerged as an offshoot of religious Zionism. Its clearest expression is Gush Emunim or, as it is known in Israel, the Bloc of the Faithful. Satmar Hasidism and the Agudat Israel bear a strong resemblance in many ways, but Gush Emunim is paradigmatic (Biale 1985; Litani 1985; Lustick 1987; Seliktar, 1983).[1] But in this case a slight adjustment must be made to the argument. For Jewish fundamentalists, it is not that history has gone wrong, it is that history *could* go wrong. As it is for Protestant fundamentalism, the RSS, and Islamic fundamentalism, so for Gush Emunim history has a sacral quality—history is God's means of communication with his people. Thus, the establishment of Israel in 1948 and its military victories in the Six-Day War of 1967 and Yom Kippur War of 1973 were signs of a providential process. Israelis had a sacred duty (*mitzvah*) to repossess and settle the land, for the land itself contains an immanent holiness. Withdrawal, therefore, would contravene God's will and represent a step backward in the messianic process of redemption. For this reason the men and women of Gush Emunim have made it their lives' work to ensure that the occupied West Bank and Gaza Strip are incorporated permanently into the State of Israel, thus hastening the fulfillment of "Jewish destiny."

The threat to the proper playing out of this redemptive history is constant. Importantly, it does not just come from the Arabs and Palestinians, but from the decadence of Western secular culture and from Israel's secular state which, as the Camp David Accords made clear, could compromise Jewish destiny for the sake of an ill-founded peace.

History, then, is at the heart of all fundamentalism. Though each fundamentalist community has its own particular vision of the nature and direction it should go, all have engaged in a quest either to put sacral history back on course or else to keep it on course. Significantly, there are places in the world where fundamentalisms are in close proximity, each maintaining opposing and contradictory views about the course and content of sacral history. The Middle East, of course, is one such place. The northwest quarter of India is another. Such proximity, needless to say, is a recipe for protracted and violent confrontation.

While the meaning of history may be at the heart of fundamentalist reaction, history is not an abstract ideal existing in the minds of theologians and philosophers. History is about a specific people in a specific place at a specific time. It is here where one may discern other characteristics of the fundamentalist phenomena.

Organized Anger

Largely because of the imperatives of the faiths themselves, fundamentalism is not just a theological reaction to modernity: orthodoxy is invariably linked to orthopraxy. This is to say, in practical terms, that all fundamentalisms are characterized, to varying degrees, by a quality of organized anger.

The issue here is one of means—the mechanisms by which the truth is defended and the forces of modernity are kept at bay. Making history right again requires the methodical mobilization of a wide range of resources. The most important of these are the resources of cultural reproduction—schools, newspapers, magazines, political advertisements, radio, television, direct mail, and the like. The reason is simple. Making history right again is, at heart, a matter of redefining the direction and meaning of history. The success or failure of a fundamentalist campaign, then, can be measured by the degree to which the cultural meanings imposed or reimposed are accepted as the official and legitimate public reality. Armed revolt and terrorist intimidation may be useful ways of getting public attention, but control over the mechanisms of cultural reproduction is, in the end, the most effective way of delegitimating the opposition's authority and legitimating one's own.

To single out the importance of symbols and the institutions that produce and disseminate them is not to suggest that the struggle is only literary in nature. The fundamentalist challenge very often incorporates the violence of military or paramilitary coercion. This is largely because of the special place given to the concept and reality of war in the fundamentalist cosmology.

It is not as though warfare is desired or eagerly sought by different fundamentalists, though martyrdom on behalf of a sacred cause does have tremendous significance in many of these traditions. War simply represents a time of testing, a sign of strength—a necessary means by which the will of Providence is worked out. It is no accident that Muslim fundamentalists view their struggle as a *jihad* or holy war against the great Satan of the United States, Israel, and the former Soviet Union. Importantly, Jewish fundamentalists share the same attitude to war. Within Gush Emunim, war is a central component to the purgative process that will bring about messianic times. Some within the movement quite literally view Arabs (including women and children civilians) as Amalekites or Canaanites that contemporary Jews, in the tradition of Joshua from biblical times, have a duty to destroy

(Seliktar 1983). (In this case, the settlement drive on the West Bank is viewed as nothing less than a military campaign. Therefore, anyone who hinders its success is considered an enemy.)

Sikh fundamentalists also view political violence as a necessary and legitimate part of a *Dharm Yudh* (religious war). Particularly after the breakdown of moderate leadership in the Akali Dal party in the late 1970s, many Sikh fundamentalists felt as though they had little effective recourse but to turn to political agitation. In the same country one may even find evidence of paramilitancy among Hindu fundamentalists, not only in the RSS but in such splinter organizations as Shiv Sena (Shiva's Army) and Bajrang Dal.

Protestant fundamentalism, by comparison to other expressions of global fundamentalism, is curiously domesticated. There is little evidence of any systemic orientation toward violent confrontation. There are numerous reasons for this having to do with its accommodation to and integration with American political culture. Nevertheless, some random anti-abortion violence and anti-secular intimidation (such as book burnings) have (long) been associated with Protestant fundamentalism. There are extremist groups scattered about the country, such as the Fundamentalist Army in southern California. Not least, the metaphor of warfare not only as applied to spiritual struggle but as applied to the struggle against the principalities and powers of this world remains one of the most potent within Evangelical Christianity in general. At the very least the language and imagery of spiritual warfare provides the rhetorical context where its translation into actual militancy becomes feasible.

The ultimate resource for coercively realizing the fundamentalist agenda is the instrumentality of the State. It is in this relationship that one may discern another central feature of fundamentalism in its global contours.

Religious Ideology and National Identity

There would appear to be, within the various manifestations of fundamentalism, a close relationship between religious ideology and national identity. This is to say that the integrity of the faith and the future of the nation are mutually entwined. The defense of one implies the defense of the other.

The case of Gush Emunim illustrates this dynamic clearly if not paradigmatically. In the religious ideology of the movement, national identity is not just a socio-cultural reality, it is a geo-political ideal. National identity is born both out of a cultural self-understanding and out of the actual land that the Jews inhabit (Lustick 1987). The popular slogan of the movement reflects this: "The Land of Israel, for the people of Israel according to this Torah of Israel."

Just as the covenant had been established with one particular chosen people, so too the covenant must be fulfilled in one particular chosen place. As Zvi Yehuda Kook, the undisputed leader of Gush Emunim until his death in 1982, put it, "The Land was chosen even before the people." Hanan Porat, one of the emerging younger leaders of the movement, echoed the solemnity of this perspective:

> For us the Land of Israel is a Land of destiny, a chosen Land, not just an existentially defined homeland. It is the Land from which the voice of God has called to us ever since that first call to the first Hebrew: "Come and go forth from your Land where you were born and from your father's house to the Land that I will show you" (see Lustick 1987, 127).

Given this view, it is hardly surprising that questions of geo-national borders "automatically assume cosmic proportions." Through the fusion of eschatological vision and political power, Gush Emunim aspires not only to assume the leadership of Zionism (altering its presently pluralistic character) but to assume control over the State of Israel itself. In this it aspires to create a religious state.

There is much the same passion for the ideals of a distinct people and a distinct place in the ideology of Sikh fundamentalism, as seen in the nationalist rhetoric of its political arm, the Akali Dal. The division of the state of Punjab into Hindi-speaking (and Hindu) Haryana and Punjabi-speaking (and Sikh) Punjab in 1966 was the first step toward the recognition of Sikhs as a nation and not just a religious community, but it was enough. As a paid political advertisement in the *New York Times* in 1971 put it (quoted in Jeffrey 1987, 61): "No power on earth can suppress the Sikhs. There are a people with a destiny. There will always be a Sikh nation. There always has been." As a result, ever since the Anandpur Sahib Resolution of 1973, the focus of political and religious aspirations within significant factions of Sikh fundamentalism has been the creation of the independent state of Khalistan.

In the Indian subcontinent, the Sikh demand for a homeland is contrasted with the objectives of RSS and its Bharatiya Jana Sangh party in its own ambition to create a pure Hindu society. It is out of this same logic that one also sees within Islamic fundamentalism a quest for an Islamic State. The notion of the Islamic State revives, in some measure, the classical ideal of the caliphate, where spiritual and political power are unified in a single office, the *khalifa* or *imam*. So too one can hear in the rhetoric of many Protestant fundamentalists a call for a "return" to a Christian America. One can find interesting variation among Christian theonomists, but virtually all view the establishment of this country, from its founding as a haven for religious dissenters to its founding documents, as the consequence of providential mediation in history. This being the case, the machinery of the state can be legitimately exercised to suppress sin and to advance the cause of righteousness and the cause of Christian faith. Among some extremists (such as the Christian Reconstructionists), the logic of theocracy extends even further, as seen in the effort to apply Old Testament law as the ideal form of governance.

In all of these cases and in others, the dualism separating religion and politics (church and state) that has so long characterized political life in the West is openly repudiated. God's dominion is indivisible and far reaching; spiritual purpose is one. Thus, fundamentalist ideology posits an organic unity between religious and political authority, its net effect being an essentially theonomic model of governance.

Scripturalism

The issue of religious authority needs to be pursued somewhat further, for it is conceived within various fundamentalist cosmologies in a fairly distinctive manner. In short, there is a certain proclivity among all fundamentalisms to base both religious authority and the rejection of modernity upon a literal reading of scriptural text. The significance of scripturalism is that it establishes very clear symbolic boundaries between good and evil, and right and wrong. It also establishes the criteria for distinguishing the faithful from the unfaithful and infidel. Given the moral and religious ambiguities that seem intrinsic to modern and post-modern thought and aesthetics, the text becomes the source of all religious and moral authority, establishing safe, definable, and absolute standards of life and thought.

In American fundamentalism the textual compulsion initially came in the reaffirmation of the Reformational principle of *Sola Scriptura*. Here the context is critical to its proper understanding. Prior to the 1850s, American Protestants, even the most pietistic, did not operate with a fully developed theology of Scripture. At best, there existed a solid, unquestioned reverence and loyalty for the Bible as the ultimate source of spiritual, religious, and moral truths.

Yet the challenge posed by literary and biblical criticism, anthropology, biology, and the social sciences unwittingly but collectively undermined this popular reverence by challenging the truths assumed by this reverence. The only recourse for those committed to the truth as inherited from earlier generations was to defend the basis upon which these truths were asserted. The logic was simple: if the faithful could successfully defend the notion that the Bible was the inerrant Word of God, to be interpreted literally as such, then they would have an adequate basis for rejecting all erroneous teachings. Modernism would be repudiated and what was going wrong with Protestant history could be made right again. The problem was that, in the effort to shore up the basic truths of Christian faith, a relatively novel doctrine of Scripture evolved, the doctrine of "inerrancy." Within a few short decades, belief in inerrancy and the hermeneutic of literalism had itself evolved as a paratheological test of true faith.

Nowhere could this be seen more clearly than in the 1910 publication *The Fundamentals*. Sponsored by two wealthy businessmen, the twelve volumes (ninety articles) were intended to check the spread of apostasy in the churches by clarifying and reaffirming the essentials of orthodox Christianity.

In Islam, the Koran plays a similar role. The very words of the Koran are not merely the meanings of human beings but are actually "uncrated"—the literal dictations of the eternal thoughts of God. As such, they are not subject to modification either through translation or interpretation. For this reason we again see an impulse toward literalism. The Koranic scriptures do not just point to ultimate truth but are themselves ultimate truth.

It is worth noting, by way of comparative-historical irony, that if anyone ever doubted the usefulness of the term *fundamentalism* as applied to the Islamic case, their doubts would have been allayed by the publication of *The Fundamentals of Islamic Thought* (Mizan Press, 1985) by the Ayatollah Murtaza Mutahhari. The volume is reminiscent of the early twentieth-century Protestant tracts not only in name but in purpose. The net effect of this Ayatollah's apologetic is nothing less than to provide a doctrinal standard for rejecting all erroneous (and, in particular, liberal and secular) teaching.

There are parallels in other faiths as well. In Theravadin Buddhism, the Pali Canon functions as a scripturalist base of fundamentalist reaction. In Gush Emunim, the literal reading of Torah operates in much the same fashion. In Rashtriya Swayamsevak Sangh, religious authority derives from a literal and politicized reading of the Bhagavad Gita. The result of this kind of scripturalism is the creation and imposition of a sharp dualism and absolutism. These qualities not only characterize theological commitments, but are translated as moral imperatives in the conduct of social and political affairs.

The Final Ironies

There would seem to be other general characteristics that most fundamentalisms have in common. For one, fundamentalism typically emerges among those faiths with a deep prophetic tradition. However, Soka Gakkai, if it can be labeled a form of fundamentalism in Japanese Buddhism, curiously does not fit that description. Another trait is that most fundamentalists are drawn from the lower middle classes, particularly those who are caught between the old order of traditional faith and the new order of modern secularity.

While important in their own right, these features are in many ways peripheral to the overriding and defining passion about the direction of history. But here we see two great ironies surrounding fundamentalist religion in its various permutations. The first irony is this: What justifies the fundamentalist impulse is the quest to overcome modernity—to put sacral history back on course or else to keep it on course. Yet what ultimately triggers the fundamentalist reaction within religious traditions is a sense of crisis in the credibility of the faith for the fundamentalists themselves. In other words, though the fundamentalist reaction, of whatever religious stripe, is legitimated by the concern for the course and content of history, its ultimate motivation appears to be a crisis in the religious self-identity of the believers themselves. Thus, modernity not only threatens to derail the course of sacral history, it also threatens the very survival of orthodox faith. Fundamentalism, then, is not born out of great confidence and bravado, but out of genuine fear about their own survivability.

A second irony follows from the first. In the attempt to shore up their own beleaguered faiths, the faiths that they so passionately defend are themselves transformed into something that may be orthodoxy in name only. In more sociological terms, the moral boundaries that long defined orthodox faith shift in such a way that the faith would become unrecognizable to previous generations. More simply, in the effort to defend the truth, truth itself is transformed.

This is seen, for example, in the struggle to establish an Islamic State (law, education, economy, etc.) in Iran and elsewhere in the context of global interdependence and the social, political, and cultural interaction that context assumes. In Protestant fundamentalism it is seen in doctrinal innovation (in the creation of the test of inerrancy) and in the reification of the concept of the traditional family. In orthodox Judaism it can be seen in the translation of religious Zionism into a new form of civil religion. These are just a few illustrations of a general tendency. In the end, the continuity with the past that fundamentalism strives so hard to maintain is broken. And it is broken in the very effort made to keep it from breaking.

Conclusion

While by no means exhaustive, the foregoing review does suggest, albeit tentatively, that there may be an empirical and conceptual basis for a general theory of fundamentalism. At the very least it suggests the need for further conceptual elaboration and empirical specification. On its own terms, then, there is legitimate call for further theoretical exploration of the fundamentalist phenomena. But the review suggests, perhaps, another truth. The ultimate significance of the fundamentalist phenomena, to the extent that one can generalize about it, may not be in what it tells us about religion as much as what it tells us about qualities intrinsic to the modern age. However one may disagree with fundamentalists theologically, morally, or politically—however one may fear their agenda—fundamentalism provides a window through which one can understand much about the modern world, particularly the pressures and strains it creates for ordinary people and the religious communities of which they are a part.

NOTES

This essay also appears as "Fundamentalism in its Global Contours" in *The Fundamentalism Phenomenon*, edited by Norman J. Cohen, copyright © 1990 by William B. Eerdmans Publishing Company, Grand Rapids, Michigan. Used by permission of the publisher.

1. Satmar Hasidism is messianic but anti-Zionist. It is true that its followers view the events of the twentieth century (the founding of Israel, the Six Day and Yom Kippur Wars, etc.) as crucial to Jewish identity, and yet they are convinced that spiritual laws prevail rather than natural laws. For those in this movement, these times still represent a period of exile for the Jews. For this reason, they oppose the existence of the secular state, secular politics, Zionism, violence, and many of the trappings of modern life, such as television, radio, and the like. Satmar Hasidism is messianic but essentially isolationist.

   Agudat Israel is also anti-Zionist, but unlike either Gush Emunim or Satmar Hasidism, it views history as indeterminate. History could go in many directions, and therefore it is important to cooperate with the secular state to help create a more just society, one that will ensure the survival of Jewish identity in the future.

   In Gush Emunim, Zionism is not just a movement but an irreversible process. True, the followers of the movement reject the nature of secular Zionism but not its effect. Though blind to the processes of religious redemption, they are still working the will of God. As for Gush Emunim, they are responding to divine initiative.

BIBLIOGRAPHY

Anderson, Walter K., and Shridhar D. Damle. 1987. *The Brotherhood in Saffron: The Rashtriya Swayamsevak Sangh and Hindu Revivalism.* Boulder: Westview.

de Bary, William Theodore, Stephen N. Hay, and I. H. Queshi, ed. 1958. *Sources of Indian Tradition.* Vol. 2 of *Introduction to Oriental Civilizations,* William Theodore de Bary, ed. New York: Columbia University Press.

Bhacu, Parminder. 1985. *Twice Migrants: East African Sikh Settlers in Britain.* London: Tavistock.

Biale, David. 1985. "The Messianic Connection: Zionism, Politics, and Settlement in Israel." *The Center Magazine* 18, 5:35–45.

Goldberg, Giora, and Efraim Ben-Zadok. 1986. "Gush Emunim in the West Bank." *Middle Eastern Studies* 22, 1:52–73.

Gupte, Pranay. 1985. *Vengeance: India after the Assassination of Indira Gandhi.* New York: Norton.

Heim, S. Mark. 1986. "Religious Extremism and Hindu Ecumenism." *Christian Century* 103:1177–81.

Hodgson, Marshall. 1974. *The Venture of Islam.* Chicago: University of Chicago Press.

Hunter, James Davison. 1987. *Evangelicalism: The Coming Generation.* Chicago: University of Chicago Press.

Jeffrey, Robin. 1986. *What's Happening to India? Punjab, Ethnic Conflict, Mrs. Gandhi's Death and the Test for Federalism.* London: Macmillan.

————. 1987. "Grappling with History: Sikh Politicians and the Past." *Pacific Affairs* 60, 1:59–72.

Kapur, Rajiv A. 1986. *Sikh Separatism: The Politics of Faith.* London: Allen and Unwin.

Litani, Yehuda. 1985. "The Fanatic Right in Israel: Linking Nationalism and Fundamentalist Religion." *Dissent*, Summer:315–19.

Lustick, Ian S. 1987. "Israel's Dangerous Fundamentalists." *Foreign Policy*, Fall 1987:118–39.

Malik, Yogendra K. 1986. "The Akali Party and Sikh Militancy: Move for Greater Autonomy or Secessionism in Punjab?" *Asian Survey* 26, 3:345–62.

Malkani, K. R. 1980. *The RSS Story.* New Delhi: Impex India.

Mishra, Dina Nath. 1980. *RSS: Myth and Reality.* Sahibabad, India: Vikas.

Newman, David. 1982. *Jewish Settlement in the West Bank: The Role of Gush Emunim.* Durham: Center for Middle Eastern and Islamic Studies, University of Durham.

————. 1985a. *The Impact of Gush Emunim: Politics and Settlement in the West Bank*, David Newman, ed. London: Croom Helm.

————. 1985b. "The Evolution of a Political Landscape: Geographical and Territorial Implications of Jewish Colonization in the West Bank." *Middle Eastern Studies* 21, 2:192–205.

Puri, Geeta. 1980. *Bharatiya Jana Sangh: Organisation and Ideology.* New Delhi: Sterling.

Saiedi, Nader. 1985. "What is Islamic Fundamentalism?" Unpublished manuscript, University of California, Los Angeles.

Schiff, Ze'ev. 1985. "The Spectre of Civil War in Israel." *The Middle East Journal* 39, 2:230–45.

Seliktar, Ofira. 1983. "The New Zionism." *Foreign Policy* 51:118–38.

Smith, Wilfred Cantwell. 1957. *Islam in Modern History.* Princeton: Princeton University Press.

Tuveson, Ernest Lee. 1968. *Redeemer Nation.* Chicago: University of Chicago Press.

Voll, John. 1982. *Islam: Continuity and Change in the Modern World.* Boulder: Westview Press.

Wallace, Paul. 1986. "The Sikhs as a 'Minority' in a Sikh Majority State in India." *Asian Survey* 26, 3:363–77.

Weiner, Myron, ed. 1968. *State Politics in India.* Princeton: Princeton University Press.

Chapter 3

Contemporary Fundamentalism: Judaism, Christianity, Islam

Hava Lazarus-Yafeh

It has become fashionable to talk about fundamentalist movements, attitudes, or leadership. Nevertheless, there exists no reasonably accurate definition of the term (it is mainly used as a synonym for fanatics or extremists), and few people seem to be aware of the fact that common denominators exist between very remote and different fundamentalist phenomena, such as revolutionary Iran, the Muslim Brethren in Egypt and Syria, the more extreme groups which split off from them, especially in Egypt, Evangelist preachers in both the United States and England, and the Jewish Ultra-Orthodox or messianic groups in Israel. Yet, although it may seem at first sight farfetched, all these and similar phenomena share many common traits and all seem to express a universal reaction to the modern Western world. In this chapter, ten common characteristics of all fundamentalist movements will be described, following an attempt to outline in a very general way some of the causes which brought about the rise of the contemporary fundamentalist phenomenon.

The Oxford Dictionary defines fundamentalism as "going back to the sources and accepting their literal inerrancy, thus reaffirming, in a radically changed environment, traditional modes of behavior and understanding." *The Oxford Dictionary of Christianity* adds the historical dimension: "A movement in various Protestant bodies which developed after the War of 1914–1918, especially in the United States. It rigidly upheld what it believed to be traditional orthodox Christian doctrines and especially the literal inerrancy of Scripture."[1]

Here we confront already one of the basic problems connected with the study of contemporary fundamentalism.[2]   Almost all studies of fundamentalist phenomena have so far been conducted within one tradition only—and suggest totally contradictory explanations of their origin and nature. Is it indeed a predominantly Protestant manifestation, as the dictionaries will have it—inconceivable in either Judaism or Islam, where the ever-developing sacred Oral Tradition seems to operate as some sort of safety valve against it? Or is it to be considered, to the contrary, a specific contemporary Islamic reaction to modernity, precisely because Islam never had the historical experience of reformation and Protestantism—as some students of Islam explain it?[3]

There can be little doubt of the fact that fundamentalism today is a worldwide phenomenon, on the fringes of all three monotheistic religions (including the Catholic church) and perhaps in nonmonotheistic religions as well. It seems to be a global wave of negative reaction to modernity and Western values, brought about by a variety of factors of varying importance in the different contexts of each one of these religions.

Some scholars contend that "extremism is the religious norm," explaining extremism (in Judaism) as "the desire to expand the scope, detail and strictness of religious law; social isolation and the rejection of the surrounding culture."[4] According to those, this orientation is usually moderated "when objectified in persons and institutions." Therefore, moderation is associated with religious prestige and strong religious commitments. Only the "decline of the religious community (and we may add, of traditional leadership) permits the breakthrough of extremist tendencies" and is "facilitated by the decline of the secular culture" with which the religious moderates are associated.

This may well fit in with the theory about the general decline of all modern ideologies such as liberalism, socialism, communism, even fascism—all of which seem to have disappointed people all over the world and generated global waves of frustration usually oriented against modernity and Western values in general. Although life has become much more comfortable almost everywhere, man has become more alienated in the modern world and his new problems more unsolvable than ever before.

This goes together with the collapse of the (wider) family, and with intensive urbanization (e.g., Cairo) and rapid secularization (Iran), and many other more specific factors in each civilization, which cannot even be alluded to here. More than a generation ago, Eric Hoffer said: "All the advantages brought by the West are ineffectual substitutes for the sheltering and soothing anonymity of communal existence."[5] In fact, Hoffer and others have already laid bare very clearly some of the deeper psychological inclinations in man which make for his zeal to be stripped of his "individual identity and distinctness"—to achieve "complete assimilation into the collective body." According to him, "faith in a holy cause is to a considerable extent a substitute for the lost faith in ourselves." In "exchanging a 'self-centered' for a 'selfless' life, we gain enormously in self-esteem" and, therefore, the discontented and frustrated would rather be part of a larger movement dedicated fanatically to a cause than shoulder their own personal freedom and responsibility. This seems to be true today for the religious fanatic movements, as it was true, two and three generations ago, for Marxism and fascism.

That the younger generation in general today consists of an especially large number of discontented persons seems to be also true, although it can hardly be proved. It may be because, as Hoffer and others suggest, "discontent is likely to be highest when misery is bearable," but also as a result of the democratization of education everywhere. The doors of many educational institutions (yeshivas [Talmudic colleges], universities, etc.) have been opened everywhere for many who—for sociological and other reasons—are incapable of making the right use of them and either fail and drop out or never get their high career expectations fulfilled in later life. Yet their new education makes them more aware of the discrepancies, and frequently arouses feelings of persecution and frustration. Seldom do educational or other authorities pay attention to these people and their distress, many of whom choose to find consolation in "going back to the sources," or the "roots," and look for the "good old times," thus becoming easy prey for the fanatic movements.

Be that as it may—and much research has still to be done to either confirm or disprove the truth of such general impressions—there can be little doubt that the leaders and members of most fundamentalist movements in contemporary Judaism, Christianity, and Islam have been affected by some of the above-mentioned factors and have reacted to them in the last generation in much the same ways. In fact, the similarities between contemporary fundamentalist phenomena in completely different societies are astonishing, and show in attitudes, terminology, religious values, and action. It seems as if modernity, instead of bringing about, as many scholars once believed, a greater resemblance between all societies, has generated only similar negative reactions in the so-called "global village" against itself, and the "going back to the sources" may be the answer to a deep human need for particularism and uniqueness in each civilization.

In this context, a further question may arise: is this contemporary rejection of modernity a new historical phenomenon, unique to modern times (perhaps designating one of the main characteristics of the post-modern era)—or is it part of a historical pattern, which will recur under certain conditions? Some scholars opt for the historical pattern and compare, for example, the medieval controversy about Maimonides' writings to present-day discussions between "rationalist" and "anti-rationalist" religious trends. To others, the contemporary scene seems unique, just as modernity itself is a unique phenomenon, although one may, of course, always draw historical parallels with earlier events. But even when taking into account only some of the technical aspects of modernity, one must necessarily admit to the uniqueness of its rejection by the fundamentalists. The fact that theological and political discussions are no longer restricted, as before, to the esoteric groups of the "learned" but have become, mainly through print and the electronic media, well known to the masses and are widely discussed in ever-growing circles, certainly deeply influences popular anti-rationalist and often "primitive" religious stands of fundamentalist movements everywhere. Their rejection of modern concepts such as the national state or the idea of democracy and democratic systems is, of course, a much more meaningful example of the uniqueness of contemporary fundamentalist phenomena.[6]

Let us now turn to enumerate briefly some features common to most contemporary fundamentalist groups in all three monotheistic religions.

A. Most of these groups constitute a counter-society, which demands intense group loyalty, and usually define themselves apart and in contrast to the surrounding "modern" or "Western" society. They are the "true" believers who cling to the "authentic" tradition, whereas the world outside, especially members of institutionalized religion, are only "nominal" believers who have either to be "reconverted" like the secularists, or are to be totally abandoned. The term "paganism" (*djahiliyya* in Arabic) abounds in all fundamentalist writings, and they all draw the same conclusion—to withdraw completely from "Westernized" society (at least spiritually, but sometimes also in practice)[7] as did some Egyptian fundamentalist groups[8] or the Jewish Ultra-Orthodox in contemporary Jerusalem. In general, "true" believers are not supposed to pray in the house of worship of their "pagan" surroundings, and for some (Jewish and Muslim) groups, it is also preferable that they be recognized by a distinctive dress.

B. This withdrawal from society includes the rejection of all "Western" ideologies and, in the case of most Jewish and Muslim groups, also the rejection of the national state and the democratic system. Modernity is seen as the great evil, born by the secular tradition and upheld by such "foreign" values as democracy. In these circles, explicit denunciations of "Western democracy" are voiced, sometimes combined with a call for the re-establishment of either the Davidic dynasty or the Islamic Caliphate. Members of some of these groups often refrain from serving in the armies of their respective countries: in Israel students of the Ultra-Orthodox yeshivas are officially exempted from military service; in Egypt the extremists refuse to take part in the "pagan state's army" and fight its wars—even against Israel. They refuse to see the war dead as "martyrs" (*shuhada*) as is customary, and declare that their war against the pagan regime of their own country is the only legitimate one and has first priority—at least for the time being. Perhaps the pacifism of some Christian fundamentalists falls into the same category. On the other hand, some millenarian Christian and messianic Jewish fundamentalists tend to overstress the religious importance of serving in the army and fighting for their cause.

Most of these groups (again, mainly Jewish and Muslim ones, because of the obvious halakhic and political character of their respective religions) have discarded former apologetic tendencies to harmonize their religious traditions with the democratic system. They call for the establishment of a Jewish or Muslim state, in which religious law will prevail (also see paragraph H). In Egypt the demand for such a national state "with the Quran as its constitution" (in itself a unique and contradictory combination of old and new concepts)[9] is being brought forward mainly by the fanatic Islamic movements and, very cautiously, also by some popular folk-preachers. The main controversy between the two lies in the means of achieving this state, whether through violence and revolution, or by long-term education. In Israel, even rabbinic officials and members of religious parties in the Knesset openly support the demand for such a halakhic state, though they denounce violence as a means to achieve it. Most of them declare openly, and sometimes give official corresponding instructions, that in any case of contradiction between the law of the State of Israel, in the name of which they officiate, and religious law—their allegiance goes to the latter![10]

C. Closely connected with this is the most virulent criticism by fundamentalists (including Christians) of institutionalized religion as a "harlot," "Satan," "apostate church," etc. In fact, the main thrust of the fundamentalist revolt is directed against the moderately compromising traditional religious leadership, which goes hand in hand with the corrupt political system. It is a striking fact that most of the leaders of fundamentalist movements in the world do *not* come from traditional religious circles, which they label traitors to the cause of religion, and have *no* traditional religious education. (This does not hold true for fundamentalist Shiite Islam in Iran where—as is well known—the revolution was led by traditional Ulama [religious authorities], perhaps because throughout the ages they had succeeded in keeping their social and economic independence from the state and could thus lead the mass resurgence against it.) Many contemporary fundamentalist leaders have some university education, especially in the sciences (such as doctors, engineers, agronomists, pharmacists),[11] a fact which may strengthen the suggestion made above about their partial absorption into the new system of education and their disappointment with it. (The fact that they have no education in the humanities, whether traditional or academic, may explain also their visceral, simplistic approach to problems of religion and belief.) In fact, some scholars discern a process of "Protestantization," especially in Islam, in the fact that the carriers of this new religious message do not come from the traditional Ulama.

D. Fundamentalist attitudes to the sciences, which have not been studied enough so far, seem to vary and are very ambiguous, in some respects even hypocritical. Fundamentalists do not resent modern arms and technology and use them freely, even while denouncing "Western" science in general (as if one could detach technology from the sciences!). It is well known, for example, that prior to the revolution, Khomeini's inciting speeches were widely distributed in Iran through tape cassettes. Islamic movements or Ultra-Orthodox groups in Israel use the same means, which are especially efficient among illiterate masses, such as in Egypt. The same holds true with regard to television, which is often regarded by fundamentalists as the "symbol" of the corruption of Western society. But while some groups totally refrain from using it, others try to spread their message through it and gain a foothold in as many programs as possible.

Some fundamentalists try to limit the use of "Western" medicine and doctors or subject them to the final decision of their religious leaders. But even of those, many (like the famous Pakistani leader al-

Mawdudi), when seriously ill, do a rapid turnabout and rush to seek help in the "Satanic" West.[12]

Evolution (versus "Creationism") is of course still the archenemy of all, challenged by fundamentalists through lawsuits and educational efforts around the world. It is a curious fact that the farfetched theory of the nineteenth-century English Puritan Gosse about the fixity of species as against Darwin's doctrine of natural selection was explicitly repeated recently by the Lubavitcher Rabbi in New York. It was also accepted, without naming Gosse and perhaps with no knowledge of him, by a well-known member of the Knesset in Israel, a university graduate, belonging to a so-called "moderate" religious party. According to this theory, there had been no gradual modification of the surface of the earth, nor any slow development of organic forms, but when the sudden act of creation took place, the world appeared instantly as a planet on which life had long existed, and in which God, as it were, had hidden the fossils in order to tempt mankind into unbelief.[13]

Biblical scholarship and the study of developments in religious thought and practice are of course repudiated by all fundamentalists, but, again, some make use of such studies when they support their own fundamentalist point of view. This has been demonstrated very convincingly by J. Barr with regard to conservative Evangelists in England, and it holds true for many other groups as well. According to Barr, "the strong hostility to modern theology and to the methods, results, and implications of modern critical study of the Bible" are one of the most pronounced characteristics of fundamentalists. Modern (Protestant) Bible criticism may be considered, according to Barr, one of the main reasons for the emergence of (Christian) fundamentalism.

This amalgamation of rejecting science in principle while using it to substantiate fundamentalist theories can perhaps best be illustrated through one of the recent legal responses (fatwa) issued by the popular Egyptian Sheikh al-Sharawi. When asked about angels and Djinn (unseen spirits who, according to the Quran, live in a separate world and sometimes interfere in ours for better or for worse), al-Sharawi unhesitatingly confirmed their corporeal reality—thereby contradicting several medieval and modernist Muslim authors. He added that one day we shall be able to see these creatures, when God permits us to invent some kind of "angelscope," parallel to the microscope, through which man can now actually see the microbes which had, of course, always been there.[14]

E. All fundamentalists share a strong, usually literal, belief in the inerrancy of their holy Scriptures. This belief has deep roots in medieval Islamic and early Protestant theology, but seems to be a more recent development in Jewish thought. The Bible is actually "reified" by fundamentalists as the infallible "Word of God," like the Quran, and as far as possible, literally explained. Later allegorical and other interpretations are almost completely discarded except when supporting the general fundamentalist approach or when inevitably needed to uphold the authority or the infallibility of the Bible itself. On the other hand, fundamentalists transform Scriptures into textbooks of contemporary history, predicting not only modern inventions and technology (in the usual apologetic way) but details of contemporary and future political events as well, turning them into eschatological details of the messianic era. Thus, for example, the establishment of the State of Israel and its wars with its neighbors (according to some also the imminent rebuilding of the Temple) are predicted by the Bible and the Quran, according to Jewish, Christian, and Muslim fundamentalists. For some (Christians, Jewish Ultra-Orthodox), these are pre-messianic tribulations; for others (Jewish mainly), already part of the messianic era itself; and for some (Muslims), though foretold in the Quran, the events have no eschatological meaning.[15]

In any case, the Bible or the Quran hold not only a central place as a source of inspiration in the religious life of the fundamentalist but become also practical textbooks for him to understand and predict contemporary and future events. Both Scriptures are designated by some fundamentalists to take the place of the constitution in the future halakhic Jewish or Shari Muslim state.

F. The strong emphasis put on the literalness of holy Scriptures as such generates a negative attitude towards the traditional interpretation of the Scriptures throughout the ages and towards the historical development of theology in general. In this respect Christian and Muslim fundamentalists are more extreme in their rejection of religious literature subsequent to the Scriptures, whereas in Jewish circles the mere revival of the study of parts of the Bible itself, as distinct from later "oral tradition," is noteworthy, and in some ways even seems to "Protestantize" contemporary Judaism. Another way to invalidate historical religious development taken by contemporary Jewish fundamentalists is to declare much of later halakhic writings (up to the sixteenth-century code of Jewish laws, the *Shulhan Arukh*) as "inspired," thus including them, as it were, in the infallible closed canon of holy

Scripture.   This, of course, shuts the gates before any historical approach to tradition.

G. All the foregoing necessarily brings about an extremely crude fundamentalist theology in all three religions, which rejects the vast and profound trove of medieval and modern religious thought cultivated throughout the ages. Divine reward and punishment, for example, are once more reduced to simple accountancy, and the fundamentalists usually feel that they are in a position to understand exactly the plans and deeds of God. (In England lightning struck a famous cathedral because of the too-liberal views of the Bishop; a tragic road accident happened to a busload of innocent schoolchildren in Israel because of a defect in the *mezuzah* parchment, and so on.) With this vulgarization of the concept of God, which has other aspects as well,[16] comes also a revival of the belief in Satan and spirits (see paragraph D) which according to some scholars usually accompanies the decline of civilization,[17] as well as a very "detailed" folk knowledge of Heaven and Hell or the Second Coming. On the other hand, many fundamentalists are also dedicated to the purging of their religion from all sorts of folk rituals (such as the worship of holy tombs in Islam) and thus oscillate between two contradictory poles. The enormous importance attached by fundamentalists to miracles, as proofs of the religious truth, in clear contrast to medieval Jewish, Christian, and Muslim thought, is also part of their simplistic theology. This usually includes the literal acceptance of scriptural miracles as well as the belief in contemporary miracles, which happen everywhere.

H. The general mood of contemporary fundamentalists—whether Jewish, Christian, or Muslim—is apocalyptic. They all expect radical changes in the near future. As Islam is, in general, less eschatologically minded than Judaism and Christianity,[18] the terminology of its radical groups is also less messianic than that of most Jewish and Christian groups. Yet, there can be little doubt that all fundamentalists yearn for the same "Kingdom of God" on earth, here and now, in clear terms of political power, not of eternal peace and spirituality. As mentioned in paragraph B, this is especially conspicuous with regard to Jewish and Muslim groups who seek to establish a state in which religious law will be enforced, according to the Torah or the Quran, and where transgression of the religious commandments such as prayer, fast, or dietary laws will be punished as criminal acts. (This is explicitly and repeatedly stated even by the more moderate "Muslim Brethren" in Egypt or by Rabbinate officials in Israel.)   Puritan standards will be imposed everywhere, especially in the realm of entertainment, the media, education, and the printed word—according to the religious law and to what fundamentalists are convinced is God's own wish. Some wait quietly for the realization of this vision by the coming Messiah, while others, especially Jewish and Muslim groups, undertake through violent and revolutionary means to carry out God's plan for mankind or, at least, to spur him into doing so Himself—through some dramatic and terrible act, as for example the destruction of the mosques on the Temple Mount.[19] Obviously, they are all led in this by unquestioned charismatic leaders, who understand best what is to be done, when, and where. In fact, belief in personal leadership as opposed to a pluralistic, democratic society, is characteristic of fundamentalism in general (see again paragraph B). There is only one version of truth, one leader, one book, one way—no doubt or self-criticism, no development or change.

It is a kind of historical irony that the rejection of Western values and modernity is expressed by most fundamentalists in typically modern, Western, political terms of a national and "constitutional" state, completely different, of course, from the Western democratic meaning of these terms.[20] Yet this terminology and the accompanying political demands are the norm nowadays among Muslim fundamentalists. In Judaism, usually only small, though very dangerous, messianic groups of activists advance them, while they seem to be almost nonexistent in Christian circles.

Various groups in all three religions advance the theory that "in the meantime" one has to stick to the group loyally, adhere to its ideals with fervor, and, in Judaism and Islam as two religions of law, observe the commandments yet more zealously than before. This, of course, widens the gap between them and the surrounding society, especially the so-called "religious" society or the older generation, who are considered by the younger to be weak in spirit and slack in keeping the commandments—even when Orthodox. Thus, while young militant Muslims do not pray in "pagan" state-controlled mosques in Egypt, as has been mentioned previously, young, even so-called "national-religious," Jews refrain from eating in officially kosher places, such as on board carriers of Israel's national airline, El Al, and prefer the *kashrut* endorsement of Ultra-Orthodox, anti-Zionist rabbis. Some even refrain from eating at their religious parents' homes, in spite of the painful insult involved.

I. It is, of course, especially important in this context to consider the general fundamentalist attitude towards women and members of other religions. Indeed, one should not be surprised by the fact that they all—with rare exceptions—share the same approach to both. Women are to be accorded high respect—if they accept their pre-emancipatory, natural state in family and society. Modern legal steps taken to ensure equality between men and women have to be revoked (and were, in fact, revoked by Khomeini in Iran) and complete separation of the sexes is advocated. In this respect, again, Western conservative Evangelists do not go as far as their Jewish and Muslim counterparts, but it seems to be no mere coincidence that no women are to be found among their higher ranks, and that they totally reject the idea of women clergy. The separation of the sexes recommended by Muslim and Jewish fundamentalists does not apply only to schools, colleges, and other institutions, but sometimes even borders on the ridiculous. Thus, for example, separate buses for women have been suggested and sporadically arranged by both Egyptian student fundamentalists, as well as by the Jewish Ultra-Orthodox in Jerusalem, while in Libya women are expected to sit in separate rows in cinemas! Polygamy is rediscovered as the true Islamic way,[21] in contrast to former Muslim modernist apologetics, for example, by the well-known Muhammad Abduh (d. 1905), who tried to prove that the Quran (Sura IV, v. 3) actually recommends monogamy.

J. Members of other religions are a source of deep concern to all fundamentalists who, as we have stated already, usually define themselves as a distinct group even against their own religious community. They reject their more moderate or liberal fellow believers as "nominal" believers only, or as "pagans," see the secularists as devoid of all values, and often consider members of other religions as the source of all evil or misfortunes that befell them. In the Middle East, where tension and strife between different religious communities are, unfortunately, rather common, fundamentalists—on every side—often inflame latent feelings of hatred and air them openly and violently.[22] But even in countries like Iran, where only very small numbers of non-Shiite Muslims reside, the same feelings of hatred show clearly, either with regard to the small communities of Iranian Bahais and Jews, or with regard to the entire wicked Christian and Jewish world. These feelings of contempt for the outsider nourish the fundamentalist's firm belief that he possesses the one existing, authentic truth. In the world of the fundamentalist, there is no place for other versions of truth or tolerance for a pluralistic society. He has to spread God's message to mankind, if necessary, even by force, and therefore each case of "conversion" to his camp, whether from the outside world or from his "pagan" fellow-believers, is always greeted by him with great joy and seems to be further proof of the authenticity of his truth. Often, the more universal the call is, the less tolerant its bearers seem to become. In Judaism and Islam, this goes together with a deliberate disregard by the fundamentalist for the clear evolvement of tolerance towards the outsider in both traditions over the centuries. Jewish fundamentalists consider Christians once more as idolaters and heathens, and reidentify present-day Palestinian Arabs with the Amalekites, who were already considered by Talmudic sages to be nonrecognizable in their times. Muslim fundamentalists forget about the rights of the "Protected People," Jews and Christians, and remember only that they have to be oppressed and despised. The rejection of Western humanistic values by both Jewish and Muslim fundamentalists makes them look for other, less human values in their own respective traditions and to extol them lavishly. This fits in well with their vision of a future religiously controlled, though not necessarily clerical, state.

Only ten characteristics have been surveyed here in order to point out the many common denominators between different fundamentalist phenomena. Of course, even in a general survey like this, the many differences emerge very clearly too, as do the varying combinations of similarity between fundamentalist attitudes in the three religions surveyed. Often Jewish and Muslim fundamentalists share some special trait (e.g., the hope for a halakhic or Shari-controlled state) which seems alien to Christian fundamentalists. Sometimes Jewish and Christian groups share a special attitude (such as millenarianism), while Christians and Muslims share others (such as their "reification" of the Bible and the Quran respectively to the exclusion of later tradition). Obviously, this is connected with the specific character of each civilization and its historical setting in past and present. Therefore, a thorough study is needed to elucidate all the points mentioned here, as well as many others, and their respective roles in each religion. Yet, the aim of this article was to stress the similarity between all, and perhaps to further a global look at fundamentalism, as well as to help define it better.

NOTES

This essay was first published in *The Jerusalem Quarterly* 47 (Summer 1988).

1. See more historical details there, and cf. J. Barr, *Fundamentalism*, 2d ed.

(London, 1984), 2. Barr deals also with parallel terms such as "Conservative Evangelists."

2. In 1986 I conducted, with the cooperation of several colleagues, a graduate seminar at the Faculty of Humanities of the Hebrew University, in which an attempt was made to address systematically the problematics of comparative research in this field. Representatives of various disciplines (such as general history, sociology, psychology, and the study of religion, especially contemporary Judaism, Christianity, and Islam), as well as guest speakers belonging to some fundamentalist movements in Israel, joined in this attempt. Though many questions were left unanswered, our understanding of the phenomenon itself seems to have made great progress, and I am very grateful to my colleagues and students for their comments on this article.

3. Cf. J. O. Voll, *Islam, Continuity and Change in the Modern World* (New York, 1982), Introduction. (Voll himself does not subscribe to this view.) See also, J. Barr, *Fundamentalism*, Foreword.

4. See Charles S. Liebman, "Extremism as a Religious Norm," *Journal for the Scientific Study of Religion* 20 (1983): 75ff.

5. Eric Hoffer, *The True Believer* (New York, 1951), 37 (see for the following quotations, 61, 14).

6. See, for example, E. Sivan, *Radical Islam, Medieval Theology and Modern Politics* (New Haven, 1985), chap. 2.

7. See E. Sivan, *Radical Islam*, and J. Barr, *Fundamentalism*, chap. 2.

8. See G. Kepel, *The Prophet and Pharaoh*, trans. from the French (London, 1985), especially chap. 3.

9. See my forthcoming "New Themes on the Agenda of Egyptian Islam—When and Where?" in *Egypt from Monarchy to Republic: Structural Continuity and Dynamics of Change*, ed. S. Shamir and I. Rabinowitz. Cf. also, E. Sivan, *Radical Islam*, chap. 2, and Hava Lazarus-Yafeh, "Political Traditions and Response in Islam," *Totalitarian Democracy and After* (Jerusalem, 1984), in memory of J. L. Talmon, The Israel Academy of Sciences.

10. See, for example, the interview with Rabbinic Judge Pardes in *Koteret Rashit* 151 (23 October 1985), or the explicit expressions of extreme religious members of the Knesset as quoted in the daily press.

11. See the tables in Kepel, *Prophet and Pharaoh*, 219–21 (and cf. Saad Eddin Ibrahim, "Anatomy of Egypt's Militant Groups," *IJMES* 12 [1980]: especially 439), and Uri M. Kupferschmidt, "Reformist and Militant Islam in Urban and Rural Egypt," *Middle East Studies* 23 (1987): 403–19; see also J. Barr, *Fundamentalism*, 19, 90ff. No study of the background of Jewish fundamentalist leadership seems to be available, but the general impression points in the same direction.

12. See V. S. Naipaul, *Among the Believers, An Islamic Journey* (Penguin, 1981), 158–59 (cf. also 80). Cf. also J. Barr, *Fundamentalism*, chap. 4, and E. Sivan, *Radical Islam*, chap. 6.

13. Cf. E. Gosse, *Father and Son* (London, 1907), chap. 5. On this topic in general (as a discussion on the limitations of modern science) cf. now "Creationism versus Evolution: Radical Perspectives on the Confrontation of Spirit and Science," *Tikkun* (A Bimonthly Jewish Critique of Politics, Culture and Society) (November–December 1987).

14. See my article on al-Sharawi in G. Warburg and U. Kupferschmidt, *Islam, Nationalism and Radicalism in Egypt and the Sudan* (New York, 1983), 281–97, especially 286–88.

15. Cf., for example, H. Lindsey, *The Late Great Planet Earth* (Lakeland, 1979), or the Moroccan author, Ahmad al-Ghumari al-Hasani's book (Arabic) about the correspondence between the Quran and Hadith sayings and modern inventions (*Mutabaqat al-Ikhtiraat al-Asriyya lima Akhbara bihi Sayyid al-Bariyya*, 3d printing [Cairo, 1963]). In Jewish circles, this is expressed in many books and pamphlets which see contemporary events as an exact parallel to Joshua's conquest of Canaan and draw messianic conclusions from this.

16. See Warburg and Kupferschmidt, *Islam, Nationalism and Radicalism*, 228.

17. Cf. A. Abel, "La Place des sciences occultes dans la décadence," in *Classicisme et déclin culturel dans l'histoire de l'Islam*, ed. R. Brunschvig and G. E. von Grunebaum (Paris, 1957), 291, Actes du Symposium International d'Histoire de la Civilization Musulmane.

18. See my book, *Some Religious Aspects of Islam* (Leiden, 1981), chap. 4.

19. See, for example, Hagai Segal, *Dear Brethren* (Hebrew) (Jerusalem, 1987).

20. See n. 9.

21. Cf., for example, al-Sharawi's book, *The Muslim Woman and the Way to God* (Cairo, 1979), and see the article mentioned in n. 14, 293. Cf. also, Saad Eddin Ibrahim, "Anatomy of Egypt's Militant Groups," *IJMES* 12 (1980), especially 428, 431.

22. On Muslim fundamentalists' attitudes towards the Copts, see, for example, Kepel, *Prophet and Pharaoh*, chap. 6, especially 156ff.

Chapter 4

Contesting Rhetorics in the PTL Scandal

Susan Harding

The story of modernity in America—or rather the version of the story that equates modernity with secularity—emerged out of late nineteenth- and early twentieth-century debates over the validity of Biblical literalism and the public worthiness of its defenders, orthodox Protestants who came ultimately to be known as "fundamentalists." The contests—which were scattered across the country in universities, public schools, seminaries, denominations, legislatures, courts, elections, the press, and local and national literatures—had unstable and contradictory outcomes. But, according to virtually every narrative (insider as well as outsider) of the struggle, after the Scopes trial in 1925, which upheld the Tennessee law prohibiting the teaching of evolution in the schools, fundamentalists "separated out." That is, they accepted their designation as unfit for "modernity" and for "modern" political discourse, which henceforth were understood to be intrinsically secular and off-limits to Biblical literalists. The definition of orthodox Protestants as "pre-modern" and their exclusion from public life were thus founding acts of this, the secularizing, version of the modernity narrative, providing both its essential binary opposition (fundamentalist and modern) and its telos (the march of modernity toward ever more secularity).

Over the next fifty years, orthodox Protestants, and even those who proudly proclaimed themselves militant anti-modernist fundamentalists, did not entirely vacate public life, but the modernity narrative that would so exclude them held together as a story, as grounds for their incomplete political and cultural segregation, and as a source of modern subjectivity. After the mid-1970s, orthodox Protestants, in particular outspoken Biblical literalists, began to break separatist taboos and with escalating success deployed their interpretive practices to an ever-expanding range of worldly targets. In 1979, fundamentalists broke the ultimate barrier and plunged en masse into the national political arena, most strikingly through the organization of the Moral Majority under the Reverend Jerry Falwell. Over the next decade, Falwell and other major televangelical preachers fashioned their fundamentalist, conservative charismatic, and evangelical followings into a national born-again constituency that left in its wake what has come to be known as "the Christian perspective on moral issues." In this context, the discursive events of the last decade constitute a rupture in the history of fundamentalism as it was constructed by the modernity narrative. Let us call it "the revolt of the excluded fundamentalist other."

The fact that fundamentalists continued to exist in the late twentieth century was something of an anomaly within the modernity paradigm, but their sudden rise to public prominence was shocking from the "modern" point of view. They not only proliferated aggressive counter-discourses—anti-worldly polemics, story genres, and public rituals attacking and subverting secular liberal discourses—but also launched a more literal "de-separation" (desegregation) process, as militant Bible believers began to colonize middle and upper echelons of mainstream political, economic, social, and cultural institutions. The events of the 1980s were utterly unexpected and unintelligible in terms of the story of modernity, and indeed, I think, must be understood, in part, as a protest against and dramatic disruption of that story. In word and deed, fundamentalists contested the elemental narrative frames of modernity, at least temporarily dislocating the boundary between fundamentalist and modern, destabilizing both subject positions, and desecularizing the public arena.

This essay discusses what at the time appeared to be the concluding episode of the revolt: the born-again telescandals of 1987 and 1988, a long year of media events launched in March of 1987 by Oral Roberts' plea for $8 million lest God take him home; taking off with the exfoliating revelations of the misdeeds of Jim and Tammy Faye Bakker and their skirmishes with Jerry Falwell; and, finally, after a lull, coming to a dramatic conclusion with Jimmy Swaggart's fall from grace.

At first blush, the scandals seem to be the "modern" dream come true: pompous, misplaced preachers brought down by their own greed, lust, and hypocrisy, a moment of predictably grotesque narrative closure on a pesky little chapter in the unfolding subtext of modernity marching on. I would like to bracket this reading of the scandals by shifting the focus from the preachers' misdeeds to the representation of those misdeeds on TV and in the newspapers, a shift which brings into view the scandalized as well as the scandalizers and suggests that the scandals (or rather the telescandals) were a continuation of the 1980s revolt against the modernity narrative rather than a confirmation of it.

Indeed, the telescandals were the moment in which the revolt reached its most fevered pitch, fragmenting the illusion of the fundamentalist whole, accentuating the similarities between fundamentalist and modern, and stripping away modernity's storied ploys, the ones that would hide it as a story and present it instead as history, as objective reportage, as "what's *really* going on." The outcome of these representational movements was more like a spectacle than a story—a narrative-free zone in which history, fiction, and the Bible were equivalent sources of narrative figures and frames, and the boundaries between religious and secular, fictional and factual, authors and characters, participants and observers were called into question, interrogated, criss-crossed, suspended, relocated, and multiplied. In other words, I am suggesting there was something distinctly postmodern about the telescandals and, more generally, about the eruption of these ostensibly pre-modern others onto the public stage.

Let me briefly illustrate what I mean: Ted Koppel represented the voice of modernity for millions of Americans throughout the born-again telescandals, which yielded sixteen blockbuster "Nightline" programs. In May of 1988, he aired an hour-long prime-time special report intended to settle once and for all, as he put it, "what this has got to do with." None of the scandalizers (Roberts, the Bakkers, or Swaggart) was present, nor were the scandalous events reviewed in any descriptive way. This particular episode in the telescandals was for exegesis, commentary, and midrash by and for the scandalized.

The title of the show, "The Billion Dollar Pie," its opening collage of talking heads, and Koppel's initial sally of remarks all had the same vector: to "unmask" televangelism, to reveal its real and vulgar business nature, rendering not just the scandalizers but all its preachers false prophets, worthy only of satire and shunning. In fact, what Koppel produced was a bald caricature of social scientific explanation, one that undermined his own ostensible detachment, that inspired a cascade of mixed metaphors, wild intertextualities, and backtalk from his guests, and began to erase the very distinction between him and "them" which he had to establish in order to have any authority at all.

In the following clip from the opening collage, Ted Koppel laid out the show's thesis while images flashed across the screen—proliferating TV ministries, a pie with money-colored filling, the birthrate declining across the century. Then religious market analyst Jack Sims vividly narrated another version of the thesis, punctuated midway by a checkerboard of talking heads from the PTL telescandal:

> **KOPPEL** *[voice-over]*: In all, there are 1,600 television ministers. Sixteen hundred. And of the $1.5 billion grossed annually by television ministries, just three of them—Pat Robertson's, Jimmy Swaggart's and Jim Bakker's—took in close to $500 million. It's a big pie, but the slices are anything but evenly divided. And because the birthrate in this country dipped sharply in the 1930s, there are fewer people in their 50s replacing those among the big givers who are dying off. The donor base is shrinking. And for televangelism, rocked by scandals, it couldn't have come at a worse time.
>
> **JACK SIMS**: Last March, it was as if the aging evangelicals were like dinosaurs that walked onto an iceberg. The end of March, when Oral announced that he was being kidnapped by God and held for ransom, the iceberg broke off and began to float south. Atop the iceberg, the aging evangelical dinosaurs began to fight.
>
> **MAN** [John Ankerberg]: The Reverend Bakker has been involved in episodes with prostitutes, and he has also been involved in homosexual incidents.
>
> **REV. JIM BAKKER, Televangelist**: If anyone has these charges against me, I want them to come forward publicly with this proof.
>
> **REV. JIMMY SWAGGART, Televangelist**: I don't appreciate preachers that get mixed up in adultery and every other type of sin that one can imagine, and them blaming Jimmy Swaggart for it.
>
> **MAN** [Bakker's lawyer, Norman Gruttman]: There is smellier laundry in his hamper than the laundry that he thought was in Reverend Bakker's.
>
> **REV. BAKKER**: There was a plot to hostilely take over the PTL by Jimmy Swaggart.
>
> **REV. JERRY FALWELL, Televangelist**: If he decides he wants to come back, he'll preside over a funeral. The funeral of his ministry.
>
> **MRS. BAKKER**: I wake up every morning wishing that they had killed me.
>
> **REV. FALWELL**: Their own clandestine behavior brought this terrible thing upon them.

> **MR. SIMS**:   But the real story of American religion is not the
> dinosaurs, it's the iceberg. It's floating south and melting, and all the
> aging evangelical electronic dinosaurs are going to die.

Jack Sims, himself a queer crossbreed—"religious market analyst"—
mixed up Darwin, Disney, and the Book of Revelation in his tale of
electronic evangelical dinosaurs in a way that foreshadowed the hybrid
scene setting and boundary blurring that ensued. Koppel greeted his
TV audience from a huge, plush, packed Memphis church and introduced his guest preachers: Jack Wimber, Jerry Falwell, E. V. Hill,
James Kennedy, Jack Hayford, James Robison, and, via satellite, on a
TV screen, Robert Schuller. Everyone (Koppel, the celebrity preachers,
the satin-robed choir, and the brimming congregation) seemed at home
in this pastiche of the religious and the secular, news and entertainment, postmodern electronics and a pre-modern God, but it was hardly
a propitious setting for a "serious discussion" of the complex conditions
that brought about the televangelical scandals. Koppel, leaving poor
Jack Sims out in the cold, abruptly shifted metaphoric gear and called
his guests "hogs at the trough" in his opening punch. Within minutes
he was caught in a quagmire of pious back talk—Falwell essentially
retorted to Koppel, "so are you." Then Hill and Hayford mystified all
by wrestling over the sinfulness of sex.

> **KOPPEL** *[on camera]*:   I must tell you that over the past couple of
> years, as many of you know, we have done a great many programs on
> Nightline on some of these problems that televangelists have been
> having, particularly the Bakkers and Jimmy Swaggart. You know
> what the sources of our information are? Not private detectives, not
> our own great reportorial skills. Other preachers. You got it. Other
> preachers. I conclude from that that what's going on here is a battle
> royale in the business world. This has got nothing to do with saving
> souls. This has got nothing to do with evangelical Christianity. What
> this has got to do with is a huge billion-dollar pie. *[Applause.]* Or to
> put it in a somewhat different sense, we've got a bunch of hogs at the
> trough here. And they see that one way of elbowing the other hog
> away from the trough is this business of sexual infidelity.
> **REV. FALWELL**:   That's true. And of course that's going on today,
> as you well know in the journalism world, the business world, and
> every vocation under heaven, which in no way vindicates or justifies
> this happening in the religious world.
> **REV. E. V. HILL, Mount Zion Baptist Church**:   This is reducing sin
> to sex. And so when you say I've sinned, everybody wants to know
> who'd you have? But I submit that there are—and you're dealing
> with it—I submit that there are some sins here in Proverbs 6:16. The

last one closes out with, "He that soweth discord among the brother-
hood." And here are the sins that God hates the most, so he wrote,
and sex ain't in it. *[Applause, laughter.]* Sex ain't in it.
KOPPEL: See, you're, you're missing—
REV. HILL: Wait a minute, let me just say it.
KOPPEL: Reverend Hill—
REV. HILL: ". . . a lying tongue—
KOPPEL: —time. Time. Just one second—
REV. HILL: —"a lying tongue—
KOPPEL *[motions "time-out" with hands]*: —hold it, hold it.
REV. HILL: —innocent blood, *[applause, laughter]* wicked imagina-
tion, running into mischief, and sowing discord. He hates these the
most, and sex ain't on the list. And we have towns and churches torn
apart because of lying lips and sowing discord, as you said, among the
ministry.
KOPPEL: Yeah. Now, what I—
REV. JACK HAYFORD, Church on the Way: I don't doubt the
validity of that list, that's scriptural, but I would recall to you, dear
brother, there's another list I read somewhere of 10, and sex is on it.
KOPPEL: What I'm trying to get at here is money. We're not just
talking about sins. We're talking about people who are competing for
millions and tens of millions of dollars. *[Applause.]*

And so the show went on, the metaphors slipping and sliding; the
preachers resisting and disrupting Koppel's withering storyline as they
drew from a spellbinding panoply of theological voices crafted through
the ages to thwart each other and to astound and stupefy unbelievers.
The show dissolved first into a mishmash of arguments among the
preachers over fine points of Scripture, doctrine, and ecclesiology, and
then into a kind of staged populist inquisition as members of the
audience stood and leveled "Biblically-based" charges against the TV
preachers, who in turn spoke back in a splendid jumble of artfully
humble voices.

Koppel never lost his composure, but he certainly lost control of the
discussion as well as his privileged position as the man who would
unmask these bandits once and for all. Surely, "TV production values"
interrupted Koppel's effort to "get a grip on the reality" behind the
scandals—that is, he himself, Mr. Modern Secularity, was torn between
story and spectacle. But the spectacularizing forces destablizing the
modernity metanarrative—on Koppel's show, in the telescandals, and
throughout the recent decade of born-again rhetorical eruptions—were
much bigger than TV. I will shortly explore some of those forces at
work specifically in the PTL telescandals—but first I would like to

contextualize them, in my own way talking back to the illusion of the fundamentalist whole and the image of the televangelical empires as pre-modern anachronisms destined for extinction. They will emerge instead as often quarrelsome, always proliferating discursive vanguards, first, of a hitherto hidden born-again world which has become a kind of frontier zone in which pre-modern, modern, and even postmodern cultural forms are intermingling and reproducing wildly, and, second, of a born-again diaspora, a movement into the unborn-again world that would blur so many of the boundaries between the two worlds that it might seem only a miracle—or a lot of money—could resurrect the myth of modernity.

Lifting Modernity's Veil

According to a 1982 Gallup poll, 35 percent of adult Americans said they were "born-again" (that is, had experienced a turning point in their lives when they committed themselves to Jesus Christ), and 37 percent held a "literal view of the Bible" (that is, considered the Bible to be the actual Word of God and that it is to be taken literally, word for word). By either criterion there are some 50 million adult Americans whom we might call "orthodox Christians."[1]   The majority are affiliated with historic evangelical denominations, Black denominations, and mainline Protestant denominations.   In recent decades the social and economic profile of orthodox Christians as a whole has increasingly approximated that of other Americans. They continue to be more concentrated in the South than in other parts of the country and more conservative politically and morally—however, they are not nearly as homogenous in this latter regard as is imagined by most outsiders.[2]

A minority of orthodox Christians—perhaps 10–15 million adults—are affiliated with pentecostal and (self-described) fundamentalist denominations and pastoral networks, and it is they who come to mind when "fundamentalism" is used in the sense of "not modern." It is they who characterize the face of orthodox Christians for most outsiders. As a whole, they do tend to be somewhat poorer and less educated—as well as still more Southern (and Southwestern) and conservative than other Americans—but it is the better-off and more educated among them who have been most politically visible and vocal in recent years, as we shall see shortly.

Fundamentalist and pentecostal groups emerged more or less independently out of late nineteenth- and twentieth-century Bible conferences and revivals, and both movements engendered new forms in the 1940s and 1950s. Billy Graham and his non-militant fundamentalist allies, relabelling themselves "evangelicals" in the late 1940s, consciously sought to engage in what they called "American culture" as they joined more mainline denominations, built substantial churches, sophisticated media ministries, well-credentialed colleges and seminaries, and a certain rather dignified political presence, most strikingly in Billy Graham's Presidential friendships. Meanwhile, Oral Roberts and his pentecostal brethren were elaborating their own novel forms. One morning in 1947 (to paraphrase Roberts), God led Oral to a passage in the Bible (III John 2) that revealed to him that God wanted his people to prosper and be healthy in this life, that "God is a good God," not a God of suffering and toil and sacrifice, but a God of well-being, comfort, and rewards in this life. So began "health and wealth theology" among pentecostals, which became the touchstone of their emerging faith enterprises and one of the wedges that opened up the "charismatic movement"—the spread of pentecostal ideas and practices into the mainline denominations during the 1960s and 1970s.

Both Graham and Roberts were pioneers in the use of TV for evangelism and faith healing, and most of the current electronic churches also had their origins in the 1940s and 1950s in relatively modest local churches and ministries. By the 1970s, hundreds of entrepreneurial pastors had parlayed their local operations into literal corporations, extending their reach far beyond church walls via radio, TV, music, and publishing operations. Until the PTL crisis, the dozen biggest electronic empires (all located in the South and California) took in over a billion dollars a year, employed over 1,000 men and women each, and paid out many millions of dollars in payroll every month. They hired ad agencies, market consultants, and corporate lawyers, and their bosses justified their six-figure salaries by saying they were paid no more than the CEOs of other major corporations.

The TV empires, then, are as much businesses as they are churches —indeed the electronic churches are anomalous, mercurial, protean creatures, at once religious, economic, and political. Far from being pre-modern relics, atavisms of an earlier age, the televangelists are a late capitalist cross-breed intertwining symbolic production, consumption, and social reproduction. They are harbingers of an emerging political economic order in which the stakes are as much collective identities, cultural ideas, and symbols as they are profits, markets, political power, and lost souls.

Most of the second generation of TV preachers are charismatics or pentecostals, and many of them, most notably Pat Robertson and Jimmy Swaggart, also mix in selected fundamentalist forms of faith, revival, and activism in the world. Jerry Falwell and Jim Bakker, on the other hand, kept the fundamentalist and pentecostal forms separate and, more than any of the TV preachers, exaggerated their distinguishing features—Falwell is Mr. Modern Fundamentalism, and Bakker is Mr. Postmodern Pentecostalism.[3]

Jerry Falwell's Empire

Jerry Falwell's world in Lynchburg, Virginia, is a very serious, solid, industrious kind of place. The language, architecture, ceremonies, and rites of daily life of Thomas Road Baptist Church communicate its singular commitment to "reach out to a world of lost and dying men and to win their souls to Christ." From the beginning, what distinguished Falwell from his fellow fundamentalists was his superhuman entrepreneurial zeal. Falwell, who comes from a family of small businessmen, got into the business of producing Christians on a whale of a scale. In 1971, Elmer Towns, Falwell's top theologian and "church-growth scientist," paraphrased Falwell's strategy in this way:

> Falwell pointed out that big shopping centers, big corporations, and big business have provided jobs and prosperity for our nation. . . . Business is usually on the cutting edge of innovation and change because of its quest for finances. . . . Therefore the church would be wise to look at business for a prediction of future innovation. The greatest innovation in the last 20 years is the development of the giant shopping centers. . . . A combination of services . . . two large companies with small supporting stores has been the secret of the success of shopping centers. The Thomas Road Baptist Church believes that the combined ministries of several agencies in one church can not only attract the masses to the gospel, but can better minister to each individual who comes.[4]

During the 1960s and 1970s, Thomas Road added one ministry after another—Falwell's church grew and grew. He built a 5,000-seat sanctuary, a school, college, and university. He turned his regional media ministry into a national enterprise with a following in the multimillions, and gradually, beginning in 1976, he came to distinguish himself as the leader of the movement organized by born-again TV empires and churches that plunged their constituents into the national political arena during the 1980 Presidential campaign and carried out what I have called the revolt of the fundamentalist other.

Like everything else, Jerry Falwell took TV literally. He used it to broadcast his church services exactly as they were performed. Later, he upscaled the services somewhat with light pop gospel tunes and select Christian celebrity singers, but he never really formatted his shows for TV, he never used TV to generate its own realities. Likewise, although his message opened up to more "current events" and "moral issues," it never strayed too far from its fundamentalist gospel core. Above all, Falwell used TV to spread the Word, the linear story of Christ's death, burial and resurrection, which offered irreversible transformation to all who would accept it. Ignoring TV's built-in preference for visually dramatic performance, Falwell seemed to be all story and no spectacle.

Through it all, Jerry Falwell and his fundamentalist allies were engaged in the business of making a distinct Christian, conservative, middle-class counter-culture and using higher education, the national news, and national politics to chip away at the cultural hegemony of its opposite number, the alleged secular, liberal middle class. This was very serious business. Jerry Falwell, his empire, and his allies stand for production, hard work, restraint, sacrifice, delayed gratification, steady growth, contained crises, hierarchy, male dominance, sexual repression, obedience to Godly others, the Word, narrative structure and authority, fixed identity, place, authenticity, depth, and centeredness.

Jim and Tammy Faye Bakker's Empire

Meanwhile, another entrepreneurial movement was emerging in pentecostal Christendom during the 1950s, 1960s, and 1970s, one that turned all those serious fundamental terms upside down. This movement, drawing from somewhat lower-class factions than Falwell's movement, reached its apogee in Jim and Tammy Faye Bakker's Heritage USA, a kind of postmodern pentecostal mecca. Their "inspirational theme park" conspicuously celebrated consumption, play, excess, indulgence, immediate gratification, wild swings of growth and crisis, anti-hierarchy, feminization, polymorphous sexuality, the godly powers of ordinary men and women, visual images, spectacle and narrative fragmentation, disposable identities, movement, artifice, surfaces, and decenteredness.

The cultural and theological reversals at Heritage USA were not accidental. The significant "cultural other" against which prosperity pentecostals fashioned their discourse and practice was not "the world" defined by the liberal, secular middle class, but the world defined by fundamentalism. The early healing evangelists of the 1940s and 1950s had themselves worked against the grain of the more fundamental voices of pentecostal church pastors, but in the late 1970s, Jim and Tammy Faye Bakker set out to build a little world in the image of their version of the "positive gospel." Jim Bakker liked to compare his kingdom to the camp meetings of his youth, and the $100 book promoting Heritage USA describes its origins in this way:

> During boyhood summers in Michigan, Jim Bakker attended camp meetings where he had his most moving spiritual experiences in an old tabernacle with a sawdust floor. Even then, looking beyond the stuffy cabins with lumpy mattresses, looking beyond the muddy swimming holes and "outdoor plumbing" he dreamed of a day when God's people could come together in beautiful, pleasant surroundings. Aware that lifestyle was changing in 20th Century America, Jim knew that drab, outmoded campgrounds would no longer appeal to Christians. . . . God impressed on Jim . . . the need to carry the spirit of the campmeeting movement into the 21st Century, and the concept of Heritage USA came into being.[5]

And so, in Fort Mills, South Carolina, Heritage USA was built, a place, a language, and a practice that performed a ceaseless, if implicit, critique, of fundamentalism's restraint, its sacrificial logic, its obsession with authority, hierarchy, and rules. Heritage USA was an ensemble of replicas, relics, facades, imitations, simulations, props, and sets drawn from Biblical Jerusalem, the Old West, small-town America, Hollywood, modern suburbs, and tourist resorts. Nothing simply was itself; everything was palpably a production, a reproduction, or a performance.

Just inside the entrance to Heritage USA, you could visit Billy Graham's "actual" boyhood home. In the study, on the wall, a series of photographs depict Billy's home being dismantled, brick by brick, and rebuilt on the edge of Heritage USA property, the displacement and appropriation of Graham's home having become part of its significance. Heritage's centerpiece was a man-made "water park" with a three-story waterslide. Nearby was the Grand Hotel and Main Street shopping mall, a hodgepodge of pastel-colored Victorian and colonial surfaces; and down the road, past the water park, and the tennis courts, condos, and campgrounds, healing and prayer were available 24 hours a day in The Upper Room, an "exact replica" of the building where Jesus and his disciples had their last supper, except that this one looked like a replica. Across the road was another self-proclaiming replica, an "ancient amphitheater" where several nights a week the Passion Play was performed, complete with special effects, new characters (mainly, Satan incarnate), and new episodes, all intended to "heighten the dramatic tension" of Christ's final days.

Church services and camp meetings at Heritage were held in the TV studio and an adjacent auditorium which in no respect resembled a church. The Bakkers never used TV to represent the traditional rituals; instead, their TV realities, including their TV personalities, broke through the screen and expanded in the empirical world. The accent was always on performance, visuals, excess, spectacle, not on words, or the Word, at least not as fundamentalists understood the Word. The linear, irreversibly life-changing story of Christ's death, burial, and resurrection, of suffering and of sacrifice, gave way to a cornucopia of miracle stories of God's healing, restoration, infinite love, and bountiful gifts.

From the beginning, Heritage troubled many Christians who noticed the internal counter-cultural message—its suppression of sacrifice theology—but few guessed how far the Bakkers had gone in the direction of antinomian heresy, of rejecting all earthly restraints. At the time of their demise, the Bakkers not only promised their partners material abundance and well-being, but were refining a gospel of infinite forgiveness, a folk theology that seemed almost to sanction sinning by guaranteeing God's perpetual forgiveness in advance.

It is not so surprising then that the two discursive traditions represented by Falwell and Bakkers' televangelical empires cast the born-again scandals in dramatically different terms. The fact that this conflict assumed center stage in the PTL crisis, however, virtually undermined the possibility that the voice of the third discursive tradition weighing into the fray, that of secular modernity, would ever get a solid grip on the telescandals.

The PTL Telescandals

The PTL scandals of 1987 and 1988 spread two grand dramas across America's TV screens. One composed of the sensational misdeeds of Jim and Tammy Faye Bakker—his night with Jessica Hahn, her blackmailing him, more sexual improprieties, gross financial misconduct, tax fraud, bankruptcy, million-dollar spending sprees, and so on. The other drama was born when Jerry Falwell's friendly takeover of PTL turned into a hostile one and launched a gaudy series of media skirmishes (known as the "Holy War") between the two professed Christian camps during which Falwell's forces and the press successively revealed, and endlessly reiterated, interrogated, and dissected the Bakkers' misdeeds before a national audience.

Roland Barthes might have said the PTL scandal was a boxing match that kept dissolving into a TV wrestling match. An orderly bout, based on the demonstration of excellence and directed, like a story, toward an outcome (the definitive downfall of the Bakkers), kept evolving into a more chaotic bout in which each moment was immediately intelligible as spectacle and the most natural outcome was baroque confusion. As Barthes put it, "Some fights, among the most successful kind, are crowned by a final charivari, a sort of unrestrained fantasia where the rules, the laws of the genre, the referee's censuring and the limits of the ring are abolished, swept away by a triumphant disorder which over flows into the hall and carries off pell-mell wrestlers, seconds, referee and spectators."[6]

Perhaps the essence of spectacle is the loss of a unitary authorial point of view, a proliferation of points of view such that stories pile up fantastically, realities clash and mingle indiscriminately, so that the total effect of everyone vying for narrative control is an irrepressible sense of events-out-of-control, of confusion, disorder, and a constant instability of genres, borders, roles, rules. The disordering forces at work in the PTL telescandal that kept it from settling into a singular storied tradition were: first, the unholy and profoundly unstable authorial alliance between the fundamentalist and journalistic points of view; second, the spectacularizing desires of the narrators themselves—their citational excesses, feuds, and histrionics; third, the ever-anarchic words and deeds of the scandalizers; and fourth, a fistful of competing sideshows, of secular scandals grabbing for public attention. Such forces spectacularize—in this instance, specifically disrupting efforts to narrate the scandals from a "modern" point of view—by destabilizing the boundary between fundamentalist and modern, by foregrounding the processes of fabrication (fabulation), and by constantly juxtaposing contradictory points of view.

Take, for example, the profusion of allusions. In measured doses, literary and historical allusions help "make sense" of events by suggesting narrative frames that, in effect, interpret characters, plots, subplots, motives, climaxes, tragic flaws, and moral meanings. In excess, they produce "a sort of unrestrained fantasia." During the PTL crisis, the Bakkers, for their part, were figured, among others, as Elmer Gantry, the Marcoses, Adam and Eve, David and Bathsheba, Ivan Boesky, Catholics buying and selling indulgences, and Gary Hart. Falwell, meanwhile, was figured (usually, he figured himself) as, among others, Protestant Reformers, Lee Iacocca, Nathan, the SEC, God in the Garden after the Fall, and Christ cleaning out the moneychangers. The scandal as a whole was compared to *The Scarlet Letter*, the sinking of the Titanic, the Book of Revelation, *Dynasty*, and the war between Iran and Iraq. Such hyperfiguration spectacularized by calling attention to the narrative process, to the narrators as "telling stories" and therefore "having a point of view," which helped break whatever spell of "truth" they might have cast.

The major narrators also kept bringing each other into focus as narrators by calling attention to their "motives," "interests," and "biases." Journalists made several attempts to "unmask" Jerry Falwell, to find evidence of his plotting to take over PTL, and constantly speculated about his "real motives" (for example, he was "out to get" the PTL TV network, or the PTL audience, or simply the free prime-time exposure). Falwell, of course, argued back that, at least when reporters turned on him, they were displaying their "secular liberal bias." In the process, the press lost some of its pretense of standing outside the fray, detached, disinterested, objective, reporting events. At the same time, Falwell's pose as a selfless man of God was compromised.

Nor were the press and Falwell above all histrionics. Ted Koppel and his "Nightline" crew orchestrated the most frenetically embroiling episode of the telescandals, a three-night series of shows in late May of 1987. The series opened with a full, heated, but indecisive, airing of the charges against Falwell. The second show was the first live interview with Jim and Tammy Faye Bakker since the scandal broke and it was pure spectacle. Twenty-three million people watched the Bakkers be themselves, with a touch of remorse and lots of "love." The series concluded, inconclusively, with a "prognosis" on televangelism featuring, of all people, Jerry Falwell.

Falwell produced his own fireworks on the morning of the third day of the "Nightline" series by calling a press conference to display evidence that the Bakkers were not truly repentant. He waved a letter from the Bakkers asking for money, homes, cars, benefits, guards, and a full-time maid, and he told a new version of that night in the Clearwater motel, exactly what Jim and his confederates, John Wesley

Fletcher and an unnamed "third man," did to Jessica. As performances go, it was still rather rhetorical, but nonetheless stunning—spectacular in a way—to hear the sordid details spill from Falwell's lips. His role as chief of Heritage USA also inspired some performances from the usually stiff Falwell, reaching a peak when he finally, on 10 September 1987, slid down Heritage Island's three-story Typhoon waterslide. After posing with (a person dressed up as) "Allie the Alligator" atop the slide, Falwell "took the plunge," arms crossed at his chest and *dressed in a business suit*, looking like he was about to be baptized . . . or buried.

The scandalizers—those about whom the narrators narrated—were another spectacularizing force, as they kept resisting and disrupting narrative frames, characterizations, plottings, and climactic moments. After every barrage of charges levelled at the Bakkers, they were still standing when the smoke cleared, smiling and chatting about God's love and forgiveness. They refused to be shamed into oblivion, escaped narrative grips, and talked back, irrepressibly, from their own point of view. They would not simply die and go away. Indeed, lingering in the wings is a potential narrative frame, which if only they could slip it into place, would produce the greatest of all spectacles. If only Jim and Tammy Faye could fashion themselves as innocent victims, slain by the forces of evil . . . they might rise again.

Finally, compounding the sense of spectacle was a backdrop of secular telescandals (Irangate, the Hart affair, the Marine spy case, Ivan Boesky, Wall Street drug raids), a whole host of lesser televangelists, hungry, waiting for the titans to fall, and the unshakable sense that we, the audiences, were inside the telescandal too—that it had caught us up, variously, and put us down somewhere else, changed imperceptibly perhaps—that just possibly, for instance, the line between the modern and the archetype of premodernity, the fundamentalist, moved in some way that made us all "different."

Of course, the story is not over. The spectacularizing forces of the telescandals did not abolish the myth of modernity; confused and confounded it, yes, but modern subjectivity actually "needs" an occasional feast of fundamentalists, for it emerges out of the contradictory processes of internalizing and expelling fundamentalist otherness. Just as surely as Ted Koppel orchestrated "The Billion Dollar Pie" as a spectacle in which his "hogs at the trough" thesis was lost in a cascading melee of excited criticism, prooftexting, and posturing, he also in the end did his best to pull his modern point of view out of the fire.

Once again let me illustrate what I mean: Koppel's evening in the Memphis church concluded with thousands of people standing up and cheering Jerry Falwell's assertion, "I do believe the Bible is the infallible Word of God." This moment, of course, bore no apparent relationship to the scandals or to televangelism; as a biting retort to a hostile question from a fellow Baptist in the audience, it further fractured the fundamentalist whole; the sight of thousands cheering the literal Bible was spectacular from any point of view; and insofar as it was "great TV," it confirmed Falwell's innuendo that Koppel was also a hog at the trough. But it was also the moment which, from the modern point of view, most categorically distinguished Koppel from Falwell, Koppel's otherwise disconcertingly cool, reasonable, and remarkably well-regarded co-author during the telescandals, by stigmatizing Falwell as an unrepentant Biblical literalist.

> **AUDIENCE MEMBER:** I have heard at least five of you on the tube, and when I hear you, you've got all the answers. I'm surprised and amazed at your humility. You know exactly how we're supposed to understand the Bible, you won't consider any other view, you know exactly who's going to be saved and who's not going to be saved. I believe that at least you, Mr. Falwell, and Mr. Robison [*both are Baptist preachers*] believe that the Bible is the totally inspired word of God, without any admixture of any kind of error. Genesis 17:7 and 8 says that God made an eternal covenant with Israel. Eternal covenant, and yet it is my understanding that both you gentlemen somehow must think he has abrogated this covenant, because you think it is your Christian duty to convert Jews. I believe there's a contradiction in this, and I'd like you to explain it.
>
> **REV. FALWELL:** All right. First of all, let me ask you this. Which Baptist church are you a member of?
>
> **AUDIENCE MEMBER:** Prescott Memorial. *[Laughter and some boos.]*
>
> **KOPPEL:** Wait, does that have some meaning?
>
> **AUDIENCE MEMBER:** What difference does that make?
>
> **KOPPEL:** Does that have some meaning? Well, I'm not sure, I'd like to know. Does it make any difference?
>
> **REV. FALWELL:** Well, most Baptists believe in the inerrancy of the Bible, do you?
>
> **AUDIENCE MEMBER:** No, I don't.
>
> **REV. FALWELL:** All right. Fine. I just wanted to know where you were. Now, the fact is I do believe the Bible is the infallible word of God. I do— *[Over half the audience, the choir, the arrayed preachers, stand up, applaud, cheer, and shout "Amen"].* . . .
>
> **AUDIENCE MEMBER:** May I respond? May I respond to that?
>
> **REV. FALWELL:** You've had your time, be quiet for a moment.

AUDIENCE MEMBER: The ovation means they agree with you, that doesn't necessarily mean you're right.

REV. FALWELL: Hush! Let me tell you something. Now. The Bible—because we do believe the Bible is the inerrant word of God, and because that Bible says Jesus is the way, the truth, the life, and no man cometh under the father but by me, Jesus doing the talking, I don't have a plan of salvation, God does, and I believe that Jews, gentiles, Moslems, blacks, white, rich, poor, all come the same way, through the death, burial, resurrection of Christ, whom we learn about in an inerrant Bible.

Shortly, Koppel said goodnight to his church guests, and then tacked on a clip for his TV audience that would be his last grasp at the modernity narrative, by way of pastor John Sherfey, a "really real" premodern preacher in a little Virginia church whom Koppel had introduced in his opening collage. With a country gospel tune in the background, we pan in on Sherfey's church from above and find ourselves sitting in the pews with Ted and John, dressed in flannel shirts and looking a little like distant cousins.

SINGER: Oh, I love to walk with Jesus like the publicans of old / when he gathered them about him and the blessed tidings told.

KOPPEL: John, I want to end where we began, right here in the pews of your church. Is there a lesson in all this that you can draw for us?

REV. SHERFEY: Yes, I think so. I think a lot of times, Ted, what I tell my people here is, don't get their eyes fastened on man. Look to God. Because man'll let you down. Of course, I do want to be a pattern, as I go in and out of this church. As I go up and down these rows, as I walk the streets of Stanley, wherever I'm at. I want to live so that I'd be a pattern for them to follow. But I still don't want them to get their eyes fastened on me, and take them off Jesus. See. Set your mind and your fixings on things above, and not on this earth. *[Short clip of Rev. Sherfey shaking hands of his people as they leave church and saying, "Bless you, Brother, and praise the Lord."]*

SINGER: I will follow / all the way, Lord / I will follow Jesus all the way / Oh I love to walk with Jesus like the man of long ago—

A touching scene, and a bit of a spectacle—Koppel and his TV crew in a little church in the hills of Virginia, concocting the image of a "good preacher" (read pre-entrepreneurial, pre-political, pre-modern, pre-postmodern) who told us the lesson of all this is that we must keep our eyes on God, not man. But visually, musically, and idiomatically,

Koppel had nonetheless reconstituted the quaint premodern fundamental other and rather unceremoniously dumped him into the Southern countryside where we may presume Koppel is telling us such folk belong.

Of course, Koppel and his co-reporters are not working alone to save the modern point of view. The meeting of the Society for the Scientific Study of Religion in November 1988 was bristling with papers tinkering away at theories of modernity, trying to patch up the holes the fundamentalists had run through. And the MacArthur Foundation has awarded millions of dollars to projects which would restore and globalize the binary opposition between "fundamentalism" and "modernity," and reconfirm upon the latter a studied, if ruffled, moral superiority.

Much money and many raconteurs can do wonders, but it seems doubtful that the secularizing version of the story of modernity can ever be put back together again. That version proposes that, when we look upon the TV preachers and their electronic escapades, we see figures and scenes from the past. In fact, it may make more sense to say we are gazing into the future.

In retrospect, religious market analyst Jack Sims provided the perfect prefatory fable to the Koppel show. With respect to the fate of the big TV preachers, he may or may not have accurately fabulated "reality," but his language, the manner of his fabulation, was indubitably precise. His wild imagery vividly conveyed the exquisite unexpectedness and improbability of the characters and events that composed the telescandals. Aging evangelical electronic dinosaurs, crawling onto an iceberg, fighting tooth and nail, as the iceberg floats south, melting, to the inevitable doom of all. The tale speaks ending, but the language, its cyborg creatures and mixed metaphors and mythic time and space, speaks beginning—the opening up of a new world composed of preposterous categorical hodgepodges and antic crisscrossings of social boundaries. Religious mingles with secular, churches become businesses, Christ dispenses grace and miracles on TV, preachers call themselves CEOs and run for President, faith healers build ultramodern hospitals, AT&T hires New Age consultants and churches hire religious market analysts, creationists call themselves scientists, and scientists discover the ineffable. If something is ending, perhaps it is the world in which the things forming these zany amalgamations were kept apart, separated, in their place, properly ordered, and moving progressively toward some end.

NOTES

The Berman Center for Jewish Studies wishes to thank Koppel Communications, Inc., for granting us permission to quote excerpts from "The Koppel Report: The Billion Dollar Pie."

1. "Religion in America," *Gallup Report*, Nos. 201–202, June–July 1982, 31–32. Gallup produced a stricter definition of "evangelicals" by calculating how many Americans met *both* criteria (born-again and Biblical literalist) *and* had ever witnessed for (encouraged someone to believe in) Christ. Seventeen percent (about 27 million adults) met all three criteria.
2. *Sojourner* magazine, for example, advocates liberal and even some relatively radical positions on issues of war and poverty. Billy Graham is viewed by most non-evangelicals as very conservative, but he made some remarkably liberal proposals in the 1980s regarding disarmament, Soviet relations, and world poverty; see his *Approaching Hoofbeats.* Nor do all orthodox Christians even agree that abortion and homosexuality are immoral. James Davison Hunter, *Evangelicalism: The Coming Generation,* documents the range of evangelical political and moral views.
3. Falwell does not "typify" fundamentalism, nor the Bakkers pentecostalism. Rather, their communities have exaggerated certain features of the cultural trappings of their religious traditions in ways that seem to parallel the dialectic between modern and postmodern cultural forms in secular architecture, literature, and popular culture.
4. Elmer Towns and Jerry Falwell, *Church Aflame* (Nashville: Impact Books, 1971), 40–41.
5. Jim Bakker and Tammy Faye Bakker, *Heritage Village Church: The Story of People That Love* (Toronto: Boulton Publishing Services, 1986), 91.
6. Roland Barthes, *Mythologies* (New York: Hill and Wang, 1972), 23.

BIBLIOGRAPHY

Bakker, Jim, and Tammy Faye Bakker. *Heritage Village Church: The Story of People That Love.* Toronto: Boulton Publishing Services, 1986.

Barthes, Roland. *Mythologies.* New York: Hill and Wang, 1972.

"The Billion Dollar Pie," The Koppel Report, aired 12 May 1988.

Graham, Billy. *Approaching Hoofbeats: The Four Horsemen of the Apocalypse.* Waco, Texas: Word Books, 1983.

Harrell, David Edward, Jr. *All Things Are Possible: The Healing and Charismatic Revivals in Modern America.* Bloomington: Indiana University Press, 1975.

———. *Oral Roberts: An American Life.* San Francisco: Harper & Row, 1985.

Hunter, James Davison. *Evangelicalism: The Coming Generation*. Chicago: University of Chicago Press, 1987.

Lash, Scott, and John Urry. *The End of Organized Capitalism*. Cambridge: Polity Press, 1987.

Marsden, George M. *Fundamentalism and American Culture: The Shaping of Twentieth-Century Evangelicalism, 1870–1925*. New York: Oxford University Press, 1980.

_____. *Reforming Fundamentalism: Fuller Seminary and the New Evangelicalism*. Grand Rapids: William B. Eerdmans Publishing Company, 1987.

"Religion in America," The Gallup Report, Nos. 201–202. June–July, 1982.

Towns, Elmer, and Jerry Falwell. *Church Aflame*. Nashville: Impact Books. 1971.

Part II

*Fundamentalism and
the Politics of the Middle East*

Chapter 5

Islamic Fundamentalism
in the Wake of the Six Day War:
Religious Self-Assertion in Political Conflict

James Piscatori

Many reasons have been given for the appearance of Islamic fundamentalism in the latter half of the twentieth century. The most obvious is the reaction to modernization: like other developing societies, Muslim societies face rural-urban imbalances, ghettoization of the cities, run-away inflation, inadequate housing and social services, and growing inequalities. The inevitable results are anomie and discontent, intensified by the manifest shortcomings of modernity itself—the devaluation of family and community, the overemphasis on wealth and status. "The world has grown strange, and people floated" is an admirable summation (in an otherwise regrettable book)[1] of the overall effects of modernity. Islam, with its relatively simple spiritual map, appears to point home.

There are also economic and political explanations for the development of fundamentalism. One such argument holds that the oil revenues of the Gulf states both generated a sense of vibrancy and provided the means for international cooperation among Muslims.[2] A more cogent explanation, however, is that, because the authoritarian nature of most Muslim political systems precludes popular participation, those who live within such systems increasingly turn to such Islamic institutions as the mosque and Shi'i mourning centers (*husayniyya-s*) as alternative outlets for political expression. Moreover, Islam's vocabulary, including such key words as *jihad* (struggle), *hijra* (migration), *shahada* (martyrdom), and *umma* (community), possesses a natural political relevance that may have helped to galvanize opposition to the political status quo.

If any one event has served to spur the recent fundamentalist trend, it was undoubtedly the Arab-Israeli war of 1967. This calamitous defeat for the Arabs produced a number of shock waves, particularly in the ranks of the Muslim intelligentsia, but it was part of a longer formative history of opposition to Zionism and Israel. Indeed, as we shall argue, the Arab confrontation with Israel has produced direct and indirect influences on Arab political and religious thought. It has, on the one hand, strengthened a secular, largely pan-Arabist current that has been developing since at least the 1940s. On the other hand, it has given new urgency to Muslim political thinking. Both intellectual responses have had the somewhat unexpected effect of turning the Arabs' attention inward, leading to condemnation of their own regimes alongside the condemnation of Israel.

The Pre-1967 Period

The 1948 War, having ended in wholly unanticipated defeat, marked an entire generation. Young military officers, fired with enthusiasm yet incompetently guided and with ill-trained and poorly equipped men under their command, would not soon forget the humiliation. 'Abd al-Nasir's *Falsafat al-Thawra* (Philosophy of the Revolution) excoriated the imperialists who imposed "a murderous, invisible siege upon the whole region, a siege one hundred times more powerful and cruel than that which encircled our trenches at Faluja."[3] But understating the injustice that the Jews and Israelis perpetrated, it emphasizes the internal inadequacies of the Arab regimes and the betrayal that sometimes eclipsed the Arabs' natural sympathy and even "affection" for the Palestinians:

> all the Arab people entered [Palestine] with the same degree of enthusiasm. They left it with similar bitterness and disappointment. Each in his own country faced the same factors, the same ruling forces that had brought them to defeat and caused them to bow their heads in humiliation and shame.[4]

The Muslim Brotherhood echoed the refrain that both foreign imperialists and inept and corrupt local elites were responsible for the Arab defeat in 1948. However, unlike the regular military, Muslim volunteer units had acquitted themselves honorably in the fighting, and this could best be explained by their commitment to Islam. Hasan al-Banna' and other leaders ultimately concluded that only through Islam—and specifically an organized Islamic political movement—would the dead hand of Western political and intellectual domination and the wickedness of miscreant rule be removed.[5]

There were those who drew the opposite conclusion, however. American University of Beirut professor Constantine Zurayq, for example, had professed a kind of romantic Arab nationalism guided by the general spirit of Islam.[6] But in 1948 he recoiled at "the disaster" (*al-nakba*) and prescribed in the end what, as a Christian liberal, would have seemed only natural to him—the separation of religion and politics. The Israelis had been victorious because their social order was predicated on a modern ideology that encouraged the growth of industrialization and valued rational inquiry.[7]

In fact, the time was conducive to growing secularization. The disillusioned junior officers staged their *coup d'état* in Egypt in 1952, and very soon the Muslim Brothers, who had welcomed the overthrow of the monarchy, came to regard the new regime as worse than the old one. Outright repression of the Islamic opposition inevitably followed. But, as in the familiar pattern of Islamic history, the *umara'*, the rulers, also used the *'ulama'*, the religious authorities, to legitimize their rule and thus ward off further opposition from the Islamic camp. There was no doubt, however, that the secular Arab nationalist ideology of 'Abd al-Nasir was ascendant.

On New Year's Day 1956, al-Azhar, the premier Islamic university, issued a legal opinion on the possibility of peace with Israel which stressed the state's concerns more than those of Islam. The *fatwa* was signed by Shaykhs Hasanayn Muhammad Makhluf (a former Grand Mufti of Egypt), 'Isa Manun, Muhammad Shaltut, Muhammad al-Tanikhi, Muhammad 'Abd al-Latif al-Subki, and Zakariya al-Barri. The four orthodox schools of law were carefully represented among these senior *'ulama'*—the Hanafi (Shaltut), Shafi'i (Manun), Maliki (al-Tanikhi), and Hanbali (al-Subki) schools. They ruled that the *shari'a*, or canonical law, does not allow the conclusion of peace with Israel because that would entail condoning the illegal act of usurpation: "Muslims may not make peace with those Jews who seized Palestinian land illegally and attacked the people and their property."[8]

A specifically Islamic note is evident in the document's call to protect the al-Aksa mosque and its sacred precinct in Jerusalem, and its frequent references to the Qur'an and Prophetic traditions (*sunna*) in its general argumentation. But more noteworthy are the explicitly political and anti-imperialist statements, reflecting official policy:

> Muslims are also legally prohibited from making it possible for Israel
> and the imperialist countries which stand behind it . . . to carry out
> those plans whose only purpose is to make the Jewish state prosper,
> live a comfortable and productive life, and continue to exist as a state
> fighting the Arabs and Islam over territory that they most cherish.

Clearly, the Baghdad Pact was the "plan" that had raised the most
concern in the document. Britain and the United States had encouraged the creation of a mutual security network among Turkey,
Pakistan, Iran, and Iraq, which was formally institutionalized in the
Iraqi capital in late November 1955. 'Abd al-Nasir saw this as a blatant
attempt of the great powers to encircle the Arab nation and to bolster
Israel. Lest other Arab states considered joining, the *fatwa* was direct:
"These alliances with Islamic countries that the imperialist countries are
calling for and working hard to bring about constitute an effort to
create dissension and to drive a wedge between the Islamic countries."
Israel itself was an imperialist pawn, created to damage Islam in its
Arab heartland and so advance "imperialist aims and purposes." One
is almost left with the impression—despite the wording—that concern
for Palestine was really secondary: "No Islamic country may go along
with those alliances or take part in them because of the great danger
that they pose to Islamic countries and to Palestine in particular."

After the June War

As disastrous as the 1948 War was, an even greater calamity occurred
in June 1967. In the wake of the June 1967 War, Zurayq agonized
over how little the Arabs had learned,[9] and generally "*the* disaster" now
sharpened the intellectual divide. The poet Nizar Qabbani excoriated
the Arabs for their useless and pompous rhetoric and, like Edmund in
King Lear, for the self-delusion that they were "villains by necessity,
fools by heavenly compulsion." The truth was altogether more
unsettling: "The Israelis conquer not our borders / but thrive on our
shortcomings."[10]

   The Syrian Sadiq Jalal al-'Azm became a sensation for his penetrat-
ing and unflinching criticism of Arab political society. In equal
measures of anger and sadness, he wrote in 1968 that the Arabs were
fatalistic and manipulable; would-be revolutionaries but in fact
demagogic conservatives; concerned with private gain rather than
public virtue.[11] In 1969, al-'Azm's *Naqd al-Fikr al-Dini* (The Critique

of Religious Thought) focused on the distortions that "the religious mentality" in particular creates and the ease with which politicians use it to maintain control over the masses.   Although Arab socialists presume that they are restructuring society, insofar as they accord great respect to religion and hesitate to reduce its role, they fail to uproot tradition and effect real progress.   According to al-'Azm, infrastructural changes count for little if they reinforce old social and class relations and ideologies.   He also criticized Arab nationalists for arguing that religion is "the true expression of the genuine pure and invariable essence of the Arab spirit over the ages."   This is a doubly false view in al-'Azm's opinion, for it equates the "backward-looking ideology" that obtains in contemporary society with all religious thought, while ignoring the fact that ideologies of all kinds are relative and changing.[12]

By the end of the 1960s, however, the tenor of the times had changed and a strong pro-Islamic ideology was on the rise.   Accordingly, such blunt secularism, like al-'Azm himself, was no longer in intellectual or political favor.   As the radical poet Adonis would write in 1982: "My era tells me bluntly: You do not belong."[13]

Three factors possibly account for the new Islamic-orientated climate.   First, 'Abd al-Nasir's military defeat put an end as well to his ideological ascendancy.   Nasirism, with its secular and socialist motifs, which had long seemed the panacea for Arab social and political ills, now appeared to be impotent or at least misguided.

Second, as regional power shifted to the Saudis, the assault on secularism found its patron.   In order to stave off Nasirist attacks on their supposed feudalism and to counter the appeal of Arab national- ism, the Saudis had advanced the idea of "Islamic solidarity."   With 'Abd al-Nasir gravely compromised, however, their kind of conservative Islamic internationalism took on a life of its own.   While it would be entirely cynical to conclude that the intellectuals' tune changed with the paymaster, there is no doubt that those writers and groups that espoused Islamic ideologies received powerful encouragement from the Saudis.   As the 1960s had been Egypt's moment in the ideological sun, the 1970s would be Saudi Arabia's.

A third factor contributing to the shift towards Islam was the loss of Jerusalem, which broadened as well as deepened the Islamic response.   For the first time, Muslim sentiment beyond the borders of the Arab world was mobilized.   There had, of course, been earlier efforts to put Palestine on the Islamic agenda, most notably at the Jerusalem Congress of 1931.   However, these were only partially successful because of the sheer difficulty in communicating across the broad expanse of the Muslim world; the suspicion that factional fighting within the Palestinian leadership would only increase with the internationalization of the issue; and the perception that British control of the Holy Land, as politically undesirable and excessively tolerant of the Zionists as it was, was not a direct assault on Islam itself.

However, by 1967, the perception had obviously changed and for Muslims everywhere the Arab-Israeli conflict acquired a concreteness it had previously lacked. Both 'Abd al-Nasir and the *'ulama'* of al-Azhar had talked of Israel as an imperialist wedge. But now the occupation of the third holiest city—that is, of sacred space—transformed the debate from the abstractions of international politics to what, in the charged universe of true believers, could only be perceived as aggression against the faith. Israel was not only in the midst of *dar al-islam*, the land of believers, but was also in control of one of its sustaining centers. From this point on, consequently, the Arabs' outrage was primarily defined in Islamic terms.

In February 1968, for example, a convocation of *'ulama'* from around the Muslim world issued a *fatwa* on the permissibility of making peace with and granting official recognition to Israel. Whereas previously the rejection of such ideas had been based on the argument that Muslim-owned land had been usurped, now the argument centered on the occupation of the holy city of Jerusalem and its Islamic sites:

> Chief among those sites is the holy al-Aqsa mosque, the first holy place in Islam and the site of the Prophet's nocturnal journey (*isra'*) and ascension to the seven heavens (*mi'raj*). [The usurpers] tore down several Muslim sites, including mosques, schools and homes, all of which were held by religious endowments (*awqaf*). They announced the schemes they had for al-Aqsa mosque and proceeded to dig under it in order to pave the way for seizing it.[14]

The Different Faces of Islam

The October War of 1973 added a sense of triumph to this outrage. Although the initial Arab successes had clearly been reversed by the time that a durable cease-fire came into effect, the overwhelming Arab perception was of a divinely inspired victory. Had not the impregnable Bar Lev line been breached and the Suez Canal crossed? Had not the Muslims stood up not just to Zionists, but also to the greatest power on earth, the United States, which had immediately and massively resupplied Israel? Moreover, this had been the war of Ramadan, a time of purification and sacrifice, when engagements bore code names reminiscent of the early Muslim community's heroic advances on the battlefield.[15]

But there were limits to this self-congratulation, for the "usurpers" remained in Palestine. Shaykh 'Abd al-'Aziz Bin Baz, an eminent *'alim* and director of the office responsible for issuing *fatwa*s (Dar al-Ifta') in Saudi Arabia, stressed that "the Palestinian problem is an Islamic problem first and last." Answering a question as to the future of this issue, he reasoned that the partial alliance of Muslim countries was harmful and that only a Muslim world united in its entirety could produce success. But achieving that kind of unity was bound to be difficult since in the past some Muslims had given non-Muslims the impression that it was exclusively an Arab problem.

For this reason, argued Bin Baz, the only way to resolve the problem of Palestine is to consider it an Islamic problem which all Muslims must unite to resolve. They must fight an Islamic *jihad* against the Jews until the land returns to its owners, the Jews return to the countries from which they came, and "pure Jews" (*al-yahud al-asliyun*) remain in their own countries under the rule of Islam, rather than the rule of communism or secularism.[16]

The *fatwa* takes a gratuitously offensive, if not unhistorical, turn at the end, but one that is characteristic of conservative opinion, especially of an older generation. The mainstream Muslim Brotherhood has displayed a particularly pronounced antipathy to Israel and often to the Jews as a people. Perhaps to demarcate its boundaries with the Egyptian government that had suppressed it, the Brotherhood has unequivocally placed Israel in the enemy camp to which the West and Communists—seen as alternating allies of the government—also belong. They are all implacable foes, working hard to defeat Islam and occupy its territory.[17] This is particularly clear in the case of Jerusalem and explains in general why the Palestinian problem is essentially an Islamic one.[18]

It is further claimed that the Jews are deceitful, greedy conspirators and aggressors.[19] Sadat's peace treaty was an invalid agreement with usurpers of Muslim territory.[20] Moreover, it had been unwise to think that negotiations with these people would succeed—only force could produce results. The Israelis had not only taken land, but, with Western support and encouragement and presumably possessing nuclear weapons, they continued to threaten and terrorize the Arabs.

"There is no hope for the Arabs out of this situation except through force."[21]

The Shi'i intellectual Muhammad Jawad Mughniyya echoed much of this hostility in his *Isra'iliyyat al-Qur'an* (Israeli References in the Qur'an). His son's foreword directly criticizes Israeli expansionism into Muslim lands.[22] Mughniyya himself, with the debacle of 1967 plainly in mind, wrote a powerful subtext based on the opposition of virtuous Palestine and iniquitous Israel. The Palestinians were victimized, while the Israelis unleashed the fires of war. Moreover, the Palestinians were constrained by adversity to move and to wander, while the new Israelis were settled and controlled Jerusalem. The Palestinian *hijra*, like the Prophet's, was an act of openness and was ennobling, but the end to the Jewish diaspora transformed the kindred spirit and ethnic identity of the Jews and created in Zionism a kind of institutionalized intolerance.[23]

It is not surprising that, in the aftermath of the Israeli invasions of Lebanon in 1978 and 1982, a hardening of Muslim opinion has occurred. Shaykh Abbas al-Musawi, who was secretary-general of Hizbullah and killed in an Israeli raid in early 1992, said that "by the very fact of its existence, the Israeli enemy constitutes a threat to the whole Islamic nation." While the Israelis were surprised to discover that *jihad* is part of the region's culture, Muslim defeatists, by spreading the myth of Israeli invincibility, have worked to Israel's advantage. This is a grave mistake, he argued, and all Muslims should renew their commitment to resistance.[24]

Muhammad Husayn Fadlallah, spiritual guide of Hizbullah, has similarly advocated forceful opposition to the Israelis. By means of force, he argued, the Israelis have come to control so central a land as Palestine, and Zionism has merged with imperialism to threaten the very core of Islamic culture.

Hizbullah's strategy of *jihad* is grounded in the premise that the presence of Israel in Palestine is illegal and constitutes an imperialist base which poses a great danger to the Arab and Islamic worlds. It must, therefore, be removed from the map completely. This is what the slogan of liberating Jerusalem represents, since Jerusalem is the Islamic symbol for all Palestine.[25] And Shaykh Subhi al-Tufayli, another Hizbullah leader, has welcomed Israeli blitzkrieg operations in the south of Lebanon on the grounds that they would escalate into what could only be considered a desirable confrontation.[26]

The sentiment that has emanated from the West Bank and Gaza Strip—particularly since the beginning of the *intifada*, or uprising against the Israeli occupation, in December 1987—is both anti-Israeli and anti-Jewish. Israel, typically scorned as "the Zionist entity," is seen as a false creation, the very antithesis of Islamic truth.[27] Created as an outpost of Western imperialism, Israel is naturally expansionist and wants to reach from "the Nile to the Euphrates."[28] The mass influx of the Soviet Jews only proves that Israel has unbounded ambitions.[29]

By way of contrast, the Muslims want only their homeland back. Hamas (Harakat al-Muqawama al-Islamiyya), the Movement of Islamic Resistance, the principal Islamist organization in the West Bank and Gaza, has defined its main goal as the liberation of the land of Palestine, while relegating the unification of the pan-Islamic community (*umma*) as a more distant objective. Hamas thus says that, unlike the Zionists with their world designs, Palestinian Muslims look to the nation (*watan*) as their focal point and regard Palestinian nationalism (*wataniyya*) as "part of the religious creed."[30]

A branch of the larger Muslim Brotherhood movement, Hamas also denounces the Jews as a people. In their view, Jews are inherently racist and are connected to an international financial network—incorporating Free Masons, Rotarians, and Lions Clubs—which exists to support their own self-interest and which exploits the labor of innocent workers throughout the world. So criminal has their conduct been that they may even be described as "Nazis."[31] The presence of Jewish troops among the Western forces that went to the holy peninsula of Saudi Arabia in 1990 in response to the Iraqi invasion of Kuwait was perceived as the vanguard of the Zionists, who have always wanted to attack the heart of Islam.[32]

As disturbing as such sentiments are, however, it would be unfortunate if one were to take them as representative of all Muslim opinion. To be sure, they probably represent the majority; yet there are two other tendencies—inwardly directed—that have also emerged and may be mitigating. First, an ambivalent voice can be heard which, while damning perhaps with faint praise, does give begrudging recognition to the strengths of Israel. Although, in a sense, this resembles the secularist critical refrain—if only we could be more like the Israelis—it is actually its mirror image. Whereas the secularists want to emulate the scientific and rational accomplishments of Israel, these Muslims want to emulate its religious commitment.

An early example of this thinking can be found in Muhammad Ghazzali's *Min Huna Na'lam* (From Here We Start), which appeared in 1948. A Muslim Brother at the time, Ghazzali appreciated that the Israeli elite, among whom were scientists accomplished in nuclear fission and others of similar acumen, had settled on the biblical name for their newly independent country, rather than another, more secular, designation such as "the Jewish Republic."[33] To Ghazzali, this was a sign that religion and material achievement could go hand in hand. Moreover, as Fouad Ajami has argued, 1967 heightened this appreciation for Israel's inner strengths, and this was used in the Arab internal debate as "ammunition" against the secularists. Thus it has been argued that "modernity and religion can be brought together, man can fight for the modern state—and definitely much better than he can fight on behalf of a thin cosmopolitan ideology such as socialism, whose slogans can be repeated without great feeling or authenticity."[34]

Second, the sense of needing to look critically inward, rather than outward at Israel, has become pronounced among a new generation of Muslim activists. Those whom Emmanuel Sivan aptly calls "the new radicals"[35] have come to regard impious "Muslim" rulers as more objectionable than the Israelis themselves. Accordingly, *jihad* to liberate one's own society of false believers and corrupt practices is worthier than the *jihad* to liberate Palestine.

Sayyid Qutb pushed modern Muslim thinking further along in this direction with his blistering condemnation of *jahili* (corrupt or ignorant) society, but it was left to his disciples to puzzle out his meaning of Islam as *haraka* or movement.[36] While Qutb had stressed the need for moral revolution as a prerequisite to the formation of such a movement, the post-1967 activists concluded that the formation of such a movement depends on seizing power. Even adherents of the Takfir wa'l-Hijra (Excommunication and Flight) group in Egypt, who advocated physical and spiritual withdrawal from the corruptions of *jahili* society, concluded that a violent confrontation with un-Islamic society was unavoidable.[37]

The question of Israel simply receded into the horizon for such activists. A re-ordering of priorities had occurred for some within the confines of 'Abd al-Nasir's jails in the mid-1960s and, when given the opportunity to redeem themselves in the eyes of the state by volunteering to fight in the 1967 War, several preferred to remain behind bars.[38] By the late 1970s, the imperative to restructure Muslim society was increasingly the primary objective. Thus, Shukri Mustafa, one of the leaders of Takfir wa'l-Hijra, bluntly said: "If the Jews or others come, our movement should not take part in combat in the ranks of the Egyptian army."[39]

In Syria, another front-line state, a Muslim Brother who was asked at his trial in 1979 why he would not fight against Israel left no doubt as to his preeminent goal: "Only when we shall have finished purging our country of godlessness shall we turn against Israel."[40] The Muslim Brotherhood, calling itself the Islamic Revolution in Syria, issued a formal program in November 1980 which explained at length the Muslim objections to the al-Asad regime. While its major concern was to explain how it would replace the regime, it also affirmed that "the true battle" was with Israel. Even while justifying this struggle with Israel, however, its immediate attention appeared to be on the Syrian government: "The Syrian regime has been brought into existence merely to act as a front to engage the people in Syria, and divert them away from their real battle with Zionists, and for this reason the regime enjoys the support of the East and West."[41]

The Brotherhood's newsletter, *al-Nadhir*, often attacked al-Asad for traveling "in the American coach" along with the Israelis but typically devoted most of its coverage to the corruption within the elite, the official encouragement of sectarianism, the excesses of the president's brother and of the intelligence services, and the failures of the nationalized economy.[42] The charter of the Islamic Front in Syria, a coalition of the Muslim Brotherhood and other Muslim groups and leaders, further enhanced this internal emphasis. Although in 1981 it pledged "support for the Palestinian brothers until their full rights are realized," this came late in the text and was brief.[43]

When the Islamic Front formed a broader-based coalition with Nasirists, dissident Ba'thists, and others, its charter of March 1982 reduced Zionism to a kind of negative measuring stick by which to gauge the evils of the al-Asad regime. When, for example, the regime refused to allow citizens to return to Hama, where thousands of casualties were sustained in a brutal crackdown on opponents in February 1982, it was accused of doing precisely what the Zionists had done in Palestine. Al-Asad himself was accused of conspiring with the Zionists to maintain his power and to deprive his archenemy, the Iraqis, of any chance of political and military success in the confrontation with Israel. Moreover, he was said to have tried to destroy the Palestinians in Lebanon and to be responsible for massacres against them. "His attitudes on the Arab and international levels were not different from his evil attitude against our people in Syria." Thus, the Syrians' responsibility was first to overthrow the government through armed struggle, and then—listed eleventh and twelfth on a list of sixteen goals—to work for the liberation of Palestine and to support the Palestine Liberation Organization (PLO).[44]

Although the PLO is headquartered in Tunisia, Muslim activists in the Maghrib have generally accorded the reform and Islamization of society clear precedence over the confrontation with Israel. To take just one example, Israel is almost entirely absent from the writings and speeches of Rashed al-Ghannoushi, leader of the Mouvement de Tendance Islamique (Islamic Tendency Movement) in Tunisia. His concern, rather, is with the over-Westernization of Tunisian society and the need, on the one hand, to establish a more balanced political, cultural, and intellectual relationship with the old imperialists and, on the other, to encourage democracy and cultural and intellectual reformation along Islamic lines at home. Committed to gradual change, however, he is ambivalent towards the Iranian revolution. While admiring the success of an Islamic movement, he is nonetheless uncomfortable with its sectarian and intolerant edge. In addition, although supporting the justice of the Palestinians' cause in terms of both Islamic rights and the national right of self-determination, he emphasizes the urgent duty of Tunisian Muslims to put their own society in order.[45]

Conclusion

The Arab response to the Arab-Israeli confrontation, as we have seen, is varied. In attempting to explain their repeated failures, some Arabs have proffered a radical criticism of their own society's shortcomings, especially the adherence to what they consider to be an obscurantist religion. Others, while not necessarily accepting this characterization, have agreed that a separation of religion from public life is desirable. There is no doubt, however, that the enormity of the defeat of 1967 fueled both pro-Islamic and anti-Israel sentiment. Within these general parameters, Muslim opinions have ranged from powerful anti-Zionism, even anti-Semitism (in the obvious sense of being anti-Jewish), to begrudging respect for Israel's strengths, to preoccupation with the un-Islamic character of "Muslim" lives.

What has remained constant, however, is the impact of the Arab-Israeli confrontation on Arab identity. Thus, Arab Muslims have been led to ask not only "how are we to deal with Israel?" but also "how do we think of ourselves?" As they search for answers, historicity, the historical validity of what they affirm to be true, becomes a secondary consideration for some of them. For these Arabs, it is easier to blame the Israelis for the sense of disorientation and anxiety that they feel than to address the problems of modernization; often it is safer to speak obliquely, censuring one's own government via denunciation of Israeli successes. Other Arabs, however, clearly recognize the defects of their own societies and are not looking for an external scapegoat. Palestine remains important to their worldview, but Islamization of their society is the prerequisite to effective confrontation with Israel.

Seen from the perspective of the *longue durée*, the Arab-Israeli conflict has sharpened Arab self-examination, even their self-criticism, which has been ongoing, often imperceptibly, for some time. However, the conflict by itself has not caused this self-examination. The emphasis and tone of Islamic fundamentalists will surely vary from place to place as they react to the crises of economic, social, and political development and modernity. Yet while the virulently anti-Israeli strand of their thinking is also undeniable and important, their rhetoric often poisonous, and their image of Jews at times distinctly unflattering, the Arab Muslim conflict with Israel seems to be somewhat more complex —and sometimes less central—than is usually assumed.

NOTES

The original draft of this chapter was first presented at a May 1989 conference, "Fundamentalism as a Political Force in the Middle East," sponsored by the Berman Center for Jewish Studies and held at Lehigh University.

1. V. S. Naipaul, *Among the Believers: An Islamic Journey* (London, 1981), 285.
2. Daniel Pipes, "'This World is Political!' The Islamic Revival of the Seventies," *Orbis* 24 (Spring 1980): 9–41; idem, *In the Path of God: Islam and Political Power* (New York, 1983), chap. 10. For a criticism of this argument, see my *Islam in a World of Nation-States* (Cambridge, 1986), 25–26.
3. Jamal 'Abd al-Nasir, *Falsafat al-Thawra* (Cairo, 1966), 63.
4. Ibid., 57. On the humiliation felt as a result of the 1948 War, see also Anwar El Sadat, *Revolt on the Nile* (New York, 1957), 108–9.
5. See, generally, Richard P. Mitchell, *The Society of the Muslim Brothers* (London, 1969).
6. Constantine Zurayq, *al-Wa'y al-Qawmi* (Beirut, 1939), especially 112–17.
7. Constantine Zurayq, *Ma'na al-Nakba* (Beirut, 1948).
8. The text of this *fatwa* was reprinted in *al-Mujtama'* [Kuwait], 28 July 1986, 17–18, on the occasion of Shimon Peres's visit to King Hasan of Morocco.
9. Constantine Zurayq, *Ma'na al-Nakba Mujaddadan* (Beirut, 1967).

10. From Nizar Qabbani's "Comments on the Notebook of Defeat," as quoted in Fouad Ajami, *The Arab Predicament: Arab Political Thought and Practice since 1967* (Cambridge, 1981), 23.

11. See Ajami's discussion of al-'Azm's *al-Naqd al-Dhati Ba'd al-Hazima*, ibid., 30–37.

12. Sadiq Jalal al-'Azm, *Naqd al-Fikr al-Dini* (Beirut, 1969), quotations (in order) at 7, 13, 17.

13. Adonis ('Ali Ahmad Sa'id), "The Desert (The Diary of Beirut under Siege, 1982)," in *Victims of a Map*, trans. Abdullah al-Udhari (London, 1984), 135 (Arabic, 134).

14. Text of this *fatwa* is republished in *al Mujtama'*, 28 July 1986, 19.

15. See, generally, Muhammad Hasanayn Haykal, *al-Tariq ila Ramadan* (Beirut, 1975).

16. 'Abd al-'Aziz Bin Baz, *Majmu' fatawa wa Maqalat Mutanawwi'a* (Riyadh, 1408 A.H./1987), 271. The *fatwa* is not dated.

17. *Al-Da'wa* (monthly journal of the Egyptian Muslim Brotherhood) (October 1976): 14–15.

18. Ibid., (December 1980): 22–25, and (December 1977): 15.

19. For example, *al-I'tisam* (monthly journal of the Egyptian Muslim Brother-hood) (December 1980): 36–41.

20. Ibid., (July 1979): 4–5; (September 1979): 55–56; and (November 1980): 34.

21. Ibid., (May 1981): 62–64.

22. Muhammad Jawad Mughniyya, *Isra'iliyyat al-Qur'an* (Beirut, 1981), 3–38.

23. Ibid., 149–50, 177–79, 192–93, 197, 203.

24. *Al-'Ahd* (weekly newspaper of Hizbullah), 11 October 1986.

25. See, generally, Muhammad Husayn Fadlallah, *al-Islam wa Mantiq al-Quwa* (Beirut, 1975); quotation in interview with Fadlallah in *Journal of Palestine Studies* 16, 2 (1987): 5.

26. *Al-Majalla*, 15–21 July 1987, 22–23.

27. See, for example, *Filastin al-Muslima* (Dhu al-Hijja, 1410 A.H./July 1990), 45.

28. *Mithaq Harakat al-Muqawama al-Islamiyya - Filastin* (mimeographed, 18 August 1988/1 Muharram 1409 A.H.), article 32, 22.

29. *Filastin al-Muslima* (Muharram 1410 A.H./August 1990), 29.

30. *Mithaq*, article 12, 11.

31. Ibid., article 28, 20.

32. See, for example, *Filastin al-Muslima* (Safar 1410 A.H./September 1990), 6.

33. Muhammad Ghazzali, *Min Huna Na'lam* (Cairo, 1948), 49.

34. Ajami, *Arab Predicament*, 70.

35. Emmanuel Sivan, *Radical Islam: Medieval Theology and Modern Politics* (New Haven, 1985), especially chap. 4.

36. Sayyid Qutb, *Ma'alim fi'l-Tariq* (Cairo, 1981), 72.

37. See Gilles Kepel, *Le Prophète et pharaon; Les mouvements Islamiques dans l'Egypte contemporaine* (Paris, 1984).

38. See, for example, 'Ali Jirisha, *'Indama Yakhuma al-Tugah* (Cairo, 1975), 48–50; and *al-'Arabi* (June 1982), 45.
39. Quoted in Sivan, *Radical Islam*, 19.
40. Quoted in ibid.
41. *Declaration and Program of the Islamic Revolution in Syria* (Damascus, 1 Muharram 1401 A.H./9 November 1980), quotation at p. 52.
42. See, for example, *al-Nadhir* 51 (19 Safar 1403 A.H./4 December 1982), quotation at p. 2.
43. *Mithaq al-Jabha al-Islamiyya fi Suriyya* (Damascus, 12 Rabi'al-Awwal 1401 A.H./17 January 1981), quotation at p. 33. It was signed by Muhammad Abu'l-Nasr al-Bayanuni, a leading *shaykh* from Aleppo and general secretary of the Front.
44. *The Charter of the National Alliance for the Liberation of Syria* (Damascus, 11 March 1982), quotations at pp. 8–9.
45. Ghannoushi's various articles are gathered in *al-Maqalat* (Paris, 1984). See especially 39–62, 75–84, 101–4.

Chapter 6

The Resurgence of Palestinian Islamic Fundamentalism in the West Bank and Gaza

Elie Rekhess

One of the most striking characteristics of the Palestinian uprising which began in the West Bank and Gaza Strip in December 1987 is the rise of Islamic fundamentalist groups. I would first like to refer to some of the reasons behind the resurgence of Islam in the occupied territories. One cannot detach the revivalism of Islam in the West Bank and Gaza from the wider movement of return to the Muslim religion evident all over the Middle East since the late 1970s. A key factor in the movement of Islamic renewal was the ideological crisis following the 1967 War. Its essence was a growing disillusionment with the Arab nationalist movement, both in its liberal constitutional form and in its more radical socialist form.

For many Arabs, the 1967 Six Day War symbolized the ideological bankruptcy of the secular political doctrines of the Arab world, many of which were shaped according to Western models. The humiliating results of the war were particularly significant to the West Bank/Gaza Strip Palestinians, who now came to be directly ruled by Israel. For them, 1967 meant a loss of land, military occupation, and loss of national pride. Faced with the hardships of military government, many found refuge in the spiritual harbor of faith. The impotence on the Arab side and the inability of the Palestine Liberation Organization (PLO) to bring about an end to the occupation sharpened the ideological crisis and led more and more people to look for explanations elsewhere. In fact, a considerable number of the new converts to Islam were former nationalist radicals, members of the PLO.

Another breeding ground for the Palestinian version of the Islamic reawakening was the continued Jewish-Muslim dispute over the places sacred both to Islam and Judaism. These clashes were interpreted as indicative of a Jewish conspiracy to take over the holy places of Islam, first and foremost Jerusalem. There was an additional cultural dimension to this reawakening. Through the return to Islam, the local population expressed its rejection of the corrupt Western lifestyle which was spreading as a result of expanding contacts with the Westernized secular Israeli society.

The socio-economic factor is especially relevant to the Gaza Strip, where the Islamic movement developed more rapidly. The traditional conservative nature of the region, a reflection of the almost exclusively Muslim population, contrasts with the West Bank, where there is a significant body of Christians. In addition, the pressing socio-economic conditions of the refugees in the Gaza Strip helped pave the way for the influence of Egyptian radical Islam.

Finally, the process of Islamic renewal was dramatically enhanced by the success of the Iranian revolution. The first Islamic fundamentalist group, the Islamic Jihad, which came to the fore in the late 1970s, was strongly influenced by the advent of Ayatollah Khomeini to power and took Iran as a model. The organization was established in Gaza by a nucleus of militant activists determined to apply Khomeini's teaching to the Palestinian scene. It was a secretive, shadowy, and terror-oriented organization. The uniqueness of the group derived from the fact that, although it was a *Sunni* movement steeped in *Sunni* traditions, it was inspired and emboldened by the *Shii* revolution of Iran and by the principle of *jihad* (holy war).[1]

The language of *jihad* was not altogether strange to the ears of the Palestinians. The more secular, Palestinian national movement had utilized Islam in the past to define its enemies and formulate modes of action against them. For example, Yasser Arafat, performing the pilgrimage to Mecca in 1978, declared the liberation of Palestine to be a commandment of Allah from which no Muslim was exempted. Accordingly, Muslim liberation was to be gained through *jihad*. Also, the Palestinian warriors in the 1960s were called *fidaiyyun*, those who are ready to sacrifice their lives in redeeming the homeland. Finally, Palestinians killed in the course of action were called *shuhada*, martyrs killed for the cause of religion and under the banner of Islam.

However, while the PLO had appropriated Islam as one element in its national political theory, the groups emerging in the West Bank and Gaza in the 1970s, particularly the Islamic Jihad, made Islam a central, predominant theme.   The Gaza-based Islamic Jihad movement, rejecting the *quietist* approach, opted for the new *Shii* interpretation of *jihad* as a symbol of militant activism.   It further adopted classical *Shii* doctrines of martyrdom and self-sacrifice in their most profound religious sense.   They were totally prepared to die for the cause, for a reward awaits in the life after death.

In 1986, members of an Islamic Jihad squad who were on trial gave the following statement: "We are members of the disinherited Islamic nation seeking martyrdom in the name of Allah against all aggression [or arrogance—the Arabic word is *istikbar*].   We attach much more importance to death than to life."[2]   This group soon gained wide notoriety through a series of daring terrorist attacks perpetrated against Israeli targets, the knifing to death of Israelis in the Gaza marketplace, hand-grenade attacks at an oath-taking ceremony at the Wailing Wall, and other such incidents.   Some of these attacks were carried out jointly with *Fatah* hit squads.

The Islamic Jihad's views on the Palestine problem and Israel derived largely from the principal tenets of the Iranian revolution.   Spokesmen for the group emphasized that Khomeini inscribed the word "Jerusalem" on the revolution's flag because of the Quranic holiness of the city.   Khomeini, they said, was working relentlessly to restore the Islamic character of Palestine and Jerusalem.   The Muslim masses of Iran, they further contended, brought Islam back to the battlefield as a counterforce to the Israeli Western offensive.[3]

Spokesmen for the Islamic Jihad described the Jews as despicable people trying to dominate the world by means of deceit, gambling, prostitution, and corruption.   The Jews could never be victorious, they insisted, because Allah had condemned them to "misery and humiliation."[4]   Israel, they contended, was nothing else but the spearhead of the Satanic forces.   It threatened all the disinherited and "served the interest of world aggression as practiced by the Great Satan, the United States of America."[5]   Israel was a direct daily threat to Muslims because it had sprung up in the heart of the Muslim homeland on the dead bodies of the Muslim Palestinian people.   Israel was, therefore, doomed to destruction.   Israel was born to die.

Following the outbreak of the Intifada, the Palestinian uprising in the West Bank and Gaza, in December 1987, the Islamic Jihad played a central role in mobilizing the Palestinian masses.   Pamphlets issued by the Islamic Jihad, proclaiming that the Islamic revolution had begun, urged the population to violently resist the authorities in the name of Islam.   Indeed, the traditional call *Allah hu akbar* (God is great, or God is the greatest) became the battle cry of the Intifada. The mosque was turned into an operational headquarters for organizing the resistance. Loudspeakers replaced conventional media. The rhetoric of radical Islam, simple and recognizable, increasingly appealed to the masses.

The Israeli authorities reacted firmly against the Islamic Jihad organization, and leading figures such as Abd al-Aziz Odeh and Fathi Shqaqi were arrested and deported. While this "iron hand" policy led to a substantial decrease in the activity of the Islamic Jihad during the first phase of the Intifada, this was not the only reason for its decline. Another Islamic movement, HAMAS, came to the fore and established itself as the leading Islamic power in the West Bank and Gaza.

HAMAS, the Arabic acronym for the Islamic Resistance Movement, represented the Muslim Brotherhood, which had been the first group to preach a return to Islamic piety in the Gaza Strip in the late 1970s. The Muslim Brotherhood, which operated through an organizational framework called *al-Mujamma*, gradually began to impose traditional Islamic perceptions on the local population. They tried to deepen the Islamic roots of society through education and community-oriented activity. Their main objective was to win the hearts of fellow Muslims and reorient the Muslim community to the righteous religious path. Occasionally, they attempted to forcibly impose their views by vandalizing liquor stores, attacking women wearing what they had regarded as immodest dress, and breaking up weddings where Western music was played. They also became more violent towards their political opponents, mostly PLO nationalists, left-wingers, and communists.

Generally speaking, and in contrast to the Islamic Jihad movement, the Brotherhood opted for the long-range, gradualist Islamic strategy. Members of the group dissociated themselves from the more activist approach towards Israel and terrorist acts against purely Israeli targets. The anti-PLO orientation of the *al-Mujamma* group partly explains why Israel tacitly ignored the group for a period of time in the late 1970s.

All of this changed when the Intifada began. The Muslim Brotherhood, outflanked and outgunned by the Islamic Jihad, soon concluded that it could no longer remain a spectator on the scene. Consequently, it, too, adopted violent *jihad*. Abandoning its support of a gradualist approach, the Brotherhood now opted for open violence and direct confrontation. Without officially or ideologically committing themselves to the Iranian revolution, they adopted the aggressive *Shii* interpretation of *jihad*.

Soon the Muslim Brotherhood set up a special military arm (HAMAS) and began to issue their own serialized leaflets, similar to those published by the Intifada's pro-PLO unified command. So successfully did they organize the resistance and mobilize the masses, that the Israeli authorities felt compelled to arrest hundreds of activists and, at a later stage, to outlaw the organization.

What was HAMAS's worldview? First, it emphasized the commitment to the principle of *jihad*. "There is no solution to the Palestinian problem except for *jihad*," HAMAS's Covenant proclaimed.[6] Second, it stressed the Islamic nature and character of Palestine: "Palestine is a *waqf* (religious endowment) land; it is a *sharia* (Islamic judicial system) ruling that any land acquired by the Muslims by force (as was the case of Palestine, occupied by the Army of Islam in the seventh century) was proclaimed Islamic endowment (*waqf*) for the Muslims. It is an eternal Islamic heritage."[7] Because Palestine is Islamic, HAMAS argued, the Jewish control over part of Palestine was a passing phenomenon which was to be rejected. It is imperative for the *Mujahideen* (the warriors of Jihad) "to kill the fighting Jews in Palestine." Thus, HAMAS adopted a strongly anti-Jewish and anti-Semitic stance. Its literature included such declarations as the following: "The Talmud teaches him [the Jew] means of theft and deceit. It [the Talmud] regards the non-Jew as an animal created in the form of a human being to serve the chosen Jew."[8]

HAMAS presented itself as an alternative to the PLO, declaring "nationalism [was] part of the religious creed." HAMAS stated that the solution of the Palestinian problem would not be achieved by setting up a secular Palestinian state but by the establishment of an "Islamic, Arab-liberated Palestine from the Jordan River to the Mediterranean Sea."[9] HAMAS rejected the PLO's concessionist, capitulating approach, which it claimed would lead to conciliation with Israel.

As we can see, HAMAS does not view nationalism and religion as mutually exclusive. While this may seem inherently contradictory to the Westerner, it is fully acceptable to the Muslim. A central feature of classical Islam is the total, comprehensive integration of state and religion. In Islam, a religiously based socio-political system, the Christian separation of church and state does not exist; the two are inseparable. The prophet Muhammad is viewed as both a prophet and a political leader of the Muslim community. The Islamic state is conceived of as a community of believers; and Allah, God, is the ultimate sovereign of the state.

Sharia, the religious legal system that provides the blueprint for Muslim society, is a comprehensive code of life which relates to every aspect of individual and communal life.   This worldview, which integrates religion and state, is the one that gives the Islamic activists in the West Bank and Gaza an ideal political model to strive for. It is this same worldview that motivates the Islamic elements elsewhere in the Arab-Muslim world.

The attitude of HAMAS towards the PLO is ambivalent. On the one hand, HAMAS speaks of the organization in friendly, brotherly terms. On the other hand, as we have seen, HAMAS sharply criticizes the PLO and continues to vehemently condemn what it regards as the PLO's conciliatory peace initiative. The ambivalence in HAMAS's attitude towards the PLO is also apparent in the reaction of Sheikh Ahmed Yassin, head of HAMAS, to the PLO's declaration of statehood in the West Bank and Gaza. He said:

> I support the idea and reject it simultaneously. I support the idea to have a state, but I am opposed to giving up the rest of my homeland Palestine. I am not against the PLO, but I am against the line of the organization which does not follow the spirit and laws of Islam. The closer the PLO becomes to Islam and the bigger the PLO's commitment to Islam becomes, the stronger my commitment to the PLO will become.[10]

What the sheikh was actually saying was that he anticipated an Islamicized PLO. He was perhaps even hinting that an Islamic takeover of the PLO was not that farfetched. In fact, it seems that HAMAS has been working towards this objective relentlessly. The movement has published its own serialized network of periodical leaflets, comparable to those issued by the PLO-oriented unified command of the uprising. Leaflet 36, for example, distributed by HAMAS in the territories in February 1989, called upon the PLO to immediately cease the dialogue with the United States and reject the idea of elections. At the same time, the leaflet provided the local population with specific dates for strikes, ordered a boycott on Israeli merchandise, and encouraged independent economic growth.

The PLO is quite alarmed at the emerging Islamic alternative. Some observers claim that one of the motives behind Arafat's staunch opposition to the West Bank elections proposed by Israel is the fear that the Islamists may win. Similar concerns were also expressed by Abu Iyyad, Arafat's deputy (who was assassinated in 1991). Addressing himself to the Israeli public in early 1989, he advised the Israelis to accept the PLO's peace initiative. Otherwise, he warned, in the near future they would be compelled to negotiate with the fundamentalists.

The PLO also undertook vigorous efforts to strengthen its Islamic profile. Sheikh Abd al-Hamid al-Saih, a religious dignitary, was appointed chairman of the Palestine National Council (PNC), the PLO's central body, comprising hundreds of Palestinian representatives. PLO spokesmen, some of whom have their early roots with the Muslim Brotherhood, tried to minimize the differences with the Islamists. Others, mainly within *Fatah*, encouraged cooperation in terror-related acts, offered operational experience, arms supplies, logistic support, and financial resources.

The Gulf War and the beginning of the political process in March 1991 accentuated the ideological and operational differences between the Islamic Jihad organization, HAMAS, and the PLO camp in the territories.

The Gulf crisis erupted at a time when the Intifada had partially stalled. The level of confrontation with the Israeli army had declined substantially due to the army's more efficient response and the arrest of leading secular and fundamentalist leaders. In addition, some measure of fatigue had begun to set in. Much of the energy that had once been expended in facing the external enemy was now being turned inward. Dozens of persons suspected of collaborating with the Israeli authorities were being slaughtered by fellow Arabs. Islamic extremists took an active part in the killing, executing not only alleged collaborators but also men and women suspected of breaking the moral laws of Islam.

The invasion of Kuwait by Iraqi forces in August 1990 was initially criticized by leaders of HAMAS. However, soon after, the Islamic circles reversed their attitude and enthusiastically supported Saddam Hussein, thus aligning themselves with the West Bank and Gaza public. The nationalist Palestinians in the occupied territories followed the directives of the Tunis-based PLO leadership and endorsed Saddam as their modern-day Saladin, a man capable of influencing the entire region and bringing about Palestinian liberation.

Unlike their pro-PLO counterparts, however, the Islamic circles emphasized the religious dimension of the crisis. The massive presence of American and Western military forces in the region, especially in Saudi Arabia, where the two most holy sites of Islam are located, and the humiliating defeat inflicted by these armies on Iraq aroused strong anti-Western sentiments within the Islamic fundamentalist movement.

The involvement of American and European troops was depicted as a modern reenactment of the Christian crusaders' assault on the Arab world and the renewal of the old religious conflict between the Muslim world and the West. In view of the "Western invasion," the Islamists began to lay increased emphasis on self-reliance and the need to reclaim the glorious past and cultural tradition of the Islamic civilization which had once dominated the world. They further urged Arabs to renounce Western—and Israeli—political and cultural domination, which had fostered secularism, materialism, and ideological bankruptcy.

The Iraqi defeat, the diminishing effectiveness of the Intifada, and the beginning of the peace process deepened the schism between HAMAS and the PLO. The Islamic fundamentalist movement came out strongly against the United States–sponsored peace process and severely denounced the Palestinians for participating in the negotiations. When the first meetings between Secretary of State James Baker and West Bank/Gaza delegates began, HAMAS hastened to label the move as an act of treason.[11] The Madrid conference and the subsequent negotiations between the Israeli and the Palestinian delegations aroused even stauncher Islamic opposition.

The Islamists challenged their PLO rivals on both the ideological and the practical levels. They contended that only free elections in the territories could determine who were the legitimate, authentic representatives of the Palestinians. Such elections, they claimed, would demonstrate the true power of Islam and would bring to the fore a loyal Muslim leadership. Unlike the secular PLO leadership, these leaders would highlight the Islamic nature of the Palestinian problem and would not consent to conciliatory, capitulatory American solutions.

When these challenges failed, the Islamic Movement resorted to extensive violence against both Israeli and secular Palestinian targets. Thus, the period since late 1991 has been characterized by an escalation of both the scope and the ferocity of violent acts perpetuated by Muslim activists, mainly members of the Islamic Jihad movement. This significant change is indicative of the growing frustration of these Islamic groups over their inability to stop the peace process, on the one hand, and their unceasing determination to forcibly impose their worldview, on the other.

To sum up, the resurgence of Islam as a pivotal factor in the Israeli-Palestinian conflict, as reflected in the Intifada, may well mark the Islamicization of the Israeli-Arab conflict. The growing strength of Islam in the West Bank and Gaza illustrates that it remains an authentic symbol of identification for Muslims in general and for

Muslim Palestinians in the occupied territories in particular. It is a powerful historical, cultural, and socio-political frame of reference which cohesively binds the local Muslim society. For the Palestinians, the Islamic alternative provides both a valid explanation for a disturbing reality and a comprehensive solution deeply rooted in their religio-political heritage. Thus, Islam offers the Palestinians a promising path for the future that is well anchored in a familiar, acceptable set of norms and values.

In an age of ideological confusion, widening socio-economic gaps, and political disarray, the Islamic formula is exceedingly attractive. While much has been said about the success and achievement of the Intifada, it is important to emphasize that the growing Islamicization of the struggle has yielded results that, from the perspective of Palestinian nationalists, are negative.   Politically and ideologically, Islamic fundamentalism has substantially eroded, if not divided, Palestinian unity. Thus, the rising tide of religious feelings in the West Bank and Gaza is indicative not only of the Islamicization of the Israeli-Arab conflict, but also of the further fragmentation of the Palestinian national movement.

NOTES

The original draft of this chapter was first presented at a May 1989 conference, "Fundamentalism as a Political Force in the Middle East," sponsored by the Berman Center for Jewish Studies and held at Lehigh University.

1.   Subsequent parts of this chapter are based on the author's article, "The Iranian Impact on the Islamic Jihad Movement in the Gaza Strip," in David Menashri, ed., *The Iranian Revolution and the Muslim World* (Boulder: Westview Press, 1990).
2.   *Koteret Rashit* (Tel Aviv), 21 October 1987.
3.   Rekhess, "The Iranian Impact," 195.
4.   Asad Bayyud al-Tamimi, *Zawal Israil Hatmiyya Quraniyya* (Arabic) (al-Qahira, n.d.), 25, 27, 30.
5.   Ahmad Sadiq, "Al-Islam wal-qadia al-Filastiniyya," *Al-Talia al-Islamiyya*, 1 December 1983.
6.   *Mithaq Harakat al-Muqawama al-Islamiyya-Filastin*, 18 August 1988.
7.   Ibid.
8.   Sheikh Salah al-Din Arqhdan, "Hukama Sahyun," *Filastin al-Muslima*, September 1989, 13.

9. *Mithaq*, 18 August 1988.
10. *Al-Nahar* (East Jerusalem), 29 April 1989.
11. *Haaretz*, 12 March 1991.

Chapter 7

Jewish Fundamentalism and the Israeli-Palestinian Impasse

Ian S. Lustick

The Arab-Israeli conflict is substantially closer to resolution now than it was 75, 50, or even 25 years ago. This is because the political division of the land between Jews and Palestinian Arabs, which is the only proposed solution to the dispute that has ever attracted substantial support from Jews and Arabs, is now the prime issue on the national agenda of both Israeli Jews and Palestinian Arabs. But another factor, religious fundamentalism, complicates even further whatever small but real chances exist to move towards a mutually acceptable negotiated peace.

As a destabilizing, extremist element in Middle Eastern affairs, Muslim fundamentalism has received wide attention in the West. The spectacular overthrow of the Shah in Iran and its consequences dramatized both the vulnerability of weakly institutionalized states and the potency of Islamic political appeals for tens of millions of Muslims, from Afghanistan to Morocco. Less attention has been given to the impact of Jewish fundamentalism, but in relation to Arab-Israeli affairs there is little doubt of its enormous influence as an obstacle to the achievement of a settlement based on political compromise.

There are huge asymmetries in the circumstances that have led to the influence of Muslim and Jewish fundamentalism in the Middle East. Obviously, Jewish fundamentalism does not exercise its influence because of the potential of its appeal to tens of millions of Middle Eastern Jews. They just do not exist. But Jewish fundamentalism has had, is having, and will continue to have an enormous impact in the region. The small numbers of Jewish fundamentalists have a power multiplied many times by their political leverage. The basic source of this leverage is the strategic position of Jewish fundamentalists in the militarily most powerful Middle Eastern state (Israel), which also happens to be not only extremely small, but organized politically in a way that offers extraordinary opportunities to energetic, ideologically committed minorities within it.

What links Jewish fundamentalist influence inside of Israel to events throughout the region is the concentration in one place—Palestine/the Land of Israel—of so much of what matters deeply to so many Middle Easterners: the Palestine Question, the Palestinian refugees, the Mosque of el-Aksa, the Dome of the Rock, the city of "el-Kuds" (Jerusalem the holy), and the nagging image of Israel as a vestige and an outpost of Western imperialism and as a non-Muslim enclave in an overwhelmingly Muslim region. All these factors, combined with a level of armaments in the hands of Israel and her Arab adversaries which approaches in many respects the weaponry available to the large European states, endow what happens there, and whoever controls what happens there, with an influence entirely unrelated to numbers of people or square kilometers. From the point of view of the Middle East as a whole, comprising perhaps the most unsettled region of a rapidly shrinking world, this justifies close analysis of Jewish fundamentalism in Israel—where it comes from, what it wants, how it thinks it can get it, and how great it expects its chances for success to be.

From a theoretical point of view, the inquiry is justified by the analytical payoff associated with finding useful comparisons among fundamentalist movements, whatever their size and sectarian affiliation. While I am unable, within the confines of the present essay, to discuss the useful comparisons that are possible, the task of defining fundamentalism is necessary both when analyzing such comparisons and when considering the specific case of Jewish fundamentalism in Israel. The problem of defining fundamentalism is seldom addressed explicitly in most studies of the phenomenon in Muslim, Jewish, or, for that matter, Christian settings.

It is absolutely necessary to define fundamentalism abstractly, not historically, and so remove it from the ultimately irrelevant etymological source of the term—the "five fundamentals" of American Protestant belief at the turn of the century. I conceive of fundamentalism as a political style. The defining characteristic of that style is that political action, dedicated towards rapid and comprehensive transformation of society, is seen to express uncompromisable, cosmically ordained, and more or less directly received imperatives. This definition, on the one hand, excludes many religious groups which are often, and rather carelessly, labeled fundamentalist: observant believers of one faith or another, traditionalists, and fanatics whose beliefs lead to withdrawal from society rather than attempts to change it. On the other hand, the definition does accommodate groups which act according to cosmic imperatives they do not describe in religious terms. Applying this definition, in other words, cultural revolution Maoists might well be seen as fundamentalists, while monks, mediators, mystics, talmudic scholars, whirling dervishes, and participants in long ecclesiastical hierarchies, regardless of how devout their beliefs or literal their acceptance of holy scriptures, would not be considered fundamentalist.

In the Israeli context, application of this definition means that the bulk of the black-coated Hasidic or "Mitnagid" ultra-orthodox Jewish communities, known as the Haredim, are not included as fundamentalists. Despite the startling electoral success of several political parties sponsored within the Haredi community, and not forgetting certain "fundamentalizing" trends among some Hasidic groups that combine messianism with concrete political action, most of these Jews, as steadfast in their faith and as observant as they may be, are not seeking to transform Israeli society via politics, so much as pursuing as great a subsidy and as great an isolation from "secularly contaminated" Israeli society as possible.

In the 1988 Israeli election, the 8 to 10 percent of Israeli Jews who belong to the ultra-orthodox community showed how effective they can be in mobilizing their people at the ballot box, even drawing some disaffected non–ultra-orthodox elements to their banners. But they do not seek, via politics, to transform society. Insofar as they are active in politics, it is primarily to help secure government subsidies for tens of thousands of lifetime seminary students and preserve their isolation from society—to keep their young men and women out of the army, and Sabbath traffic, as well as lewd advertisements, out of their neighborhoods. Moreover, many of these people are uncomfortable with the very idea of Israel as a Jewish state, let alone the fundamentalist principle that the State of Israel is a holy instrument of God. These ultra-pious Jews, the Haredim, have always been, and continue to be, outside of the mainstream of Jewish life in Israel.

It is impossible to understand Jewish fundamentalism in Israel without considering the great national schism over what to do with the territories occupied by the Jewish State in 1967—the West Bank and the Gaza Strip (or Judea, Samaria, and the Gaza District, in the parlance of the Jewish fundamentalists). Jewish Israel is deeply and almost exactly evenly divided on whether the territories should be permanently ruled by Israel or returned, wholly or in part, to Arab rule in exchange for peace.

Annexationists claim that Israel needs the territories for security purposes, to prevent terrorism, and to give the Israeli army maneuvering room in time of war. Anti-annexationists argue that the occupation breeds terrorism and that ending it can reduce the likelihood of war. In any case, they contend, modern weaponry reduces the importance of territorial expanse and increases the value of demilitarization agreements.

Annexationists argue that the West Bank and Gaza are so tightly interdependent with Israel economically and infrastructurally that withdrawal would subject the Israeli economy, and the 250,000 Israelis who live in the territories (including expanded East Jerusalem), to intolerable dislocations. Those who favor territorial compromise point to the continuing cost of the occupation, the millions of man-hours spent in policing operations, the damage done by tens of thousands of semi-legal Arab laborers to the traditional Zionist conception of a Jewish working class, and the enhanced opportunities for trade and investment that would be associated with a peace agreement.

Anti-annexationists also argue that, demographically, Israel will cease to be Jewish if it absorbs the 1.8 million Arabs in the territories, adding them to the 750,000 Arabs living now within Israel itself. They point out that there are already more Arab children in the area between the Jordan River and the Mediterranean Sea than Jewish children. Annexationists, however, contend that demographic trends can be misleading, that the large numbers of Russian Jews moving to Israel will solve the problem, and that regardless of whether Israel relinquishes the territories or not, it will have to deal with a large discontented, internal Arab population.

On the ideological level, annexationists argue that withdrawal from the heartland of biblical Israel and the abandonment or dismantling of settlements would be a betrayal of the Zionist principles upon which the state was founded. Anti-annexationists stress that equally important Zionist principles of creating a Jewish working class, a model society, and achieving peace with the Arabs are betrayed by the employment of tens of thousands of semi-legal Arab laborers from the territories, continuation of the occupation, and its corrosive effects on the country's moral spirit.

As you might expect from this summary and partial list of claims and counter-claims, the average Israeli is likely to be confused, uncertain, and frustrated—not knowing how to choose among so many convincing but contradictory arguments about the very essence of his nation's future. It is partly to this sense of confusion and worry that the Jewish fundamentalists, who express no confusion or doubt whatsoever, owe their political power. Jewish fundamentalists agree that the disposition of the West Bank and Gaza (Judea, Samaria, and the Gaza District as they term them) is the single most important issue facing the country. But for them, the real issues are not security, demography, economics, or politics, but a metaphysical question of transcendent importance. For the majority of Jewish fundamentalists, the disposition of the territories is an explicitly religious question—whether or not the process of God's redemption of the Jewish people, and of the world as a whole, including the advent of the Messiah himself, will be brought to its glorious conclusion in the relatively near future, or whether it will be tragically delayed or even halted.

Before explaining the beliefs of Jewish fundamentalists in greater depth, let me provide a brief assessment of the extent of their power and appeal on the Israeli political scene. The organizational core of the fundamentalist movement is Gush Emunim (The Bloc of the Faithful)—an umbrella organization of approximately twenty thousand devoted activists. Their ideas are fully or partially represented in the Israeli Parliament by the National Religious Party, Moledet, Tzomet (together holding ten percent of the Knesset's seats), and by many members of Likud.

The core of Gush Emunim is the more than 150 settlements established in the West Bank, the Gaza Strip, and the Golan Heights since 1967. However, the recruitment pools for the movement within Israeli society include the religious youth movement "Benei Akiva," a network of paramilitary seminaries, the religious educational system, new immigrants, and many middle-class Israelis with strong political commitments to expansive versions of Labor Zionism or to Revisionist Zionism. Though officially non-partisan, Gush Emunim is actively supported in the national political arena by important cabinet ministers, and more than 35 percent of the Parliament, representing half a dozen political parties. Electoral support for parties supporting Gush Emunim is strong among Israel's "Oriental Jews," those who immigrated from, or whose parents immigrated from, Asian and African countries.

Gush Emunim itself has never had a "formal" membership list or an elected leadership. Nevertheless, it has spawned its own settlement building and sustaining organization—"Amana" (Covenant). Its settlements are organized within Yesha (Salvation), the Association of Local Councils in Judea, Samaria, and the Gaza District. Aside from sponsoring the publication of *Nekuda*, an "in-house" monthly journal, Yesha gives Gush Emunim a semi-official governing body, elaborate administrative and economic resources, and direct involvement in the implementation of government policies in the occupied territories. Gush Emunim also includes overlapping groups dedicated to specific objectives, including propaganda, legal affairs, immigration, political outreach, and security.

The influence of the fundamentalist movement, for which, as I have indicated, Gush Emunim serves as the central organizing focus, is reflected in each week's headlines, where the obstacles to peace associated with Israeli settlements in the occupied territories are unremittingly evidenced. Established primarily by fundamentalist activists, these settlements, and the political support they can muster among Israeli annexationists, pose difficult and even frightening problems for any government inclined towards a policy of trading land for peace—including the Labor-led government formed by Yitzhak Rabin after the July 1992 elections. This fundamentalist influence is also reflected in Israeli opinion polls. Ultranationalist and religious fundamentalist beliefs, attitudes, and political programs, which were regarded as crackpot extremism by the vast majority of Israeli Jews in the late 1960s, are currently embraced by 20 percent of the Israeli-Jewish population. Another 10 to 15 percent gives strong support to the key Gush demand that absolutely no territorial concessions be made in the West Bank and Gaza Strip.[1]

Another telling indication of Gush Emunim's impact comes from a June 1987 survey of 22 leading Israeli figures from across the political spectrum. They were asked to name the person who has had the greatest impact on Israeli society in the last 20 years. Rabbi Moshe Levinger, the most prominent ideological guide of the fundamentalist movement today, tied with former Prime Minister Menachem Begin for first place in this survey.

In many respects Gush Emunim, a highly energized minority movement emphasizing pioneering values and a grand vision of Zionism, can be compared to the kibbutz movement of the pre-state era. Before 1948 the kibbutz movement, kibbutz members, and the socialist-Zionist leadership associated with the kibbutzim provided the Yishuv (Jews living in Palestine) with its most salient models for Jewish patriotism, Zionist commitment, civic duty, and spiritual guidance. To the present generation of Israelis, Gush Emunim, its "pioneering settlers" in the West Bank and Gaza, and the charismatic and rabbinic leaders that it has raised to prominence are the most salient such models available.

What are the elements of the Jewish fundamentalist belief system that give such prominence, such decisive, overriding significance, to Jewish political rule over the whole Land of Israel? Where did the movement come from? Is it a logical extension of Zionism? These are some of the questions, discussed at length in my book, *For the Land and the Lord: Jewish Fundamentalism in Israel*, that I will touch on in this essay.

Jewish fundamentalists in Israel refer to one man, Rabbi (Rav) Zvi Yehuda Kook, who died at 91 in 1982, as "our teacher and master." Zvi Yehuda was the charismatic founder of contemporary Jewish fundamentalism. In 1967 he was an obscure rabbi in a dilapidated, forgotten yeshiva, or seminary, in Jerusalem. In 1977, with the Prime Minister of Israel kneeling before him, he sealed an alliance between Jewish fundamentalism, in its pursuit of messianic redemption, and the political fortunes of Israel's right wing—the Likud. When I say kneeling, I mean this quite literally. Let me quote a description of a little-known but revealing incident that occurred shortly after the Likud's victory over the Labor Party in 1977 Israeli elections:

> When Begin was chosen as Prime Minister he came to visit Zvi Yehuda. He came as if to Canossa, as if this man, Zvi Yehuda, was God's representative. Suddenly the Prime Minister kneels and bows before Zvi Yehuda. Imagine for yourself what all the students standing there and watching this surrealistic scene were thinking. I'll never forget it. I felt that my heart was bursting within me. What greater empirical proof could there be that his fantasies and imaginings were indeed reality: You could see for yourself that instead of treating him as if he were crazy, people looked upon him as something holy. And everything he said or did became something holy as well.[2]

Although for the time being, at least, Gush Emunim has lost the powerful and direct influence over government policy it enjoyed under the Begin and Shamir governments, a future Likud victory will bring its voice back to the center of power. Just as important as that influence is the basic challenge Jewish fundamentalism has posed, and continues to pose, to the liberal, social democratic ethos that prevailed in Israel and in the Zionist movement for more than 60 years. I witnessed the vitality of that challenge during a visit to Israel in 1988.

During the most promising period of Secretary of State Schultz's peace initiative, upwards of 80,000 Israelis met to demonstrate on behalf of a peace treaty involving recognition of Palestinian rights and withdrawal from occupied territories. I was there, and was impressed. But the very next night, in the same place in Tel Aviv, Gush Emunim organized a counter-demonstration, labeling peace as surrender and withdrawal from any parts of the Land of Israel as betrayal. There were over 150,000 Israelis at this demonstration.

I also attended a ceremony commemorating the sixth anniversary of Zvi Yehuda Kook's death. It was held at the greatly expanded and refurbished "Merkaz Harav" Yeshiva where the Gush Emunim was born. Both the Chief Rabbi of Israel and Prime Minister Yitzhak Shamir delivered impassioned speeches to the enthusiastic crowd, jammed shoulder to shoulder within the sanctuary of the yeshiva. They pledged their faithfulness to the memory of Zvi Yehuda Kook and their commitment to honor his injunction to put the unity of the whole Land of Israel above all other concerns.

Here I would like to discuss several of the basic assumptions enumerated in my book, which undergird Jewish fundamentalism. The first, and perhaps the most important, is the fundamentalists' view of the Jewish people as utterly unique—not just different from other peoples in the way that each people is singular in its cultural characteristics and history, but different qualitatively from all other peoples. I wish to stress that this represents a complete reversal of classical Zionist ideology. The basis of Zionism was the belief, arrived at by Zionism's founders in the late nineteenth century, that anti-Semitism was caused by Gentile perceptions of Jews as weird, as abnormal. The Zionists traced this belief, which triggered feelings of fear and hatred in non-Jews towards Jews, to the fact that Jews lived in an "abnormal way," separated from their neighbors, a strange minority everywhere, and a majority nowhere. If Jews could have a state of their own somewhere, and be a majority there, they could be "normalized." There would still be Jewish minorities in other countries just as there would be German or Irish minorities, but anti-Semitism would cease; through their state the Jews would become, in the famous Zionist phrase "*goy kekhol hagoyim*"—a nation like any other nation.

For Jewish fundamentalists, this idea of Jews becoming normal is delusional. For them, Jews have been created as intrinsically abnormal—special, chosen for a mission in the world that lifts them above the norms, laws, and categories applicable to other peoples. If Zionism was right to bring Jews back to the Land of Israel, it was misguided in its understanding of why it was doing so—not to "normalize them," but to set the stage for the continuation of the Jewish people's special role as God's assistant in the redemption of the world. In this process, the non-Jews (including the Arabs, but certainly not only the Arabs), indeed all the *goyim*, can be expected to fight against the Jews, thereby reflecting only the recalcitrance of the non-chosen towards the message of redemption brought by the chosen.

In this context, we can understand the point made by Rabbi Shlomo Aviner, head of the "Crown of the Priests" Yeshiva in Jerusalem, a disciple of Zvi Yehuda Kook, who explained that while God requires other, normal nations to abide by abstract codes of "justice and righteousness," such laws do not apply to Jews. To his people Israel, God speaks directly. His commandments, in the context of a covenanted relationship with the Jewish people, take precedence over all appeals to universalist ethics:

> Ours is not an autonomous scale of values, the product of human reason, but rather a heteronomous or, more correctly, "theonomous" scale rooted in the will of the Divine architect of the universe and its moral order.[3]

> From the point of view of mankind's humanistic morality we were in the wrong in [taking the land] from the Canaanites. There is only one catch. The command of God ordered us to be the people of the Land of Israel.[4]

Thus does Jewish fundamentalism utterly reject the traditional Zionist image of Jews as a normal people, bound by and rewarded accordingly to the same laws and principles of national self-determination that are applied to other nations. Far from seeking formulas allowing Jews and the Jewish state to fit in with and be accepted by the family of nations, Gush Emunim is proud to emphasize one of its favorite verses in the Bible which refers to the Jews as "the people that dwells alone, and that will not be counted among the nations."[5]

Another important part of Gush Emunim's worldview is the fundamentalist understanding of current history as the unfolding of the redemption process. A key element in Jewish fundamentalism, as in any fundamentalist movement, is the belief that its adherents possess special and direct access to transcendental truth, to a true vision of the future course of events, and to an understanding of what the future requires.

For Jewish fundamentalists, history is God's means of communicating with his people. Political trends and events contain messages to Jews which provide instructions, reprimands, and rewards. Political and historical analysis, properly undertaken, is equivalent to the interpretation of God's will. In combination with religious texts, this analysis guides the continuing struggle towards Redemption. This general approach is well illustrated by the divine messages which Jewish fundamentalists discern in three key events: the Holocaust, the Six Day War, and the Yom Kippur War.

Fundamentalists tend to see the Holocaust, the destruction of six million Jews by Nazi Germany during World War II, as an example of God's discipline—"a commandment written in blood upon the soil of Europe."[6] God thereby instructed his people that the Emancipation, in which so many Jews had placed their hopes for a future of equality within a liberal democratic Europe, could not provide Jews with an escape route from the burdens of their Covenant.[7] Thus, the Holocaust is seen as God's way of coercing his chosen people back to the Promised Land and of convincing them of the cosmic urgency of its complete reunification—the whole people of Israel in the whole Land of Israel. Best known for this interpretation of the Holocaust is Rabbi Menachem Kasher, who argued that the Holocaust, which entailed the destruction of more Jews than the loss of the First and Second Temples combined, must be understood as the "birthpangs of the Messianic Age [which] fell upon our generation and thus opened for us the way to Redemption."[8]

In general, Jewish fundamentalists believe that the wars of 1967 and 1973 show that God speaks to Israel not just through disaster, but through deliverance. The Six Day War, by which Israel came into possession of the Temple Mount in Jerusalem and the core areas of the biblical Land of Israel, as well as the enthusiasm and excitement about the land which it awakened in many Jews, are seen as God's signal that the process of Redemption has begun. The completedness of the Land, a prerequisite for the completedness of the Jewish people, is also a prerequisite for the completedness of the Redemption of the entire world.

Any doubts that Jews may have had about the meaning of that victory and the continuing struggle with the Arabs should have been, according to fundamentalists, wiped away by the 1973 war, launched against Israel by Egypt and Syria on the holiest day in the Jewish calendar—Yom Kippur. The awful casualties suffered and the final victory won are both seen as God's reminder to Jews: to abandon conceptions of the Arab-Israeli conflict as a "normal" political dispute; to therefore avoid trusting in any negotiated peace agreements; and to trust only in God and in the unique destiny of the Jewish people. Peace, in the fundamentalist view, will only come with the Messiah, with the culmination of the redemptive process. But that process itself cannot be completed if parts of the land are relinquished, or if parts of the land are left unsettled by Jews.

Jewish fundamentalists believe that all events reflect the will of God and that the center of his interest in the world is the unfolding Redemption of the land and people of Israel. Again, during my 1988 visit to Israel, I was reminded of this principle of fundamentalist belief in a conversation I had with the then secretary-general of Gush Emunim, Daniella Weiss, in her hilltop home in a settlement on the West Bank. It was the day of the giant rally in Tel Aviv, and she was anxious about amassing a large enough crowd to make the proper impression, both in Israel and abroad. I asked her how she could work so hard in the mundane aspects of political life and still see what she was doing in cosmic, redemptive terms. She responded by explaining what she called "parallel thinking." "Listen to the roaring wind," she said, pointing to the window.

> On the one hand I am worrying about how the weather might interfere with the turnout for our rally. But then, at that moment, I understand that God is providing the bad weather so that our spirit can be tested and demonstrated that much more effectively to all of Israel when we appear, against all odds, in our large numbers.[9]

These and other unquestioned assumptions of Jewish fundamentalists make it possible to understand why Gush Emunim sees every suggestion or initiative that might bring Arabs and Israelis to the bargaining table, every perception of moderation in the Arab or Palestinian position, not as an opportunity to be examined carefully as a possible move towards peace, but as a danger, a "test" of the Jewish people. To Gush Emunim, the attraction which negotiations have for many Israelis and their willingness even to consider Arab proposals for peace reveal their spiritual weakness and the distance the Jewish people still must travel to achieve the national discipline required to accomplish its redemptive tasks.

Jewish fundamentalists characterize their movement as *the* authentic representation of Judaism, of Jewish values, and even of what Zionism was always meant to be. The movement's many opponents in Israel characterize it as a freak and tragic aberration that has nothing to do with the universalist, tolerant, and liberal values which they see as at the core of Judaism. Both are wrong—the fundamentalist impulse is an authentic one in Judaism. The Redemption of the world is, in Jewish cosmology, closely connected to Jewish rule over the whole Land of Israel. In the name of these beliefs, two great and catastrophic revolts were launched against Roman rule in Judea in the first and second centuries of the common era. Millions of Jews were killed in these revolts, Jewish independence in the land was ended, and the Temple destroyed. But, although the rabbis have strived, for good reason perhaps, to suppress and de-emphasize the role of mysticism and activist messianism in Jewish life, the authenticity of these fundamentalist outbursts and the beliefs which led to them cannot be denied.

Thus, Jewish fundamentalism must be seen as *an* authentic expression of Judaism, if not *the* authentic expression of it. It arose, essentially, as an unintended result of the success of Zionism. The return of the Jews to their land insured that the myths and memories of rule over the whole "promised land," of the need to rebuild the Temple, of the imperative to help God inaugurate the messianic age, and of the vision of the Jews being recognized by all, not as a nation like any other nation, but as the center of God's universe, could no longer be neutralized as they had been in the diaspora. Traditional rabbinic injunctions against conjuring the Messiah and the traditional belief that God, alone, will accomplish the return to Zion did not stop the Zionist movement from appropriating the powerful Jewish motifs associated with return to the "promised land." However, the return to the Land of Israel, the reunification of Jerusalem, and the conquest of the biblical heartland of the West Bank made the view that secular Zionism was itself somehow the instrument of the messianic redemption increasingly credible in religious circles.

Nevertheless, fundamentalist critiques of Zionism as but a stage in a grand redemptionist drama have thrived, while the ideas and institutions of mainstream Zionism have withered. Despite its impressive achievements, Zionism has fallen decisively short of its goal—Jews are neither secure, nor at peace. Jewish life has not, in the classical Zionist parlance, been "normalized." Whatever the reality, Jews in Israel perceive themselves as surrounded by hostility. This evokes all too recent memories of destruction, an abiding Jewish distrust of non-Jews, and a profound desire for categorical guarantees for the future.

In a very real sense the struggle within Israel over withdrawal from the territories in return for peace, the struggle over whether Jews can order their national life to conform with the dictates of international politics, is a recapitulation of the struggle which Jews fought among themselves in Roman times. Could Israel live, as others did, under Rome, or only under God? The incompleteness of Zionism's success has reopened this Pandora's box. Can it be closed? Can Jews in their own land resist this time, as they could not two thousand years ago, the temptations of what Gershom Sholem called "the blazing landscape of redemption"? Can they resist this temptation in favor of more pragmatic, imperfect, but infinitely less dangerous political alternatives?

NOTES

This chapter was first presented at a May 1989 conference, "Fundamentalism as a Political Force in the Middle East," sponsored by the Berman Center for Jewish Studies and held at Lehigh University.

1. Despite the stunning upset by the Labor Party and its dovish allies in the July 1992 elections, a careful review of the electoral results shows that if all competing lists are taken into account (including three fundamentalist lists which did not receive enough votes to pass the minimum representation threshold in the Parliament), those lists running on platforms inclined toward permanent incorporation of the territories received more Jewish votes than did anti-annexationist lists.
2. Daniel Ben Simon, "Merkaz HaRav: Gush Emunim Developed Here," *Haaretz* (14 April 1986), 8. Cited in Ian Lustick, *For the Land and the Lord: Jewish Fundamentalism in Israel* (New York: Council on Foreign Relations, 1988), 37.
3. Rabbi Shlomo Aviner, "Messianic Realism," in *Whose Homeland: Eretz Israel Roots of the Jewish Claim* (Jerusalem: Department for Torah Education and Culture in the Diaspora, World Zionist Organization, 1978), 115–16.
4. Shlomo Aviner, "The Moral Problem of Possessing the Land," *Artzi* 2 (1982): 11. *Artzi* is a scholarly and ideologically oriented fundamentalist journal, edited by Rabbi Yoel Ben-Nun, that has appeared irregularly since 1983.
5. Numbers 23:9.
6. Harold Fisch, *The Zionist Revolution* (New York: St. Martin's Press, 1978), 85.
7. Ibid., 18, 86–87.
8. Menachem Kasher, *The Great Era* (Jerusalem: Torah Shlema, 1968), 32.
9. Daniella Weiss, interview with author, Kedumin, 13 March 1988.

Chapter 8

The Politics, Institutions, and Culture of Gush Emunim

Ehud Sprinzak

Zionism and Judaism

Gush Emunim has always seen itself as the revitalizer of Zionism. In its 1974 manifesto the Gush said:

> Our aim is to bring about a large movement of reawakening among the Jewish people for the fulfillment of the Zionist vision in its full scope. . . . The sources of the vision are the Jewish tradition and roots, and its ultimate objective is the full redemption of the Jewish people and the entire world.[1]

Gush Emunim obviously feels that historic Zionism died out in the Israel of the 1950s and 1960s, and that Israelis now live in a crisis born of the fatigue that followed the partial implementation of Zionism in the State of Israel. This crisis has led to the weakening of the pioneering spirit, to an unwillingness to continue the struggle against the pressures of the outside world (especially the Arabs), and to the growth of a materialistic society in which the needs of the individual have superseded the national mission. Gush members want to overcome the present Israeli decadence by restoring the pioneering and sacrificial spirit of the past.

The attempt to reconstruct Zionism is only part of a larger Gush Emunim project: the Judaization of secular Israel. Most Gush leaders are reluctant to admit that secular Zionism has been deficient since its inception and was consequently *bound* to decline. Rav Kook [Rabbi

117

Abraham Isaac HaKohen Kook], though impressed by the deeds of secular Zionists, never endorsed secular Zionism. He would have preferred to see a religious movement lead the modern Jewish return to Eretz Yisrael. Since there was no such movement, and since he was moved by the early pioneers, he devised a unique kabbalistic ploy, the *sacralization of the profane*, that is his religious legitimation of secular and atheist Zionism.[2] Gush Emunim, while formally loyal to Rav Kook's reasoning, does not operate however under his constraints. Its leaders are aware of the great weakness of modern Zionism, as well as of their own power and potential. Thus, aside from a formal approval of secular Zionism for its past achievements, they are critical of most of Israel's present Zionist movements and parties. And Israel's conventional foreign policy, based on considerations of international interests and opinions, often raises their ire.

Gush Emunim's greatest conflict with modern secular Zionism is expressed in its critique of the Zionist theory of normalization. Both Leo Pinsker and Theodore Herzl, the nineteenth-century thinkers who formulated the classical doctrines of political Zionism, argued for "Jewish normalization." They believed that anti-Semitism was a product of the abnormality of Jewish life among the Gentiles and that the existence of a Jewish state, to which all the Jews would immigrate, would eliminate the hatred of the Jews and solve the "Jewish problem." Once Jews had a state of their own, they and the rest of the world would recognize them as normal human beings and their state would function like any other member of the community of nations.[3]

The normalization approach was never popular in Gush Emunim. Rabbi Zvi Yehuda Kook was known for his great hostility to Gentiles, especially Christians. He was responsible for Gush Emunim's suspicion and hostility toward other nations and for its repeated insistence on preserving the "honor" of Israel.[4] Gush Emunim's first manifesto read:

> Any framework or international organization whose resolutions imply the humiliation of the honor of Israel has no right to exist and we consequently do not belong there. We must leave that organization and wait for the day when the honor of Israel would rise again and the truth among the nations will be uncovered.[5]

The normalization theory was utterly rejected after the Yom Kippur War. From a Kookist perspective, the war should not have taken place. The miraculous Six-Day War had, according to these people, shown God's great interest in a quick redemption. If so, the Yom Kippur War implied the opposite. There could be only one explanation for this war: it was the final attempt of the Gentiles to stop the coming redemption of the Jews. It was a struggle against God Himself. Rabbi Yehuda Amital's essay, "The Meaning of the Yom Kippur War," helped shape the thinking of many Gush members in those difficult days:

> The confusion and sense of unease which followed the Yom Kippur War exposed a deep crisis. This is the crisis of the very Zionist idea in the Herzlian thinking . . . . Herzl sought to solve the "Jewish Problem" for the Jews and for the nations of the world. . . . When Israel will have his own homeland and state, it will obtain its proper place in the family of nations. No room would remain for anti-Semitism. . . . But now, just as Zionism celebrates its practical victory, its ideological conception is in a total disarray. The Jewish Problem has not been solved and anti-Semitism has not disappeared but has grown worse. . . .
>
> The dreams of normalization have been exposed as hollow. The State of Israel is the only state in the world which faces destruction. . . . The vision of the prophet—"a people that dwells alone and that shall not be reckoned among the nations"—is fulfilled in front of our eyes in the most physical sense. The earthquake people speak about in these days is not a result of the weakening of security or political thinking but a consequence of the failure of the ABC of the Zionist nationalist theory.
>
> But there exists another Zionism, the Zionism of redemption, whose great announcer and interpreter was Rav Kook. . . . This Zionism has not come to solve the Jewish Problem by the establishment of a Jewish state but is used, instead, by the High Providence as a tool in order to move and to advance Israel towards its redemption. Its intrinsic direction is not the normalization of the people of Israel in order to become a nation like all the nations, but to become a holy people, a people of living God, whose basis is in Jerusalem and a king's temple is its center. . . . What is revealed in front of our eyes is the beginning of the fulfillment of the vision of the Prophets regarding the return to Zion. The steps are the Messiah's. And although these are accompanied by pains, the steps are certain and the course clear. . . . It is time Zionism becomes the Zionism of redemption in our consciousness too.[6]

Amital's negation of the very heart of secular Zionism was one of many indications that the Gush intended to "reawaken" Zionism somewhat more radically than the public had thought. Gush Emunim has been less interested in a new religious-secular synthesis than in a religious transformation of secular Zionism in ways that in fact deny its essence.

Gush Emunim is a special kind of religious movement, orthodox collectivity whose very essence is the paradox, the unresolved tension between the sacred sin and the obsolete religiosity.

> Zionist fulfillment stands tainted by the reinvigoration and institution-alization of profanity and sin which go against the living according to the Torah and which are understood as the falsification of the truthful faith. This is a secular victory which is by itself a very frustrating dissonance. At the same time Zionist fulfillment implies a totally contradictory element—the fulfillment of the obligations of the Torah and the actualization of an article of belief, i.e., of a religious peak. In its struggle with this contradiction Kookism reaches an "idealization of secularity," which is understood as a lofty expression of the religion.[7]

The Kookist paradox should not deceive the observer regarding the true nature of Gush Emunim. The repeated references to the movement's strong attachment to secular Zionism are misleading, for they tell only part of the story. The movement should not be seen as a religious offshoot of the secular Zionist movement, but as a very successful religious raid into the heart of secular Israel. Many Gush members have moved toward Jewish ultraorthodoxy, which supports this assessment. Facing a growing number of blocks on the road to redemption, frustrated Gush members do not join *kibbutzim* or go to development towns to strengthen the foundations of traditional Zionism, but turn instead to ultraorthodoxy and the Torah, convinced that the Torah, not the Israeli army, will save the nation from its troubles.[8]

The State and the Rule of Law

Kookist theology is distinguished by its great respect for the State of Israel and its institutions, the government, the Knesset, and the army. Gush Emunim's legendary document, the prophetic sermon that Rabbi Zvi Yehuda delivered at Merkaz Harav on Israel's nineteenth birthday, just before the Six-Day War, emphasizes that the State of Israel is holy:

> And against what was said, "Is this the state envisioned by our Prophets?" I say: This is the state the prophets envisioned. Of course, this is not the state in its completion, but our prophets and their successors said that the state is going to be like that: the seed of Abraham, Isaac, and Jacob will settle and establish there a reality of

settlement and an independent political government. . . . It has now been nineteen years of development. . . . We are honored to witness the wonders of God and His secrets—in construction, agriculture, policy, security in matter and spirit. . . . The real Yisrael is the redeemed Yisrael, the kingdom of Israel and the army of Israel.[9]

According to the rabbi, Israel and its institutions are legitimate not only because they rely on the support of the people of Israel and are duly constituted, but mainly because they represent the will of God. Israel won its independence not because the Zionists mustered the military and political power to beat the Arabs and win international legitimacy, but because God wanted it that way. Being constituted by God, the state deserves the halakhic status of a "Kingdom," and consequently ought to receive the allegiance of all its citizens and the respect of all the present religious authorities.

This definition of the State of Israel is the great theological divide between Gush Emunim and Israel's religious ultraorthodox. The Gush does not approve of either the extremists of Neturei Karta and the Satmar Hasidics, who consider the State of Israel an apostasy and a direct rebellion against God, or the ultraorthodox Agudat Israel, which participates in the conduct of Israel's public affairs but denies halakhic status to the institutions of "the Zionists." Gush Emunim's principled commitment to the sanctity of the State of Israel was restated strongly by Rabbi Moshe Levinger when the Jerusalem District Court imposed severe punishments upon the members of the Jewish Underground:

Following the conclusion and the verdict of the underground trial, it is our duty to remember that the State of Israel and all its institutions, just like her sky, land, and fruits, are all holy. . . . The establishment of the State of Israel means a state and all that comes with a state and is related to a state's existence, schools and synagogues and the institutions responsible for the public life of the state, the government, the Knesset, the courts, the police, the security services and even the prisons are all part of the Israeli statism which is being renewed with the help of God. Thus, when we are about to react—and there is room for reaction—to the conclusions and the verdicts, we have to do it from a position of respect for the people, the land, the state and its institutions, especially those that leave us bitter. This is because a deep and truthful commitment to values shows in time of crisis, when it appears that reality looks hard and cruel.[10]

This glorification of the State of Israel explains why, despite the Gush's many confrontations with the government, the police, and the army, there have been relatively few severe incidents and why the movement has rarely been considered in Israel as a seditious or rebellious organization. However, it does not explain the huge number of Gush Emunim's illicit and extralegal operations. What, in practice, does this glorification of the state mean? How does the movement perceive legitimate as opposed to illegitimate political participation?

It is one thing to avow a deep respect for political institutions and quite another to translate this attitude into compliance with the law. In the case of Gush Emunim the gap seems rather broad. There are two keys to the understanding of the intense extralegal behavior of Gush Emunim: one is the difference between the sacredness of the *State* of Israel and of the *Land* of Israel, and the other is Gush Emunim's legal philosophy.

What we might call "the Gush Emunim doctrine of sacredness," suggests that the State of Israel is not as holy as the territory of Israel. The state is never mentioned as part of the "holy trinity"—the Land, the People, the Torah of Israel. Furthermore, unlike the holiness of the trio which is absolute and eternal, the sanctity of the state is relative and conditional. "The land and the state," writes Rabbi Jacob Ariel in *Nekuda* [Gush-Emunim-oriented magazine],

> are two values whose location in the right place in our scale of values is of great importance and of many practical consequences. Which of them comes first, which is preferable to the other, which is the means and which is the end? . . . The land is not a means for the state but the state is a means for the land. The land is the goal and the state is nothing but the means to achieve this goal. . . . Eretz Yisrael is an absolute entity whose essence does not depend on any political factor (and) the virtue of the state of Israel in Eretz Yisrael is its ability to fulfill the obligation of settling Eretz Yisrael with no constraints or limitation. An Israeli state which limits or inhibits the settlement of Israel by its people loses both its virtue and importance, and in the final analysis its moral and legal authority altogether. In the public struggle being waged on this scale of values, which determines the relationship between the land and the state, the very existence of the state, its uniqueness, Jewishness, and destiny are at stake. Those who place the state in its right position in this struggle—as a tool to secure the sovereignty of the people of Israel over its land—are the ones who secure the continuation of its development, growth, expansion, strength and invigoration.[11]

Ariel's argument provides the rationale for Gush Emunim's great confrontation with the Labor government in the mid-1970s over the issue of settling Samaria. Its extension to include the absolute prohibition of surrendering Eretz Yisrael territories justified the 1982 extralegal settlement operations in Sinai. The argument and the operations were backed by Rabbi Zvi Yehuda Kook's rulings that any prohibition of settlement in Eretz Yisrael by the government of Israel was null and void, and that the preservation of the integrity of the Holy Land was a sacred obligation, a case of *Yehareg Uval Yaavor* (be killed rather than sin).

But there was another element—*Gush Emunim's disrespect for the rule of civil law*. Gush Emunim, like several other political groups in Israel, has never respected the rule of law as a principle of good government. Most of its leaders have always been hostile to formality and order, and see no virtue in proper procedures or obedience to the law. Pioneering, self-sacrifice, taking risks, and breaking new ground are the qualities they admire in the early Zionist who settled the land without asking permission. Rabbi Yoel Ben-Nun, the most moderate and civil of all Gush Emunim ideologues, once responded to a query about the Gush's respect for the law:

> It is shocking that Yigal (Allon) speaks about the law. When he makes a decision no law bothers him. When he decided that Hebron (the first Jewish settlement in the Park Hotel) had to exist and it needed arms, he saw to it that arms were moved, under the table, from Kfar Etzion to Hebron. Stealing chickens from the henhouse is a norm the Palmach introduced.[12]

Here Ben-Nun linked the illegalism of the Palmach—the paramilitary units of the Labor movement during the British Mandate—with the extralegalism of Gush Emunim. He intended no irony; he was expressing strong conviction that Gush Emunim on the hills of Samaria in the 1970s was just like the young *kibbutzniks* on the hills of the Galilee in the 1920s; any government of Israel that barred Jewish settlement in Eretz Yisrael was to be equated with the British Mandate government that, in 1939, issued the White Paper barring Jewish settlement and immigration. It was also to be put in the same category of the Zionist authorities in Palestine in the 1920s and 1930s, who were reluctant to permit daring settlement operations in remote areas for fear it would hurt the reputation of the movement and create indefensible settlements.[13]

Settlement of Eretz Yisrael territories is, according to Gush Emunim, the most distinguished Zionist and Jewish virtue. Neither law nor any principle of good government can match it.

Gush Emunim's consensus regarding the permissible and the illegitimate was broken following the 1984 discovery of the Jewish Underground. Suddenly it was learned that the extralegalism of several distinguished members of the movement extended to premeditated killing of Arabs. The first reaction seemed to be general shock and disbelief throughout the settler community, but when the dust cleared, there were clearly two ideological camps within Gush Emunim—those "who understood" the underground and those "who refused to understand" it.

The halakhic issue at stake was whether the underground constituted *Merida Bamalchut* (a revolt against the kingdom). Rabbi Yoel Ben-Nun, who led the attack on the underground, was very resolute:

> The state is the foundation and the government is the authority for conducting war against Israel's enemies. There are no private wars, and no rules of war are applicable for a private individual, neither from a general moral perspective nor from a moral-halakhic point of view. . . . Every revolt against the kingdom is also a revolt against God.[14]

While Ben-Nun and his camp were extremely candid about their opposition to the operations of the underground, many of the supportive authorities, and those who "understood" its activities, remained silent. The real controversy within Gush Emunim was conducted in bitter closed sessions, and was revealed only in 1986.

The ones who spoke in support of the underground were rather cautious. Rabbi Israel Ariel, who was to become the spokesperson for the most radical wing of the movement, responded in the same issue of *Nekuda* to Yoel Ben-Nun's charges. He argued that since the government of Israel was never elected directly by the people, as required by the *halakhah*, but rather indirectly, it did not fulfill the conditions of Jewish law for a fully legitimate kingdom. He further reminded his audience that Rabbi Zvi Yehuda Kook had made a distinction between state and government:

Rabbi Zvi Yehuda . . . did not define the prime minister as a king, not even as a judge, but as "judgelike." When Prime Minister Rabin made his reprehensible statement that he did not care if we reached Hebron with a Jordanian visa, he criticized him severely and said: "He who does not care about Eretz Yisrael, Eretz Yisrael does not care about him." Would anybody call Rabbi Zvi Yehuda an opponent of the government's authority? . . . What else do we need than Rabbi Zvi Yehuda's announcement that in the case of Judea and Samaria no concession will be made and that "it will not pass without a war"? This was said in front of the students of the yeshiva and was published in the press. Would anybody dare call Rabbi Zvi Yehuda "a rebel against the kingdom"?[15]

While Gush Emunim's theoretical commitment to the sacredness of the State of Israel has not changed today, its practical commitment has been eroded. The Gush settlers, bitter about the government's inability to defend them against Arab violence on the roads of Judea and Samaria, find it hard to respect the government. Rabbi Zvi Yehuda Kook is gone, and the "post-Kookist" Gush is in no position to keep the old orientation alive. Though there are several successors to Kook's "moderate" legacy, they do not carry his authority. The dominant line in Gush Emunim now seems not to glorify the sacred state, but rather to challenge the government in the name of Eretz Yisrael and its future.

The Palestinian Question, the Arab-Israeli Conflict, and the Fate of the Israeli Arabs

Gush Emunim's position on "the Palestinian question" is sharp and unequivocal: the problem does not exist and is no more than a vicious ploy by the Arabs, who want to destroy the State of Israel, furthered by leftist Jews who refuse to see the Arabs' true intentions. Eretz Yisrael in its entirety belongs to the Jews by divine command. The Arabs, whoever they are, have no collective right over the land, and the issue, if there is one, is of individuals who must find a way to live under Jewish rule. The universal principle of self-determination—even if it might have some relevance in other places—does not hold in Eretz Yisrael.

The key question, then, is not, What should be done about the Palestinian nation? but rather, What should be the status of Arabs living in Eretz Yisrael in the age of redemption? Gush Emunim's only official answer to the question was formulated in its 1974 manifesto:

> The Arabs of Eretz Yisrael and other alien minorities living there ought to be given the complete private and legal rights every person deserves. These include the right to emigrate, to own property, to free trial and all the other individual civil liberties. These rights cannot be abrogated, except for direct security reasons. The possibility of granting Israeli citizenship to every alien resident who will be ready to assume all the obligations involved (including service in the IDF [Israeli Defense Forces] or a substitute) should be examined. Nevertheless, it is recommended that the emigration of those who are not ready to receive Israeli citizenship for nationalist reasons will be encouraged by propaganda and economic aid.[16]

This vague statement, which was based on the Torah concept of *Ger Toshav* (alien resident), was sufficiently broad and undemanding to encompass various positions on this sensitive issue in the early days of Gush Emunim. When outsiders insisted upon a clearer statement, Gush spokespersons responded with the famous "three alternatives"—choices that should be presented to Israeli Arabs: (a) to acknowledge the legitimacy of the Zionist doctrine (Gush Emunim's version) and thereupon to receive full civil rights, including the right to vote and be elected to the Knesset (and to serve in the army); (b) to honestly obey the laws of the state without formal recognition of Zionism and in return receive the rights of resident aliens (but no political rights); or (c) to emigrate to Arab countries with economic assistance provided by Israel.

As long as contacts between the Gush settlers and the Palestinian Arabs were limited before the 1978 penetration of Samaria and the beginning of the massive settlement of the West Bank, these general statements satisfied the members of the movement; Gush Emunim sincerely hoped that most of the Palestinians would learn to live with the Jews and opt for the *second* alternative. But this hope was not fulfilled, and the growing Jewish-Arab violence has made it increasingly necessary to translate the abstract halakhic position on the issue to concrete suggestions and policies.

The moral and political sensitivity of the issue has made unanimity impossible; different parties *within* Gush Emunim adhere to three different proposals for the status of non-Jews in Israel: limited rights, no rights, and total war and extermination. While the positions are usually stated as reaction to actual events, each is anchored in an authoritative interpretation of Scripture.

The first, most liberal, position sticks to the Gush's original "three alternatives." Limiting Arab rights stems from the conviction that the notion of universal human rights is a foreign ideal that, like other European non-Jewish values, has no meaning in the context of the Holy Land. In the Bible, non-Jewish inhabitants of Palestine were accorded the status of resident aliens, enjoying some privileges but never obtaining rights equal to those of the Jews:

> We are obliged to grant the *Ger Toshav* (alien resident) civic rights, and also a decent social respect and an option to buy houses and land in the country. This implies, of course, that he accepts the authority of the state of Israel and agrees to be a loyal and devoted citizen, which includes the seven commandments of Noah's sons—which are the fundamental laws of human morality. . . . It is however clear that we cannot allow the transfer of Eretz Yisrael lands to the Gentiles of other states, who certainly do not qualify as *Gerim Toshavim*.[17]

Note that even the liberal spokespersons of Gush Emunim no longer talk about granting full *political* rights to loyal Arabs, preferring to leave the issue undefined. But at least they recognize that not all Arabs are dangerous and that many deserve to be treated humanely. Most of the leaders of Gush Emunim and most members share this view. But even among them there are shades and variations—some would use very tough measures against seditious and violent Palestinians, while others call for moderation and restraint.

The second position on the status of non-Jews amounts to a denial of all rights, since Arabs are hostile to the Jewish rebirth in Eretz Yisrael and always had been. Proponents of this position do not oppose the doctrine of *Ger Toshav*, but they argue that consistent Arab hostility makes it illusory and irrelevant. Their conclusion is very close to the notorious Kahane position of expulsion. [Meir Kahane, founder and leader of the extremist, quasi fascist Kach party, whose racist ideology advocated that Arabs living in Israel be pressured to leave, and that only those accepting the status of resident aliens be allowed to remain.—ED.]

> The Arab hostility towards the Zionist venture has been proven beyond doubt in many decades of bloodshed, and there is no sign of any change in this hostility or for a reduction in its intensity. . . . The idea that maintains that it is possible to settle within areas of dense

Arab population, to expropriate its land, to hurt its national feelings and also to obtain its sympathy by quoting old Arab tales, cannot but make one laugh. Once and for all we have got to clarify to ourselves and to explain to the nation that in Eretz Yisrael either the Arabs or the Jews can live, and not the two of them together.[18]

A poll of West Bank rabbis found 64 percent of them favoring this solution.[19]

The most extreme solution, extermination, was expressed in an essay by Rabbi Israel Hess published in the official magazine of Bar-Ilan university students under the title "Genocide: A Commandment of the Torah." Hess likened the Arabs to the biblical Amalekites, who were deservedly annihilated. The Amalekites, according to Hess, were both socially and militarily treacherous and cruel. Their relation to the Jews was like the relation of darkness to light—one of total contradiction. The Arabs, who live today in the land of Israel and who are constantly waging a treacherous terrorist war against the Jews, are direct descendants of the Amalekites, and the correct solution to the problem is extermination.[20]

Hess's position, relatively isolated, has not been repeated by any Gush Emunim authority. But the Amalekite analogy exists in the minds of a Gush Emunim minority and sometimes appears in conversations and on the pages of *Nekuda*. A Kedumim settler, David Rosentzweig, in a small research project found that in the last 50 years several distinguished authorities had used the analogy when speaking of the unending Arab hostility toward the Jews.[21] And Haim Tzuria, a Shavei Shomron settler, wrote in his article "The Right to Hate" that "a hatred of any enemy is not a sick feeling but a natural and healthy one." He continued,

In each generation we have those who rise up to wipe us out, therefore each generation has its own Amalek. The Amalekism of our generation expresses itself in the extremely deep hatred of the Arabs to our national renaissance in the land of our forefathers.[22]

Gush Emunim is aware of the political sensitivity of its views; its spokespersons consistently refuse to discuss the future of the Arabs in Judea and Samaria after the "expected" annexation of the West Bank. They say that their mission is to solve not the Arab question but the Jewish problem on the general principles found in the Torah and *halakhah*; in due time Almighty God will take care of the details in his mysterious way.[23]

The Invisible Realm of Gush Emunim

Though Gush Emunim originated as an extraparliamentary organization often acting extralegally, its leaders always wished for formal recognition by the Israeli authorities. The reasons were both ideological and pragmatic.

On the ideological level, most of the founders were sincerely devoid of political ambitions; they were less interested in the organization than in its calling. They believed that the settlement of Judea and Samaria was the obligation of the government and not of volunteers. In the early years the Gush considered itself as only a temporary structure that would fade away the moment the Israeli government stepped in and legalized the settlement of Judea and Samaria.

On the practical plane, the heads of the Gush wanted legalization, for they knew that they could not change the demographic balance in the West Bank without official backing. They were fully aware that their early squatting drives were only beginnings, a symbolic proof that a Jewish settlement in every part of Eretz Yisrael was possible and legitimate.

Most of these early aspirations have by now been completely fulfilled, perhaps beyond the wildest dreams of the Gush leaders. There have been difficulties and crises of ideology and leadership, but from a political, organizational, and economic perspective the Gush has been extremely successful. It is, therefore, not erroneous to speak of the Gush Emunim *invisible realm*, a highly sophisticated political, economic, and cultural network, which dominates the life of nearly 100,000 settlers in Judea, Samaria, and Gaza, controls the yearly distribution of hundreds of millions of dollars, and significantly influences Israel's decisions. This Gush Emunim conglomerate is "invisible," since only a few of its institutions are obviously part of Gush Emunim.[24] The activists of the movement have been able to impart their political thinking to many non-Gush people and institutions, and to control several small but highly important communal positions, thereby assuring that they make the critical decisions.

One reason for Gush Emunim's success is that its activists have moved adroitly from spontaneity to organization without losing their flexibility. In terms of organization, the movement has gone through three stages: *spontaneous single actions, institutionalized licit and illicit drives,* and finally *full official and state-supported operations.* Each new stage has involved more people, bigger resources, greater proximity to the centers of power, and fuller political legitimacy. Though the political and ideological development of Gush Emunim has been marked by crises and setbacks, its economic and administrative organization has been built up slowly and methodically.

The formative years of Gush Emunim, from 1967 to 1974, were the most important. These were the years when each squatting effort erupted with no grand strategy or highly organized backing. The return to Gush Etzion, the occupation of Park Hotel in Hebron, the early operations of Gariin Elon Moreh [the religious nucleus established in the yeshiva at Kiryat Arba to spearhead the settlement of Samaria— ED.], and the illicit settlement of Keshet in the Golan Heights all took place with no established procedures. Highly devoted individuals and groups felt that they had to act, with or without official support, and they did so.

But as isolated and unorganized as the pioneering Emunist squatters were, they did have three institutionalized sources of support: Yeshivat Merkaz Harav, the Bnei Akiva youth movement, and the Land of Israel Movement. None was fully geared to the specific needs of the settlement Gariinim [small groups of people, usually young, who intend to establish new settlements—ED.], but they all rendered moral and material assistance.

Merkaz Harav was probably the single most important support, a solid source of manpower and moral backing. According to many sources, Rabbi Zvi Yehuda Kook turned the yeshiva into a settlement command post. The yeshiva students who lived under his spell were unequivocally encouraged to join the new settlements.[25]

Similarly, the Bnei Akiva movement and several of its yeshivot backed the new pioneers. The number who actually moved to the West Bank in the pre-Gush era was very small, but a movement of many thousands stood behind them. Settlement leaders like Hanan Porat and Rabbi Moshe Levinger, who were also persuasive speakers, became the idols of a whole Bnei Akiva generation. They and several other speakers traveled throughout the country, and their message electrified the youth. Most of the Bnei Akiva organization was supportive too—teachers, heads of yeshivot and branches, and the Bnei Akiva representatives in such influential institutions as the Jewish Agency and the World Zionist Organization.[26]

Although the unorganized new settlers proved themselves skilled politicians, their lack of political organization led them to depend on the elderly activists of the Land of Israel Movement. The settlers were the darlings of the LIM journalists, writers, and politicians. The notables visited the small settlements, wrote about them, spread their message, and legitimized their actions among the secular public. First and foremost among the LIM admirers was Eliezer Livneh, who constantly communicated with their young rabbis and praised their activities in private and public.[27] Former generals, diplomats, bureaucrats, and professors showed their support. Long before the formal establishment of Gush Emunim, its future activists were already entrenched in Israel's public life.

The second stage began in 1974 with the formal establishment of Gush Emunim. Its first manifesto suggested a platform for the political, ideological, and spiritual takeover of the nation, but the operational meaning of the act was much smaller: the routinization of the practice of the first Gariinim and its formalization. No longer was the creation of a settlement Gariinim to be left to the daring imagination of individuals; an established organization was to plan the activities, logistics, and propaganda. Gush Emunim formalized a *Mazkirut* (executive secretariat), *Mate Mivtzai* (an operational command), and *Moetza* (public council).

The Mazkirut was an ordinary executive committee whose job was to oversee policy matters and coordinate daily activities, but the Mate Mivtzai was a unique Gush Emunim structure. Its task was to prepare and carry out Gush Emunim illicit operations, which mostly involved unlicensed squatting. Since these operations meant outmaneuvering the army, the police, and the other West Bank authorities, the Mate recruited men of great skill and ingenuity—reserve officers, practiced hikers familiar with West Bank topography, veteran illegal settlers from the Mandate period, and logistic organizers.[28] Since Gush Emunim has never had a written constitution, the structure and names of these organizations occasionally changed. An extended Mazkirut was later added and professional departments were established for settlement, *Hasbarah* (public relations and education), organization, and finance. A small *Aliya* department was also added later.

The institutionalization of Gush Emunim in the mid-1970s was not a refutation of its earlier spontaneous character. On the contrary, the same Merkaz Harav core group continued to inspire the Gush and control it with no bureaucratic constraints. Neither rules of formal membership nor a constitution was adopted. No general vote was ever taken and no procedures for legitimate or illegitimate Gush Emunim operations were ever written down. The heads of the movement did whatever they thought fit and moved swiftly from one sphere of action to another.[29]

Instead of dealing with hampering procedures, the Gush devoted all its time to operative matters.   Thus while constantly launching settlement drives, and jousting and bargaining with the authorities, the movement was also able to invest great energy in building the Gush infrastructure.   Gush branches were opened all over the country to broadcast the message of the movement as widely as possible and recruit supporters and future settlers.   In hundreds of *Hugei Bait* (small sessions in private homes), Gush people preached the new gospel. Local volunteers not only announced their commitment to settle in the West Bank, but also actively recruited future colleagues.   Gush activists penetrated organized groups like synagogue communities, religious PTAs, and Bnei Akiva alumni circles, greatly facilitating their organizational tasks.[30]

This massive operation, which was not widely reported in the press, involved very little expense.   A Gush Emunim branch was usually a small apartment with a telephone.   A skeleton Gariin was a devoted individual or a small group of friends who would spend all their free time talking to people and future followers.   Favorable Bnei Akiva chapters and friendly Yeshivot Hesder with larger assets and resources were especially good locations for strong Gush branches and Gariin-im.[31]

In this second stage, the Gush established a settlement department. While struggling to maintain their few existing strongholds, mostly in military camps in the West Bank, the leaders of Gush Emunim also started to work on an ambitious plan to settle all of Judea and Samaria. Experts in geography, demography, agriculture, and settlement were asked to help develop an operational program; the result was the 1976 Yesh Plan.   Though the Yesh Plan was supplanted two years later by Gush Emunim's Master Plan for Settlement in Judea and Samaria, it had established the new Gush Emunim settlement concept.   There were to be three types of settlements: villages of a few hundred people, towns of several thousands, and cities with tens of thousands of residents.   The main objectives were strategic—to introduce hundreds of thousands of Jews to the area, to occupy all the strategic strongholds in the mountains, and to secure complete control of the main roads. The resettlement of ancient biblical locations was given a lower priority, though was nevertheless considered important.[32]

The third organizational stage of Gush Emunim began in 1977, when the Likud, under Menachem Begin, won the elections.   Though Gush Emunim was a small voluntary movement, it had two important psychological assets: nearly ten years of settlement experience and a

healthy skepticism about the ability of the government, any government, to provide for the settlement of Eretz Yisrael. Further, Gush
Emunim had the will and the means to push through their demands
and were sure that God was behind them. Therefore, though a more
sympathetic government had come to power, the Gush did not
dismantle its settlement department and leave the job of settling the
West Bank to the friendly Ministry of Agriculture. Its leaders established, instead, Amana (Covenant) as their official settlement movement
and initiated, two years later, a non-Emunim umbrella organization,
Moetzet Yesha (the Council of the Settlements of Judea, Samaria, and
Gaza). These two institutions, accorded full recognition by the new
government, became the foundation of Gush Emunim's political and
economic power.

The Evolution of Amana

In 1977, though the movement had big plans, it had only three
settlements of its own: Ofra, Kedumim, and Mishor Edomim. There
was just one certain way of changing this situation—to establish a
recognized "settlement movement" with the full backing of Israel's
Ministry of Agriculture and the Department of Rural Settlement of the
World Zionist Organization (WZO).[33] Likud's official recognition of
Amana was not a mere legal act that could be obtained by any
individual land developer; recognition meant that Amana's activities
were considered essential for the nation, part of state-supported
Zionism. In the past, such recognition had been accorded only to
pioneering settlement organizations, the *kibbutzim* (collective) and
moshavim (cooperative) movements. Therefore it was extremely
important for the extralegal zealots of Gush Emunim to become
legitimized as partners in this exclusive club.

There was another incentive. Being officially recognized entitled
Amana to large state and WZO budgets, as well as to many other
benefits such as secure positions for its members in Israel's settlement
bureaucracy and a say in decisions of many official circles. It also
meant the right to the paid professional assistance of Israel's top
settlement experts.

Amana took advantage of all the benefits official recognition
implied. It was run by a Hanhalah (Directorate) of thirteen people and
a large representative council made up of members from all the
movement's settlements. The heads of Amana, veterans like Hanan

Porat, Uri Elitzur, Uri Ariel, and Moni Ben-Ari, realized that the Gush's informal methods were not suitable for a big settlement organization with money and land. They wrote a short constitution for Amana, which, for the first time in the history of Gush Emunim, introduced democratic procedures. According to the constitution every settlement is entitled to two delegates at the Amana council, and the council was made the final authority on all matters within the movement's jurisdiction. The Hanhalah and the organization's influential secretary-general are elected by the council.[34]

The establishment of Amana expanded development opportunities for Gush Emunim but led, paradoxically, to the decline of the movement's guiding secretariat. Eager to shed their image of illegal adventurism, the leaders of the Gush sought the status of a fully legitimate Israeli settlers' movement. Once they decided in 1979 not to establish a political party of their own, they saw no need to continue Gush Emunim formally; now Rabbi Levinger could spend more time in Kiryat Arba, Benny Katzover in Elon Moreh, and Hanan Porat in the Knesset.

Amana took over the Gush offices in Jerusalem and guided a massive Gush Emunim settlement drive. In 1978 it submitted an ambitious plan to the government calling for the settlement of 100,000 Jews in the West Bank within ten years. This program underlay the Drobles-Sharon settlement plan that became the official policy of the World Zionist Organization and Israel's Ministry of Agriculture.[35]

With the government settling urban areas close to the Green Line (the pre-1967 border), Amana could concentrate on establishing new ideological settlements in unattractive but strategic spots in Judea and Samaria, usually in areas with heavy Arab populations or far from urban centers. Constantly keeping the settlement of Judea and Samaria on the national agenda, Amana worked diligently to create new Gariinim, attract industries to the new settlements, and train new settlers for jobs that could support them in their new locations. Amana also developed an absorption and immigration section to attract new immigrants to Emunim's future settlements. It has been so successful that potential settler groups not necessarily identified with the ideology of Gush Emunim have occasionally asked to join it.

Amana's major innovation was the *Yishuv Kehilati* (a communal settlement), a concept developed in the 1976 Yesh Plan. Previously, most settlements supported by the government or WZO were based on an egalitarian socialist ideology—either collective (*kibbutz*) or cooperative (*moshav*) agrarian-industrial endeavors. But Gush Emunim was never socialist, and most of its members had a middle-class mentality. The conception of redemption that drove them to the West Bank had a nationalist, not socialist, content. The Likud was also far from socialism: *kibbutzim* and *moshavim* were identified with its political archrival, the Labor movement.[36]

Furthermore, water and arable land were too scarce on the West Bank for many *kibbutzim* and *moshavim*. The *Yishuv Kehilati* overcame these limitations. While insisting on the communal character and shared responsibility of the settlement, it gave its members great economic freedom. Amana settlers own their property individually and are free to leave or sell it.[37] While the old Labor socialist settlements had been encouraged to become self-reliant and self-sufficient, many members of Amana settlements, up to 80 percent, commute to work across the Green Line every day. The only time Amana exercises formal control over individual settlers is in the selection process. Only individuals who identify with the movement's goals, pass sophisticated tests of suitability for communal living, and endure long interviews with psychologists and social workers are admitted.[38]

The Local and Regional Councils

While Amana transformed Gush Emunim, it was the Israeli government that laid the foundations for the movement's invisible realm. On 20 March 1979, six days before the signing of the peace treaty with Egypt, the military government in the West Bank signed Order 783 establishing three regional councils in the area. Two more councils were added later; all five are governed by the regulations governing Israeli regional councils. In March 1981, Order 982 set up five municipal councils in the West Bank. That order largely duplicated the Israeli Municipal Ordinance, so West Bank municipalities, like their Israeli counterparts, can levy taxes, supply municipal services, nominate officers, and employ workers; the West Bank councils also enjoy planning and building-licensing powers.[39] The Israeli settlement areas were declared "planning regions" and the councils were designated "special planning commissions."

These acts of the Begin government were intended to strengthen Jewish control of the area and ensure the permanence of the settlements. But they accomplished an additional and unintended task: for all practical purposes they gave Gush Emunim control of the entire Jewish endeavor in the West Bank. Even though the Gush has never supplied more than 20 percent of the West Bank settlers, its leaders, by virtue of their experience, public image, and competence, were appointed to key executive positions in most of the new municipalities and regions. Former illegal settlers and candidates for arrest were now state officials with large budgets, powers, and responsibilities. Amana's small staff and budget were supplemented by hundreds of paid official jobs under its control.

By April 1988, there were 48 community settlements incorporated in Amana. Its Emunist settlers numbered about 12,000 to 15,000 (about 2,500 families). The WZO investments in these communal settlements alone came to $80,000 per family. There were other supporters of Gush Emunim in towns such as Kiryat Arba, Ariel, Efrat, Ma'ale Ephraim, and Ma'ale Adomim. Gush members head five out of the seven regional councils and exert considerable influence in the towns. Great sums of government money have enabled these municipalities and councils to employ large staffs and provide services of every description.

Meron Benvenisti estimates that in 1983 per capita grants to regional councils were $230 in Gush Etzion, $245 in Mate Benyamin, and $357 in Samaria—two or three times as much as grants to regional councils in Israel proper—Mate Yehuda (the region west of Jerusalem adjacent to Mate Benyamin) $86; Sha'ar Hanegev, $126; and Upper Galilee, $97. Grants-in-aid provided more than half the total income of the Jewish local authorities in the West Bank—Elkana and Ariel, 52.8 percent; Ma'ale Adomim, 60.8 percent; and Kiryat Arba, 68.8 percent. By contrast, local councils in depressed areas within the Green Line received grants in the following proportions: Rosh Ha'ayin, 44 percent; Or Yehuda, 36.8 percent; Or Akiva, 28.9 percent.[40] These huge sums of state money amount to preferential treatment for the settlers in the West Bank by the Likud coalition and give Gush Emunim leaders a formidable financial and political base. [The new government led by Yitzhak Rabin has declared a halt on construction of militarily non-essential settlements and will most likely reduce the amount of financial support to Gush Emunim.—ED.]

Building Political and Economic Power

The solidification of the invisible realm of Gush Emunim was completed in 1980 with the creation of the Yesha Council, the representative organization of the Jewish settlements in Judea, Samaria, and Gaza.

From its inception the Yesha Council was designated to become the political arm of the Jewish settlers in those areas.[41] It was conceived by Israel Harel, a journalist, who realized in 1979 that the legitimized Jewish settlements created a new and expanded power base for Gush Emunim.

Gush leaders had been underscoring their demand for more land with a long hunger strike, and Harel realized that he was observing a new Israeli geopolitical entity that was different from the rest of the country, with existential interests of its own. Only 20 percent of the settlers were Gush members, so its critics argued that the Gush could not speak in the name of the entire body. Nonetheless, the movement's leaders were convinced that despite their minority status they could maintain political hegemony in the area.

Unlike Amana and the regional and local councils, the Yesha Council had never sought official state status. It was a voluntary legal association intended to represent the entire Jewish population of the West Bank and Gaza in Israel's public and political life.[42] Each settlement, whatever its political affiliation or size, elects two representatives to a general council whose job is to formulate the political position of the settlers on relevant national issues. The real power in the council is entrusted to the Hanhalah, a directorate made up of the heads of the regional councils of Judea, Samaria, and Gaza and several officeholders who sit *ex officio*. Special committees meet regularly to submit recommendations to the general council, on legal and political matters, as well as for security, economic, education, and information issues.

While the Yesha Council has limited its activities to politics, its heads and those of Amana and the most influential regional councils have aided their movement through their power of the official purse. In the last nine years they have set up a myriad of profitable "development corporations" that have helped build the area. While bidding for contracts issued by the councils, the members of the boards of the corporations have been either the heads of the same councils or their neighbors and associates from Amana. Using machinery supplied by public funds, such as buses or heavy mechanical equipment, they have been able to compete rather favorably against private corporations.

Seeing the success of the development companies, Amana cooperated with two regional councils to create a large West Bank corporation that would attract major outside partners. The new venture, SBA, established its own insurance company and took up major projects such as building a science park in Ariel. It also moved into the home-construction market in both the West Bank and Gaza. It plans to establish several subsidiary firms specializing in a variety of industries and investments.[43] The overseers of the new company, major Gush figures, aim for economic independence from the government, so that in case of conflict they could proceed on their own. In a *Nekuda* interview, Dr. Yosef Dreizin, the executive director of SBA, discussed his desire to follow the historic model of the Zionist Labor movement. Starting in the 1920s, it developed an independent Jewish economy in Palestine, which facilitated the struggle against the British and the Arabs, and later became the solid foundation of the Israeli economy.

> We have in front of us the Histadrut's industries without their faults. We told ourselves: let us erect economic institutions in construction, industry and other fields that could become in the proper time an autonomous system. This will assure the continuous development of the area with no relation, or direct relation, to the political system which may become hostile.[44]

Gush Emunim figures continue to dominate the key institutions in the West Bank and Gaza, despite the growing number of the non-Emunist settlers, for the simple reason that the entire settler community benefits from the arrangement. No other group in Israel has recently received so many benefits and allocations. The West Bank leaders have obtained for their constituency the privileged status of all three of the most preferred groups in Israel—*development towns, pioneering settlements, and confrontation settlements*. Instead of asking the authorities to create a special category, these leaders have insisted on their inclusion in *all* the existing categories.

This combined status, confirmed by both government and Knesset, makes the settlers eligible for huge subsidies and concessions. It has also made them almost completely immune to financial cutbacks, even in times of severe austerity. Benvenisti has rightly observed, "It is politically impossible to revoke their status, only to change the entire system of Israeli subsidies. The powerful pressure groups which rely on continued preferential treatment would not allow that, even if they are opposed to settlement in the West Bank."[45] Thus, though the majority of the settlers are not religious and probably do not share the messianic beliefs of Gush Emunim, they need the movement's extensive political skills as much as it needs their support. This interdependence is not likely to disappear soon. The main reason that Israelis continue to move to the West Bank, even during the *intifada*, is the unmatched incentives offered to the settlers. Since only the Gush activists can make sure that this situation continues, the movement's decreasing proportion among the population is unlikely to affect its informal political power. [Under the present Israeli government of Yitzhak Rabin, the construction of new settlements has been limited and, consequently, Gush Emunim projects significantly reduced.—ED.]

The Cultural Infrastructure of Gush Emunim

A relatively unrecognized, but essential, part of the Gush Emunim invisible realm is its substantial cultural and educational infrastructure, whose development started long before the legalization of most West Bank operations and the official recognition of Amana.

Yeshivat Merkaz Harav in Jerusalem has always played a crucial role, especially after 1967, when it became the center of a new dynamic movement. Rabbi Zvi Yehuda Kook, its head, achieved national prominence, and its graduates became the most prestigious group in religious Zionism. Almost every talented Bnei Akiva graduate wanted to study in Merkaz, or at least to be taught by its graduates. And because Merkaz Harav aimed to convert the entire nation to the new "Eretz Yisrael Judaism," it has become preeminently a missionary order. Graduates like Haim Drukman and Tzfania Drori have established Merkaz-oriented yeshivot outside of Jerusalem; others have simply taken over existing institutions throughout the country. The first order of business of most Gush Emunim settlements has been to establish a yeshiva. Hard-core Gush Emunim seminaries such as the Kiryat Arba Yeshiva of Rabbis Eliezer Waldman and Dov Lior have become emulated models.

The nucleus in Jerusalem was expanded immensely. The Yeshiva Gdola, the traditional four-year post-secondary institution, has been joined by a Yeshiva Letzeirim (a Merkaz prep school), a *Kolel* (an advanced seminary for married male students), two research centers, and numerous institutions for young children of the students and staff. A special youth movement called *Ariel*, more pious and devoted to the Land and the Torah than the old Bnei Akiva, was started. A whole Merkaz enclave was created in the Jerusalem neighborhood of Kiryat Moshe, a milieu of total commitment in which hundreds of teachers and students live with thousands of their family members. Merkaz graduates who leave Jerusalem are encouraged to consider the yeshiva their second home and to constantly return for lessons and consultation.[46] Money is apparently no problem, for the school's growing prestige has attracted big donors. And Merkaz enjoys the strong backing of the National Religious Party and financial aid from Israel's Ministry of Religion—a fiefdom of the party.

Two other important Kookist-Emunist institutions have become powerful instruments of culture dissemination: the Noam Schools and Machon Meir. The Noam Schools are selective elementary schools that place great emphasis on transmitting the Eretz Yisrael message to young children. They are considered an elite alternative to the ordinary state religious schools, and are an important socialization agent. Their high quality attracts many non-Emunist parents eager to give their children a first-class education. Many of them later find themselves parents of young Gush settlers.

Machon Meir is a popular adult institution that provides short and informal religious courses. Its branches, which are now spread all over Israel, attract Jews from Israel and abroad, young and old, who want to learn about Jewish religious orthodoxy in an open and pleasant atmosphere. Though few of the thousands of people who take such courses every year stay, repent, and join the formal Kookist course of ordinary yeshiva life, many leave with a feeling for Gush Emunim and the entire Eretz Yisrael theology.

Most of the teachers and administrators in the Noam Schools and Machon Meir are Merkaz Harav graduates and their confidants. These institutions, like the other Merkaz organs, are thus solid economic bastions of the invisible realm.[47] The lives of many thousands of people depend on their success and prosperity. Thus, the Emunist message, in addition to being an article of faith, is also their prime source of funds.

Nowhere does the economic function of the cultural institutions associated with Gush Emunim stand out so clearly as in the movement's infrastructure in the West Bank. Under the Likud administration, the Ministry of Education and Culture was headed by Zevulun Hammer of the National Religious Party (NRP). During his first years in office he was an ardent supporter of the Gush. Hammer's ministry established an elaborate educational network in the West Bank in which the religious section was especially promoted. There are such schools in almost every West Bank settlement, even the small ones—136 of them were registered in 1983–84 (70 kindergartens, 35 primary schools, 5 high schools, 10 yeshivot, 14 kolelim, and 2 religious colleges). A separate teacher-training network, branches of the Bnei Akiva youth movement, and libraries were all financed by the state.

The West Bank educational system has thus become one of the settlers' main sources of income. Benvenisti has calculated that in the Mate Benyamin region, a Gush Emunim stronghold, 10 percent of the total labor force (including women) worked in teaching and administration. He showed that the disproportionate state expense per capita on education had become particularly glaring considering the underutilization of the system: "In 1984–85 there were 16 pupils at the Mt. Hebron elementary school; 72 pupils in six elementary classes in Ofra; 80 students in junior high and high schools in Kedumim; and 95 students in grades 7–10 in Kiryat Arba."[48]

A special section of this institutional complex comprises the Eretz Yisrael midrashot. These are short-term learning centers, whose main purpose is to conduct short courses for visiting groups on such subjects as Judaism, Zionism, and the teachings of Rav Kook, as well as on the wildlife and geography of Eretz Yisrael. The midrashot have never been officially denoted as Gush Emunim organs, since they are under the state's Ministry of Education, just like similar institutions within the Green Line. Nevertheless, most of the West Bank midrashot are located in strongholds of Gush Emunim and were established during Zevulun Hammer's administration. The person designated by the Ministry of Education to oversee the midrashot and other institutions was none other than Rabbi Yohanan Fried, a prominent Gush Emunim veteran. Rafael Eitan, the IDF chief of staff, had earlier put Fried in charge of the Jewish education program of the IDF.[49]

While the Eretz Yisrael midrashot have not become a major source of income, they do provide many part-time jobs for students on leave from Merkaz and other yeshivas. And since tens of thousands of Israelis pass through these institutions each year, they are one of the most effective education agents of the Gush.[50]

A more serious effort is the growing academic complex of Midrashat Kedumim, or the Judea and Samaria College. Under Gush veteran Zvi Slonim, it seeks to compete with the nation's *secular* colleges and to become, one day, an alternative to the Hebrew University of Jerusalem and other such "leftist" centers. At present, Midrashat Kedumim is an adult-education center, with courses taught by sympathetic professors from Bar-Ilan, Haifa, Tel Aviv, and the Hebrew Universities. Two research institutions are also part of the growing Kedumim conglomerate; their main purpose is to document the settlement project in Judea and Samaria—and to become the Eretz Yisrael counterpart of the famed Van Leer Institute, which is known for its leftist orientation.[51]

Defending the West Bank Settlers

The invisible realm of Gush Emunim has evolved a district security and defense organization. Almost from the beginning of the Israeli occupation there were security problems in the West Bank. Because of anti-Jewish terrorist and guerrilla attacks, the settlements were designated "confrontation settlements"; special military orders authorized their guards to defend them with force. Many Jewish residents of the West Bank are, in fact, soldiers "on extended leave"—mainly religious students combining military service with advanced Talmudic study. In every settlement one settler is appointed "security officer" and receives a salary from the Ministry of Defense or the Israeli police. The result is that the settlers are directly involved in defense and security matters that were originally handled by the army and the military government.

In 1978, Israel's chief of staff, General Rafael Eitan, initiated a policy making each settler community in the West Bank responsible for securing the area and defending itself. Hundreds of settlers were transferred from their regular army units to the West Bank, to protect their own settlements and to secure roads and public property. Every settlement was required to have a fixed number of soldiers, including officers. They were to perform their active duty on a part-time basis while leading normal civilian lives.

In addition, regional mobile forces equipped with armored personnel carriers policed the Palestinian population. Large quantities of military equipment, including sophisticated weapons, have been stored in the settlements under the complete control of the local commanders.[52]

Eitan probably saw the regional defense system as the best and cheapest way to secure the settlements against Arab attacks; the concept was familiar from prestate days, when the border settlements and *kibbutzim* necessarily defended themselves. Nevertheless, one cannot ignore the dangerous potential of a semi-independent armed force should strong disagreement with government policy arise. When the settler community debates its future in the event of major territorial concessions by the government, a minority reportedly favors armed resistance.

This group, though small, appears to be much larger than the isolated group that resisted the army in Yamit in 1982. Several of the Jewish Underground members were ranking officers in the reserves, and one, Yeshua Ben Shoshan, was a captain on active duty. According to unconfirmed but persistent rumors, none of the responsible officers of the Israeli army knows exactly how many arms are stored in the settlements' caches, and no one dares check. While there is no doubt of the loyalty of the vast majority of these soldiers to the State of Israel and to the army, the potential existence of a small seditious element should not be disregarded.[53]

Settler violence and vigilantism reached crisis proportions in the summer of 1985. In June, the Israeli government exchanged prisoners with the Syrian-controlled PFLP General Command headed by Ahmed Jibril. Eleven hundred and fifty Arab prisoners were released in exchange for three Israeli soldiers. Six hundred of the freed Palestinians were allowed to return to their homes in Israel and the West Bank. Most of the freed Arabs had been serving sentences of 15 to 20 years, but a few had been serving life terms for some of the most abominable terror acts in the preceding 20 years. Since many of the freed terrorists had been responsible for the deaths of their friends and students, the entire settler community was stunned. The Arab sector saw the exchange as a major victory and gave the freed prisoners a hero's welcome all over the West Bank.

This was too much for the settlers to take—while 25 of their men were serving prison terms for defending the settler community against Arab terrorism, the "real" perpetrators of the bloodbath, as they viewed it, were being freed. Waves of armed settlers roamed the West Bank, usually at night, intimidating the local communities and ordering released prisoners to leave the country at once. Backed by the majority of Israelis, they were not stopped for weeks. There were very few acts of outright violence in these raids, but the settlers made it very clear that no one, not even the army and the government, was going to stop them from defending their families and their ministate.[54]

Since 1985 there have been repeated eruptions of settlers' vigilantism. If Arabs threw rocks at an Israeli bus in Judea and Samaria—an act that had become quite common in the area even before the *intifada*—local vigilante road guards would respond swiftly and harshly. They used to enter the neighboring Arab village, smash car windows, break into houses, and warn the local residents against collaboration with the saboteurs. A *Washington Post* correspondent quoted a member of such a group: "The army is not doing its job so we are helping them. . . . Arabs are afraid of us. You can see it on their faces. They know we have no problem protecting ourselves. The stick is the best weapon, not the gun. The Arab knows you will think twice before using the gun, but not to smash his face with a stick."[55]

Aspirations for Legal Autonomy

Gush Emunim's drive for autonomous institutions goes beyond the administrative, economic, cultural, and military areas; there have been signs that some of its authorities are thinking in terms of autonomous legal institutions as well. An early article in *Nekuda*, written by Rabbi Yehuda Shaviv of Yeshivat Har Etzion, suggested that Gush settlements should not follow the typical Israeli court system, but adopt instead a system of rabbinical courts that would rule according to Torah law:

> I was recently told that there is an intention of establishing courts of justice in the settlements of Judea and Samaria. . . . I am afraid that if the new system is made by the ordinary lay institutions we are going to have ordinary courts and stand at a danger of getting less than what we bargained for. Have we only come here to revive desolate mountains, placing on them settlements that live by the common norms? It appears to me that many of us came over to establish a new framework of life not just in the economic material sense, but also the social spiritual. . . . I think that one of the most impressive creations here may be the revival of the institution of *communal court*. This institution, apart of its legal authority, is bound to become a comprehensive moral-halakhic authority.[56]

While no action has been taken on the Shaviv proposal, many Gush members would have loved to see Knesset law supplanted by Torah law and *halakhah*. It was therefore not surprising that in 1985 the regional council of Mate Benyamin established a rabbinical court to resolve financial issues according to *halakhah*. As the announcement of the court's establishment explained,

> The revival of the Israeli nation means also the return of the law of Israel and the management of financial issues between a man and his peers according to the Torah and not according to the law imagined by the Gentiles. It appears proper that settlements that are instituted by the Torah should follow this path, for the law is from God.[57]

Given Gush Emunim's evolution in the direction of political, social, and cultural autonomy, it is hard to disagree with the conclusion of Giora Goldberg and Efraim Ben Zadok that an unprecedented process of territorial cleavage between old Israel and the occupied territories has been in the making for quite some time.[58] While it is hard to predict the end result of this process, it is clear that the leading force in this cleavage, Gush Emunim, has placed itself in a position of power and influence unusual for a movement that probably numbers about 15,000. Recently Gush Emunim has begun broadcasting "positive" messages of patriotism and Zionism from a ship in the Mediterranean—a clear sign that the Gush intends to expand its involvement further, and to move into new territories of influence and control.

NOTES

This chapter is reprinted from Ehud Sprinzak's volume *The Ascendance of Israel's Radical Right*, pp. 114–37. Copyright © 1991 by Oxford University Press, Inc.

1. "Gush Emunim: A Movement for the Rejuvenation of Zionist Fulfillment" (Hebrew) (a Gush Emunim early pamphlet, n.d. [1974]), 1.
2. Cf. Gideon Aran, "From Religious Zionism to Zionist Religion: The Roots of Gush Emunim," in Peter Medding, ed., *Studies in Contemporary Jewry* II (New York: Oxford University Press, 1986), 402–6.
3. Cf. Amnon Rubinstein, *From Herzl to Gush Emunim and Back* (Tel Aviv: Schocken Publishing House, 1980), chaps. 1–2.
4. Aran, "From Religious Zionism," 226–32.
5. "Gush Emunim: A Movement," 6.
6. Rabbi Yehuda Amital, *The Elevations from Depths* (Hebrew) (Allon Shvut: Yeshivat Ha-Zion Association, 1974), 41–43.
7. Aran, "From Religious Zionism," 402.
8. The process of "blackening" [the growing strength of the ultra-Orthodox or *haredim*, often characterized by their black garb—ED.] has become a reason for grave concern among Gush Emunim circles. Cf. Dan Be'eri, "Zionism: More Than Ever Before," *Nekuda* 95 (21 January 1986): 8–10; Avraham Nuriel, "The Ultraorthodoxization of Religious Zionism," *Nekuda* 105 (9 December 1986): 18–19; Yosef Ben Shlomo, "Indeed, the Flame of Redemption Burns Deeply in Their Bones," *Nekuda* 110 (27 May 1987): 35. See also, Daniel Ben-Simon, "An Alien Fire: Yeshivat Mercaz Harav," *Ha'aretz*, 4 April 1986, 4–6.
9. Rabbi Zvi Yehuda Kook, "This Is the State the Prophets Envisioned," *Nekuda* 86 (26 April 1985): 7.
10. Rabbi Moshe Levinger, "They Are All Holy," *Nekuda* 89 (7 July 1985): 7.
11. Rabbi Jacob Ariel, "The Land and the State," *Nekuda* 28 (15 May 1981): 3.
12. Interview with Rabbi Yoel Ben-Nun, 24 April 1976.
13. Cf. Ehud Sprinzak, *Every Man Whatsoever Is Right in His Own Eyes: Illegalism in Israeli Society* (Hebrew) (Tel Aviv: Sifriyat Poalim, 1986), 124–26.

14. Rabbi Yoel Ben-Nun, "Yes, an Autocritique," *Nekuda* 73 (25 May 1984): 13–14.
15. Rabbi Israel Ariel, "Is It Really a Revolt Against the Kingdom," *Nekuda* 73 (25 May 1984): 16.
16. "Gush Emunim: A Movement," 6.
17. Rabbi Shlomo Aviner, "On the Completion of Eretz Yisrael," *Artzi* 1 (1982): 28–34.
18. Yedidiya Segal, "Neither Arabic nor Arabs," *Nekuda* 9 (16 May 1980): 12.
19. Cf. Rabbi Israel Rosen, "Yesha Rabbis: To Encourage Arab Emigration," *Nekuda* 115 (November 1987): 37.
20. Cf. Rabbi Israel Hess, "The Genocide Ruling of Torah," *Bat Kol* (the Bar-Ilan students' paper), 26 February 1980.
21. Cf. David Rosentzweig, "A Time to Break Conventions," *Nekuda* 75 (6 July 1984): 34.
22. Haim Tzuria, "The Right to Hate," *Nekuda* 15 (29 August 1980): 12.
23. Interview with Daniella Weiss, 4 March 1985.
24. For an early analysis of the invisible realm of Gush Emunim, see Ehud Sprinzak, *Gush Emunim: The Politics of Zionist Fundamentalism in Israel* (New York: The American Jewish Committee, 1986), 18–22.
25. Cf. Aran, "From Religious Zionism," 348–62.
26. This is based on numerous interviews conducted with many former Bnei Akiva activists and a conclusive interview with National Religious Party veteran politician Eliezer Shefer, 9 April 1980.
27. Interview with Yoel Ben-Nun, 29 April 1976. On the relationship between the Land of Israel Movement and the Gush Emunim settlers, see Zvi Shiloah, *The Guilt of Jerusalem* (Hebrew) (Tel Aviv: Karni, 1989), 58–61, 114–23.
28. Interview with Yoel Ben-Nun, 29 April 1976.
29. Interview with Yoel Ben-Nun, 26 February 1978.
30. Interview with Yoel Ben-Nun, 30 June 1976.
31. Interview with Gershon Shafat, 1 July 1979.
32. Cf. *A Master Plan for the Settlement of Judea and Samaria* (Gush Emunim publication, 1978).
33. Cf. Danny Rubinstein, *On the Lord's Side: Gush Emunim* (Hebrew) (Tel Aviv: Hakibutz Hameuchad, 1982), 60–62.
34. Cf. Ehud Sprinzak, "Gush Emunim: The Iceberg Model of Political Extremism," *Medina Mimshal Veyehasim Bein Leumiim* 17 (Fall 1981): 48.
35. Cf. Meron Benvenisti, *The West Bank Data Project: A Survey of Israel's Policies* (Washington, D.C.: American Enterprise Institute, 1984), 52–60.
36. Cf. Sprinzak, "Gush Emunim: The Iceberg Model," 31.
37. Cf. David Newman, "Spatial Structures and Ideological Change in the West Bank," in David Newman, ed., *The Impact of Gush Emunim: Politics and Settlement in the West Bank* (London: Croom Helm, 1985), 175–81.
38. Interview with Amana activist Yoram Adler, 10 October 1979.
39. Cf. Benvenisti, *West Bank Data Project*, 39–49.

40. Cf. Meron Benvenisti, *1986 Report: Demographic, Economic, Legal, Social and Political Developments in the West Bank* (Jerusalem: The Jerusalem Post, 1986), 56–57.
41. Cf. Yehuda Litani, "The Mass of Yesha," *Ha'aretz*, 26 December 1980; Israel Harel, "Chosen, Not Self Selected," *Nekuda* 11 (27 June 1980): 7.
42. Interview with Israel Harel, 20 June 1985.
43. Cf. Benvenisti, *1986 Report*, 58–62.
44. "An Interview with Dr. Yosef Dreizin, the Director General of S.B.A.," *Nekuda* 68 (13 January 1984): 6–7.
45. Meron Benvenisti, *1987 Report: Demographic, Economic, Legal, Social, and Political Developments in the West Bank* (Jerusalem: The Jerusalem Post, 1987), 63.
46. Cf. Aran, "From Religious Zionism," 299–301.
47. Ibid., 302–5.
48. Cf. Benvenisti, *1986 Report*, 54–55.
49. Interview with Rabbi Yohanan Fried, 1 March 1985.
50. Interview with Avi Gisser, director of *Midrashat Ofra*, 20 June 1985.
51. Yair Sheleg, "Rest and Peace," *Nekuda* 94 (20 December 1985), 7.
52. Benvenisti, *West Bank Data Project*, 41.
53. Ze'ev Schiff, "The Military Potential of the Settlers," *Ha'aretz*, 15 November 1985.
54. Cf. Benvenisti, *1986 Report*, 73–76.
55. Glenn Frankel, "Israel and the Palestinians," *The Washington Post*, 1 June 1987, A16.
56. Rabbi Yehuda Shaviv, "To Establish Communal Courts," *Nekuda* 25 (13 March 1981): 4, 15.
57. Cited by Yehuda Litani, "Double-edged Sword," *Ha'aretz*, 21 February 1985.
58. Cf. Giora Goldberg and Ephraim Ben Zadok, "Regionalism and Territorial Cleavage in Formation: Jewish Settlement in the Administrated Territories," *Medina, Mimshal Veyehasim Bein Leumiim* 21 (Spring 1983).

Chapter 9

Jewish Zealots: Conservative versus Innovative

Menachem Friedman

When zealot groups in Israel are discussed, two diametrically opposed religious-political viewpoints—Neturei Karta and Gush Emunim—are considered the two poles on Israel's religious map. In this chapter, these groups are shown to be manifestations of two types of fundamentalism: "conservative" in the case of Neturei Karta, and "innovative" (or revolutionary) in the case of Gush Emunim.

Because the concept of fundamentalism originally evolved within the framework of the history of Christianity,[1] the term cannot always be used in the same way with reference to non-Christian religions, such as Judaism or Islam. We use the term to define a religious outlook shared by a group of believers who base their belief on an ideal religious-political reality that has existed in the past or is expected to emerge in the future. Such realities are described in great detail in the religious literature. And the fundamentalist believer is obliged to use whatever religious and political means are necessary to actualize these realities in the here and now.

Both conservative and innovative fundamentalism refer to the traditional Jewish religious conception of Jewish history, which is said to be in a state of dialectical tension between "Exile" and "Redemption." However, although Redemption signifies an ideal religious-political reality, paradoxically, within contemporary Orthodox Jewish society, the exilic past, particularly that which evolved in Eastern Europe, is viewed nostalgically as the very model of Jewish life. Thus, conservative fundamentalism looks to the past; any deviation from the idealized Jewish society, whether on the religious-social or religious-political plane, must be fought. From this perspective, conservative fundamentalists condemn as "deviant" the Jewish reality in the State of Israel today.

Radical or innovative fundamentalism, on the other hand, sees a diametrically opposite "reality," one in which the State of Israel today exists in a condition that is categorically different from the exilic state. Although radical fundamentalists do not view the reality of the State of Israel today as a sign of complete Redemption, they do perceive it as a signal that the period of the "footsteps of the Messiah" is beginning. Thus, images and precepts that are part of the traditional Messianic literature sometimes assume radical "new" significance for innovative fundamentalists.

Although Neturei Karta cannot really be regarded as a formally organized movement,[2] more attempts than ever before are currently being made to organize those who identify with its religious-ideological views in an institutionalized framework. These attempts have been increased since the deaths of two Neturei Karta founders and leaders, Amram Blau[3] and Aharon Katzenelbogen,[4] who, by virtue of their personalities and work, succeeded in spontaneously rallying many of those who had identified with the entire Neturei Karta ideology and practices, or had joined the group because they agreed with one or more of the issues it was fighting for. The deaths of Blau and Katzenelbogen created a vacuum that exacerbated existing differences and tensions between Neturei Karta, which represents the extreme isolationist view that rejects every form of contact with the political-economic Zionist establishment, and the Edah Haredit,[5] another ultra-Orthodox group that rejects the aspirations of Zionism in Palestine by adhering to the principle of "isolationism."

The increased tensions arose because, as an organized community, the Edah has been forced to make some compromises with the political-economic reality of the State of Israel in order to ensure that its members receive the full complex of communal services. This is in contrast with Neturei Karta which, despite attempts to become more structured, remains a fairly loose, mostly spontaneous association of people who define themselves as "zealots" in the terminology of traditional Judaism. Whereas the Neturei Karta to a certain degree is a protest group, its zealotry goes much further than mere protest. Deeply rooted in the Jewish religion, zealotry expresses the tension between a religion based on ancient sacred writings and the reality that characterizes the Jewish religion in today's world.

Neturei Karta first appeared in the wake of the political developments of the 1930s, when the conflict between the Jewish *yishuv* and
militant Arab nationalism was becoming increasingly violent and the
Nazis were rising to power in Germany. These developments impelled
Agudat Israel,[6] the extreme anti-Zionist Jewish religious-political
movement that until then had included Neturei Karta leaders, to
reconcile itself to some forms of political cooperation with the Zionist
leadership in Palestine. This signified a major turning point for Agudat
Israel, which had opposed Zionist *yishuv* institutions from the beginning
of the British mandate, when the Agudah and the Edah were identical
in Palestine. Agudah-Edah activities aimed at delegitimizing Zionist
efforts to establish a new secular Jewish society in *Eretz Israel* found
their most stringent expression in the "exodus" of both from the
organized Zionist communities (*knesset Israel*) and in the establishment
of the Edah as an anti-Zionist group on its own. But, after the riots of
1929 in Palestine and the worsening economic and political position of
Jews in Poland and Germany, Agudat Israel saw no choice but to
identify with the minimum demands of the Zionist *yishuv*, in order to
ensure Jewish immigration, especially for their own members.

The problems of European Jewry notwithstanding, Amram Blau
and Aharon Katzenelbogen, who were then the leaders of Tzeirei (the
Young Guard) Agudat Israel, remonstrated against the Agudah for
having betrayed its fundamental principles in abandoning isolation by
cooperating with secular Zionist organizations and institutions.
Originally calling themselves Ha-haim (Life), they adopted the Aramaic
name Neturei Karta (Guardians of the City) in 1939, when Blau and his
circle published a proclamation against a fundraising campaign—in
actuality a tax—for defending Jews against the Arab Revolt of
1936–1939. The name derives from a passage in the Jerusalem
Talmud (Hagiga 76:B) that calls religious scholars rather than armed
watchmen the guardians and true defenders of the city. In their
proclamation the group argued that, as religious students and scholars,
they (Neturei Karta), and not the defense units of the Zionists (*Hagan-
ah*), were the guardians of the city, as the latter desecrated the Sabbath
in public and did not observe the dietary laws of *kashrut*, in line with the
secular character of Zionism. Amram Blau and his friends raised this
challenge both verbally and in writing. They even raised it physically,
when they took to the streets to interfere with attempts to collect the
"defense" money.

Although secular Zionists were the proclaimed enemy, Agudat Israel
became the principal target of the Neturei Karta protest. For, in the

eyes of Neturei Karta, the Agudah was unwittingly helping legitimize the Zionist organization by cooperating with this effort. When Edah Haredit elections were held in July 1945, Neturei Karta, in cooperation with some Edah leaders, obtained control over its institutions and ousted the representatives of Agudat Israel from this body.

Although Neturei Karta and the Edah expressed the same political-religious point of view after July 1945, they still differed in organization and function. The Edah was and still is a communal organization with its own bureaucracy, whose main function is to provide its members with communal services, in particular with regard to *kashrut* and personal status (marriage and divorce). Yet, paradoxically, the very same isolationist principle that dictates providing separate religious and communal services has forced the Edah to accommodate itself to "Zionist-atheist" institutions in order to have the wherewithal to do so.

After the State of Israel was established in 1948, political reality as well as financial need dictated some form of cooperation with the state. For example, even the most extreme and anti-Zionist elements are not prepared to relinquish government sanction of marriages, as without it the Edah could not take any binding legal measures against a member who leaves his wife and children. Although some protracted and enervating procedures for applying pressure are always available in such a community, the outcome is not at all certain. They therefore must accept formal authorization from the Ministry of Religious Affairs in order to perform legally binding marriages and to grant divorces. Further, the provision of separate Edah *kashrut* services necessitates municipal and sometimes also governmental licenses (e.g., for slaughtering houses), as well as arrangements with Zionist enterprises and corporations such as Tnuvah (a Histadrut affiliate), which supplies most of the country's dairy products, fruit, and vegetables. Moreover, having its own bureaucracy has almost inevitably led the Edah to make further concessions in its isolationist principle when it fights for its economic interests by trying to gain a greater share of the Israeli food market for ultra-kosher products. As long as the standard of living in Israel remained low, these tendencies were hardly noticeable. But by the mid-1960s, as it rose and the *haredi* (ultra-Orthodox) community sought to share in it, an increasingly sharp controversy developed between Neturei Karta and Edah leaders.

The controversies between Neturei Karta and the Edah, between these two and Agudat Israel, and between all three and secular Jewish society provide the background and context for the activities of radical extremist elements in Neturei Karta and related groups, whose acts of religious zeal often take on a verbal and physical violence. Paradoxical as it may seem, these activities are directed not only against the secular Zionist but also against recognized, accepted rabbinic authorities and distinguished leaders of the ultra-Orthodox groups. Again paradoxically, these expressions of tension between groups are based on the shared historiosophical and historiographical views of *yahadut haredit*: *haredi* Judaism. It is only with this knowledge that we can understand such acts of religious zeal and their dialectical nature, for it is my thesis that this particular social context fosters conservative fundamentalism.

Without elaborating on the development of the term *yahadut haredit*, the historiosophical and historiographical principles that determine the social confinement of this society are formulated in a brief and somewhat simplified manner.

1. The term *Jewish nation* is meaningful only within the context of the mystical unity of Israel, the Torah, and God. Thus, Jewish identity has meaning only when there is faith in God, as well as in the Torah (both written and oral) as the expression of his absolute will. The Torah must therefore be obeyed by observing the halakhic commandments as interpreted by the *gedolei ha-Torah* (Torah sages) of every generation.

2. The historic destiny of the Jewish people derives from the special relationship between the Jewish nation and God, as described in the biblical quote, "Not like the other nations is the house of Israel." The Jewish nation cannot escape its special historic destiny of Exile and Redemption, both of which are basic concepts of Jewish existence. And Agudat Israel, Edah Haredit, and Neturei Karta all define Jewish existence in the current political reality of Zionism and the State of Israel as being in a condition of Exile. Whereas the adherents of Zionism define it as "the return of the Jewish people to history," ultra-Orthodox Jews view it as a revolt against the "not [being] like other nations." The *haredi* viewpoint, perforce, leads to viewing Zionist attempts to control Jewish history as a mutiny against God. This viewpoint leads to its isolationist principle and policy toward Zionist institutions and the State of Israel. Hence, every deviation from this policy, if justified at all, is justified on pragmatic grounds alone, in other words, *a posteriori*.

3. The way of life that developed in traditional Jewish communities, especially in the Ashkenazi communities of Central and Eastern Europe before the process of modernization and secularization (*haskalah*) began, is viewed as the fullest expression of Jewish society. Thus, *haredi* ultra-Orthodoxy takes this traditional Jewish society as its standard for

determining the legitimacy of Orthodox Jewish life in the modern reality. From this point of view, *haredi* ultra-Orthodox religiosity to a large extent can be defined as "neo-traditionalism," a term used here deliberately because *haredi* religiosity is certainly not consistent with traditional religiosity. Although one finds traditional religionists, whose adherence to the traditional way of life is absolute and who make no attempt whatsoever to adjust to modern society, *haredi* Jews seem to be able to deviate from tradition when necessary. However, it should again be stressed that any changes in traditional ways of life are justified only *a posteriori*, generally as a concession to social or personal imperfection.

Haredi society therefore is viewed hierarchically, in accordance with the degree of adherence to the old way of life. Since adherence to tradition as expressed in outer appearance (traditional garments, beard, side-locks), speech (Yiddish), and the education of children (*heder*) is considered the most legitimate, Neturei Karta who follow the traditions of the old Ashkenazi *yishuv* in these respects are not merely the best representative of the isolationist approach, but also the embodiment of extreme and uncompromising loyalty to the traditions of "Israel of old."[7]

Haredi self-identification therefore is determined not only by its special historiosophical and historiographical points of view but by the awareness of the degree to which these have been deviated from on the political, religious, and social levels. Thus, *haredi* society is characterized by continuous feelings of self-delegitimation, guilt, and weakness *a posteriori* in the face of Zionist reality. These feelings determine the strength of Neturei Karta as a *radical religious group*. To a large extent they also determine its dialectical relation with all of *haredi* ultra-Orthodoxy, as well as, in a sense, with religious Jewish society in general.

But radical though they may be, these paradoxical and complicated relations place Neturei Karta and similar groups in the camp of conservative fundamentalism. This is because Jewish traditional society is their context of reference and they consider themselves living in conditions of Exile, which limits their use of power to traditional "exilic" means of behavior. Religious groups such as Neturei Karta express their radical viewpoints in activities that they call *zealotism*, viewing this as a legitimate religious phenomenon in the context of Judaism. The classical example of such religious zeal is that of Pinhas, son of Elazar, son of Aaron the Priest, who killed both Zimri, son of Salu, "a chief in the Simeonite family," and Cozbi the Midianite, daughter of Zur, before the entire congregation of the children of Israel.[8] The Talmudic commentary on this event provides the following sociological analysis of Pinhas' act.[9] Although God praises Pinhas in the Bible, the Talmud justifies his deed only *a posteriori*. The ambivalent attitude toward such direct, violent acts may be sensed in the discussion between the Talmud sages. The Talmud says that if Zimri had killed Pinhas, he would not have been punished, "for he [Pinhas] is a persecutor." And when a man chases his fellow with a weapon in his hand, he who takes the life of the pursuer does not have to be punished, as he has in fact saved the lives of those being pursued. However, a deed such as that of Pinhas can be justified only "if it was committed spontaneously, in a mood of uncontrollable anger."

Despite the ambivalence of the halakhic sages, they recognize that such outbursts are inevitable expressions of religious emotion. But, as it is described in the Talmud,[10] the story reflects another important aspect of the "zeal syndrome": the tension between zealots and their leaders. By acting in front of the entire congregation, Pinhas demonstrated the weakness of the leader Moses. Indeed, it is one of the crucial aspects of this syndrome that, whatever their intention, zealots always end up challenging the established religious leadership. Even though their anger is directed at sinners, it ultimately implies criticism of the established leaders, however respected they may otherwise be.

Numerous examples of religious zeal, manifested in acts of verbal and physical violence against "sinners," can be found in various historical contexts. However, such acts are more likely to occur during periods characterized by secularization, when religion has lost control over the behavior of the people. For example, the old Ashkenazi *yishuv* in Jewish Jerusalem at the turn of the century provided a particularly favorable climate for religious zealots. The process of change and modernization that took place in Jerusalem toward the end of the nineteenth century, triggered by the activity of Western European Jewish philanthropic organizations with reformist tendencies, made possible the development of an economically and socially strong class of intellectuals (*maskilim*). But, although this new way of life was regarded an antithetical to the tradition of the old *yishuv*, the religious leadership was too weak to take serious action against it. The difficult economic and political situation also compelled them to rely upon these deviators from tradition to maintain contact between them and the philanthropic organizations. However, precisely this weakness of the religious leadership allowed the zealots relative freedom of action.

Within the social structure of the old *yishuv*, among rabbis who possessed authority and were respected in the traditional Jewish world, the zealots were able to find religious authorities to be their patrons and to sanction their activities. From this point of view, such figures as Rabbis Y. L. Diskin and J. H. Sonnenfeld played a very important role in the phenomenon of religious zeal in Jerusalem. This patronage had economic significance, too. For the rabbinic scholars who sanctioned the activities of the zealots enabled them to assume a relatively independent position in the economic structure and power centers of their society by supporting them while they devoted their time to religious activities. Thus, the tradition of religious zeal that developed in Jerusalem constituted a source of direct or indirect subsistence by allowing zealotism to become a "profession." And this structure has remained the same in essence down to this very day.

An analysis of zealot activities demonstrates that they are facilitated by three levels of participation on the part of their community:

1. *Active zealots.* Unlike Pinhas, who acted alone, the zealots' acts of verbal or physical violence usually are influenced by the group. In other words, those who act against either "sinners" or rabbinical authorities, by shouting, protesting, blows, or vilification usually act as a group, with mutual encouragement.

2. *Sympathizers or passive zealots.* Public sympathy for zealotry is a complex phenomenon, with sympathizers ranging from those who support activists wholeheartedly and publicly, yet do not dare to join them, to those who object to the acts themselves, yet refrain from doing anything that might lead to the identification or arrest of the perpetrators because they identify with their final aims.

3. *Rabbinical patrons.* Recognized and respected rabbinical authorities legitimize zealous acts. They are especially necessary when such acts are directed against other rabbinical authorities.

The relationships among these three groups are neither static nor fixed, but rather dynamic. Nor are they harmonious; indeed, they are subject to permanent tension stemming from the violent and unpremeditated nature of some zealous acts.

Against such a social reality, violence is inherent to acts of religious zeal. Indeed, in the case of Pinhas, the archetypical zealot, the violence led to death. This has not been the case with *haredi* zealots, whose violence is confined mostly to verbal or written harassment and the destruction of property. Although people have been hurt by stones thrown at cars traveling on the Sabbath, this has not resulted in any fatal injury. Moreover, the zealots have never taken up weapons or used any other means deliberately aimed at killing people.

The reasons for this restraint are critical to our understanding of the distinction between conservative and innovative fundamentalism, as one of the factors that lead *haredi* zealots to exhibit restraint is their awareness of mutual Jewish responsibility, which is strengthened by their very affinity to Jewish tradition. However, they express this in a very curious manner. Even when they are explicitly stating their hope that the mutinous and atheistic State of Israel will vanish, they add:

> This Lord of the Universe . . . knows how to lead His world in mercy and benevolence and to remove the obstacles and delays of the coming of the Messiah [an allusion to the State of Israel] without, Heaven Forbid, hurting anyone in Israel. . . . He who passed over the houses of Israel in Egypt and saved those who waited for redemption shall also show us wondrous things at the time of future redemption.[11]

This quote, by one of the main supporters of the zealots in Jerusalem, is evidence that, despite all their differences with other Jews, there is a clear sense of a common Jewish fate in a hostile world.

The affinity of extremist zealots for the complex social structure that constitutes Orthodox society in its entirety, and their dependence on it as well as on recognized religious authorities, inevitably keeps their activities within tolerable confines. And, because they do not serve in the army, extremist *haredi* zealots usually are not familiar with the use of firearms. In fact, as a very small and visible minority, they can be easily harmed themselves.

Finally, the extremists have no political ambitions in terms of reaching positions of power within Israeli society. On the contrary, they want to continue to live in Exile as a minority protected by the powers that be. The central religious import of the concept of Exile in traditional Jewish society is not as a mere political-geographical one delineating relations between Jews and the society and sovereign political framework that surround them. It is essentially religious in that it determines the historical framework of Jewish existence as the basis of the unique relationship between the Jewish people and God. According to kabbalistic tradition, notably that of the Lurianic Kabbalah, the reality of Exile encompasses the Divine system itself, which has been "damaged," as it were, and requires "restoration."

To define the historical reality as one of Exile is to evoke much of halakhic significance that does not admit elaboration within the present framework. Fundamentally, however, defining the political reality as one of Exile serves as a mechanism of adaptation to the unique conditions of Jewish existence on both the political and religious-halakhic planes. Therefore, not only are Torah laws relating to or bound up with Temple rites sequestered from day-to-day Jewish life in Exile, but the entire network of precepts dealing with relations between Jews and gentiles is perceived as not binding in accordance with the Jew's political experience as a persecuted minority.[12]

Two levels of simultaneously existing religious rulings are discernible within this framework. One bears an affinity to the political reality of Exile, and the second relates to a utopian "reality" that either existed in the past or is destined to emerge in the future, when "Israel's hand shall be high." The reality of Exile enables political-social ideas from the non-Jewish world to be absorbed and adopted while preserving a binding and fundamental affinity to religious-political precepts that are completely opposed to such ideas. Indeed, ever since the emergence of the modern era, Jewish society has been characterized by the existence of two different worlds, which demand contradictory systems of social-cultural norms.

Without going too deeply into the different interpretations given to Exile by various groups of *halakhah*-bound Orthodox Jewry, some remarks are called for on the Jewish society in *Eretz Israel* as it evolved through the agency of the Zionist movement. Secular in nature, the Zionist movement sought to establish a sovereign Jewish society that would be "modern" not only on the technological plane but also, and perhaps chiefly, on the culture-value plane. In such a democratic society, it was envisioned, non-Jews would enjoy full personal and religious equality, in contrast to the discrimination and persecution that Jews and Jewish culture had suffered in non-Jewish societies. These basic concepts were first put to the test in *Eretz Israel* in the formative stage of Zionism, when the religious-political question of women's right to vote for institutions of self-government arose after Britain took over Palestine.[13] The two positions of principle adduced on this issue were the modern-secular view, which could not accept discrimination against women as it conflicted with the political-social values of modern society, and the religious outlook, grounded in *halakhah* and in the values of the traditional religious society. This question was not resolved in the religious community as a whole, as it split along the lines of Zionist and anti-Zionist identification. The anti-Zionists, who rejected Zionism as

an attempt to annul the state of Exile by secular-political-material
means, viewed the enfranchisement of women as a substantive
expression of secular Zionism. As such, they refused to take part in the
Jewish institutions established at the outset of British mandatory rule
in Palestine.

Notwithstanding halakhic pronouncements by rabbinical authorities
whom it also accepted, the religious Zionism that found expression in
the stand of the Mizrachi movement[14] relied upon halakhic rulings of
other authorities, who acquiesced in the secular Zionists' stand on this
question. Although the Mizrachi movement's "decision" on the issue of
women's enfranchisement did not follow from its obligation to *halakhah*,
it viewed itself as true to its commitment to both the Jewish people, the
Torah, and God, on the one hand, and to the national goals of the
Zionist movement, on the other. This is what led to their imbuing the
Zionist enterprise in *Eretz Israel* with a "positive" religious definition in
terms of the traditional concepts of Exile and Redemption, and of what
underlies the fundamentalist religious innovation of religious Zionism.
This principle of religious Zionism vis-à-vis Exile and Redemption,
which was concealed and downplayed in the past, is highly visible in the
radical religiosity of Gush Emunim's Zionism.

Paradoxically enough, within the framework of the dialectic
between Exile and Redemption, the ability of religious Zionism to cope
with the secularization process undergone by Jewish Palestine was
almost inevitably grounded in the religious conception of the uniqueness of Jewish history, of being "not like all the other nations." In other
words, it was based on a principled religious outlook holding that the
historical process, as it evolved in Palestine, implied a change in the
state of Exile or the transition to the state of Redemption. Hence, the
"secularization" of the Jewish community in Palestine, as part of a
reconstructed sovereign Jewish society, could be perceived and
explicated both in terms of the sanctification of the entire historical
process and as an essential part of a Divine plan for the redemption of
the Jewish people by extricating them from the state of Exile.

These concepts were given their full expression in the writings of
Rabbi Abraham Isaac Ha-Kohen Kook.[15] Though religious Zionists
did not necessarily accept all or even part of Rabbi Kook's religious
philosophy, such realities of Jewish existence as World War II and the
establishment of the State of Israel as a sovereign political entity were
perceived as an inherent part of the process of Redemption. In other
words, the fact that the State of Israel offered Jews a place for
ingathering from Exile was enough to accord religious legitimization to

it and even to the secular Jewish society existing there. These same basic principles, however, also became the rationale for another kind of political radicalism and fundamentalist religious positions derived from Jewish "writings" relating to Redemption.

The Six-Day War was a turning point in the political expression of religious radicalism. If Israel's 1948 War of Independence is viewed as a Zionist war for the establishment of an emergent secular Jewish state, the Six-Day War can be defined as a Jewish war that reflected a substantive historical change in dialectic between Exile and Redemption. For, whereas the Six-Day War did not necessarily constitute total and absolute transition from Exile to Redemption, it marked the point at which a substantially different religious reality came into existence.

The background to this development stems from social changes in the Israeli polity, as well as from such historical circumstances as Israel's rapid and astonishing victory over Egypt, Jordan, and Syria, which brought all of *Eretz Israel* under Jewish rule. Now that places denoting the Jewish people's essential affinity to *Eretz Israel*, such as Jerusalem with the Temple Mount at its center and Hebron with its Tomb of the Patriarchs, had come under Jewish rule, a new geopolitical reality was created. And the young religious-Zionist elite that encountered this new reality was ready to accord the war and the situation it generated an existential-religious meaning through which the State of Israel became the Land of Israel and the Zionist state the Jewish state. This concatenation of events led to the emergence of Gush Emunim, a movement that regards itself as religious-Zionist in its fulfillment and within whose framework expression has been given to fundamentalist concepts that represent what I term *innovative fundamentalism.*

Religious Zionism represents an attempt to combine a modern way of life with observance of *halakhah* as it has traditionally been interpreted. The consolidation of modern religiosity inevitably entailed selecting the traditions and practices that conformed to this new way of life. Thus, some traditional elements were excluded and observance of such central Jewish commandments as prayer, Torah study, and premarital chastity became less stringent. The pattern of life that emerged from this basically spontaneous and socially activated process might be termed one of diminished religiosity.[16] Although this religiosity allowed religious Zionist Jews to play a role in the developing society and its economy without affecting their self-identification as Orthodox Jews, there was no ideological development in this atmosphere. Once the intensive pioneering activity of prestate *Eretz Israel* leveled off, and the rise in living standards facilitated the establishment of high school *yeshivot,* religious Zionist youth became aware of the painful contradiction between their parents' way of life and what they felt was prescribed in the halakhic literature they studied. The helplessness of parents in the face of direct and indirect criticism from their children began a delegitimation of parents that has had social and political repercussions. Whereas some of the national religious youngsters who graduated from high school *yeshivot* were absorbed by ultra-Orthodox "great" *yeshivot,* others went on to those that were more in line with the principles of religious Zionism. The oldest and most important of these latter *yeshivot* was the Merkaz Harav Yeshivah of Rabbi Abraham Isaac Ha-Kohen Kook. Under the direction of his son Zvi Yehudah Kook, Merkaz Harav presented young people with a worldview that offered a meaningful religious existence in the State of Israel in accordance with Zvi Yehudah's interpretation of his father's teachings.

Rabbi Abraham Kook's historiographic views are directly opposed to those of *haredi* ultra-Orthodoxy. His doctrine perceives the historical reality of his generation as more complex and essentially dialectical. In this view the reality defined as "the footsteps of the Messiah" is considered part of the historical development toward future Redemption, because it views secular-Zionist society as playing a positive and crucial role in the Messianic process, which is also essentially dialectical in nature.

Although Rabbi Kook's use of the concept "the footsteps of the Messiah" was not intended to express an innovation in religious-Zionist policy, it constituted a turning point in Jewish religious thought. Indeed, extremist zealot fears regarding the potential for innovation and change are not without basis, since the concept was meant to help religious Zionism integrate into Zionist society and politics in *Eretz Israel* as a "junior partner." Thus, as a religious-political manifestation, Gush Emunim reflects changes in the religious-Zionist community in *Eretz Israel* on two levels:

1. On the plane of historical consciousness within the framework of the dialectic between Exile and Redemption, Gush Emunim reflects an awareness and inner sense of confidence that the "history" of the Jewish people has already passed the incipient stage of the "footsteps of the Messiah"—although it is still not clear exactly how far Jewish history has advanced in the stage of Redemption.

2. In the normative-halakhic sphere, Gush Emunim essentially signifies the criticism and rejection of "light" religiosity and a concomitant commitment to the strict and stringent religiosity demonstrated,

paradoxically enough, by the ultra-Orthodox standardbearers of "anti-Zionist" religiosity: the Haredim.

A comparison of the conservative religious radicalism of *haredi* Neturei Karta and the innovative radicalism manifested by various circles within Gush Emunim reveals many structural similarities. Fundamentally, both forms base themselves on the same "writings" and see themselves as committed to the same halakhic-midrashic-kabbalistic literature. However, as Neturei Karta unequivocally defines the historical reality as a state of Exile, it regards any deviation from the "traditional" way of life as constituting a "revolt" against Divine Providence. In contrast, by designating the current historical situation a state of Redemption, Gush Emunim broadens the historical frame of reference to encompass the "utopian realities" in traditional religious literature, which lay down different norms, especially in the political-religious sphere.

Indeed, the religious radicalism of Gush Emunim encompasses features that were of only theoretical import in the stage of Exile but that suddenly became "compatible" with the new political situation as interpreted by Gush Emunim's religious leaders. However, in areas relating to "normal," day-to-day life, Gush Emunim manifests a clear tendency to reject "diminished religiosity" in favor of the "strict religiosity" characteristic of today's Haredim, of which Neturei Karta is an integral part. However, the "innovative" religious radicalism of Gush Emunim sometimes finds itself in polar conflict with conservative fundamentalism, the differences between them relating to elements central to the Jewish faith; for example, to the question of a Jewish religious presence on the Temple Mount. Moreover, as we have seen, the relations between groups such as Neturei Karta and religious authorities accepted by ultra-Orthodox Jewry places restrictions on their freedom of action as well. For the dialectic that characterizes these relations is an integral part of the self-identity of members of these groups as traditional Jews committed to heeding the instructions of "Torah sages."

The radical-religious groups who feel that the fundamental change after the Six-Day War denotes a new religious-historical experience are bound along a new track from the outset. Their certainty that there is a reality that differs substantively from the traditional one, one that is as experiential as it is imbued in consciousness, must encompass elements of a religious-political activism that will find little if any legitimation in religious authorities outside their own frameworks. Moreover, this certainty, which derives its sanction from the political reality of Jewish control over all of *Eretz Israel,* requires the legitimation of religious authorities who are even more of an anathema to Orthodox Jewry. Yet, it is precisely the gap that inevitably exists within a political reality that is both the very actualization and symbol of extrication from the states of Exile and Redemption which is expressed in Israel's democratic character. This tension will no doubt become increasingly intolerable as time passes. "Painful" contradictory realities, such as Muslim worship on the Temple Mount, are liable to push groups of individuals into seeking renewed sanction for what they feel is the character and essence of current Jewish history. And the need for repeated sanction of the inner reality of Redemption in the face of the more complex and less unequivocal political reality bears within it the possibility of a religious innovation that has the potential of thrusting radical religious groups into confrontation with the Jewish religious establishment.

NOTES

This chapter is reprinted from *Religious Radicalism and Politics in the Middle East,* edited by Emmanuel Sivan and Menachem Friedman, by permission of State University of New York Press. ©1990 State University of New York.

1. G. Herbert, *Fundamentalism and the Church* (Philadelphia, 1957); R. Hofstadter, *Anti-Intellectualism in American Life* (New York, 1963).
2. Neturei Karta (Guardians of the City, in the religious-spiritualistic sense) emerged against the backdrop of the confrontation between the Zionists and anti-Zionists in Palestine under British mandate during the *yishuv* period (1917–1948). See M. Friedman, *Society and Religion: The Non-Zionist Orthodoxy in Eretz-Israel* (Hebrew) (Jerusalem, 1978), especially 365–66. See also N. Lamm, "The Ideology of Neturei Karta According to the Satmar Version," *Tradition* 13 (1971).
3. Amram Blau died on 5 July 1974.
4. Aharon Katzenelbogen died on 13 December 1978.
5. A community in Jerusalem, which incorporates within it those who do not recognize the State of Israel as a legitimate Jewish political entity. Founded in 1918, the Edah Haredit evolved into an isolationist religious community representing the religious elements that rejected the aspirations of Zionism in Palestine.
6. Agudat Israel initially was organized in 1912 as part of the struggle against the processes of change and secularization undergone by the Jews in

Europe since the second half of the eighteenth century. Chiefly represent-ed in this movement were traditional-religious groups that objected to any change in the traditional Jewish way of life. After the establishment of Israel, this movement adopted a more moderate political stance, and it now takes part in the country's political life.

7. For an expanded treatment of this subject, see M. Friedman, "Haredi Jewry Confronts the Modern City," in *Studies in Contemporary Jewry* 2 (1985).
8. Numbers 25:1–15.
9. *Babylonian Talmud*, Sanhedrin 81a, 82b.
10. Ibid.
11. *Der Id* (Yiddish weekly of Satmar Hasidim, published in New York City), 11 May 1984.
12. Many illustrations of this can be found in J. Katz, *Exclusiveness and Tolerance: Jewish-Gentile Relations in Medieval and Modern Times* (London, 1961; New York, 1962).
13. For a detailed treatment of this subject, see Friedman, *Society and Religion*, 146–84.
14. Hamizrahi (short for "spiritual counter" in Hebrew), founded by Rabbi Isaac Reines in 1902, expressed the desire of Orthodox circles in Judaism to be integrated into the activity of the Zionist movement and to adapt to the values and ways of life of modern society, while also maintaining a binding affinity to *halakhah*.
15. Rabbi Kook served as the first chief rabbi of Palestine (1921–1935). On his philosophical outlook, see especially Z. Yaron, *Mishnato shel ha-Rav Kook* (Jerusalem, 1974).
16. For a detailed treatment of this subject, see M. Friedman, "The NRP in Transition: Behind the Party's Decline," in *The Roots of Begin's Success: The 1981 Israeli Election*, ed. D. Caspi et al. (London and New York, 1984), 141–68.

Chapter 10

Withdrawal and Conquest:
Two Aspects of the Haredi Response to Modernity

Gerald Cromer

Secularization is the process by which sectors of society and culture are removed from the domination of religious institutions and symbols.[1] This occurs both at the institutional level (e.g., the separation of church and state) and, perhaps more importantly, at the level of human consciousness. As a result of this secularization of consciousness, an increasing number of individuals look upon the world and their own lives without the benefit of religious interpretations.[2] As far as they are concerned, God, if not dead, is at least irrelevant.

It must be pointed out, though, that secularization does not only affect those who abandon their belief in the divine; it also has a crucial influence on the faithful. Having become what Peter Berger[3] so aptly calls a cognitive minority, they are forced to choose between two options—accommodation and defense.[4] In the first case, an attempt is made to reach some form of *modus vivendi* with the secular majority; in the second, all efforts are directed towards avoiding its deleterious influence.

However, this dichotomy must not be allowed to hide an important similarity between the two approaches. Despite their protestations to the contrary, advocates of defense, often called fundamentalists, are not simply the standard bearers of old religious traditions; they are, rather, responding to those who have made some form of accommodation with modernity. Thus, defense as well as accommodation is a response to the changing situation. According to Eric Sharpe,[5] this reaction can be divided into three stages. First, there is a rejection of accepted traditional authority. This is followed by an attempt to adapt tradition to the contemporary world, i.e., to try to find a *modus vivendi* between them. This leads, in turn, to a reaction by the "true believers." While claiming to preserve the authentic traditional faith, they, in fact, espouse an extreme interpretation of that tradition in response to those who have rejected it or adapted it to modern currents. Consequently, "fundamentalism is as much a product of the secularization process as the liberalism it is determined to abolish."[6]

Judaism provides a classic example of this process. The hegemony of traditional Judaism came to an end with the Emancipation. Rejecting traditional religious authority, Jews were free to choose new ways, both religious and secular, of being Jewish. The growing popularity of these alternatives (e.g., liberal Judaism and Zionism) led to the advent of Orthodox Judaism, i.e., the movement consisting of those who persisted in their traditional behavior in spite of the emergence of different modern forms of Judaism. But, as Jacob Katz has clearly pointed out, "the claim of the orthodox to be no more than the guardians of the pure Judaism of old is a fiction. In fact, orthodoxy was a method of confronting deviant trends, and of responding to the very same stimuli which produced those trends."[7]

Research studies of ultra-Orthodox or *haredi*[8] communities in Israel[9] and the Diaspora[10] have generally emphasized the extent to which its adherents segregate themselves from both non-Jews and non-observant Jews in order to avoid being contaminated by them. This defensive response, it has been argued, arises out of a fear that any form of contact is more likely to endanger the traditional community's existence than attract the surrounding society to its way of life. Recently, however, a number of observers have drawn attention to a new mood amongst *haredi* Jews.[11] The "trauma of erosion" that had generated a defensive position has given way to a feeling of superiority or triumphalism. No longer satisfied with simply defending those within the fold from the perils of modernity, rabbinical and political leaders are determined to take the offensive against secular society. The *haredim*, to use Charles Liebman's terms, are using strategies of withdrawal and conquest at one and the same time.[12]

The present chapter tries to analyze these *haredi* strategies by examining three major spheres of communal activity—education, parliamentary legislation, and extraparliamentary protest. My aim is not to give a detailed history of these activities, but simply to illustrate the way in which the *haredim* have in each case engaged simultaneously in withdrawal and conquest, and to analyze the dialectical relationship between these two responses. Before doing so, however, it is necessary to describe, albeit briefly, the attitude of the *haredi* community to secularism in general and secular Zionism in particular.[13]

Background

The black garb of *haredi* Jews gives the impression of a homogeneous community. However, as Amnon Levy has pointed out,[14] the trained observer can distinguish between different groups of *haredim* according to the kinds of clothes they wear. The *haredim* community is "full of variations and full of color; there are all shades of black and white."[15] And this heterogeneity is by no means limited to outward appearance. Each group also has its own ideological stance on a wide variety of issues.   Of particular importance are the differences of opinion concerning secular Zionism and the State of Israel.

The Edah Haredit[16] and the Neturei Karta[17] are the most extreme in this respect. They both adopt an avowedly anti-Zionist stance. According to their way of thinking, Divine Providence placed the people of Israel outside the natural laws of causality and subjected them instead to a divinely ordained pattern of reward and punishment. Consequently, the Jewish people are obligated to pursue a path of political quietism and wait patiently for the coming of the Messiah: "Unless the Lord builds the house, its builders labor in vain. Unless the Lord watches over the city, the watchman keeps vigil in vain."[18] According to this perspective, any human effort to "hasten the end" constitutes an interference in the realm of the Divine. Thus, in the view of the Edah Haredit and the Neturei Karta, the Zionist attempt to return to history was, and for that matter still is, a collective revolt against the Kingdom of Heaven.

Clearly, therefore, those *haredim* who are anti-Zionist oppose the State of Israel not only because it is a secular entity; they object to the very existence of a Jewish state prior to the coming of the Messiah. Even if it were to be run according to the Jewish law, such a state would constitute a "defilement of the Torah." In fact, the whole idea of a *halakhic* state is regarded as a contradiction in terms, for in such a state the observance of the Torah would be based on a rebellion against one of its most basic tenets—to quietly await the coming of the Messiah.

The vast majority of *haredim*, however, are non-Zionists rather than anti-Zionists. Adopting a much more pragmatic stance towards the Jewish state, those *haredim* who support the various political parties make a clear distinction between secular Zionism and the state to which it gave rise. While rejecting the former, they grant to the state de facto recognition. Nevertheless, as far as these non-Zionist *haredim* are concerned, the Jewish state is devoid of any religious significance per se and is completely unconnected to the question of redemption.

In contrast to the Edah Haredit and the Neturei Karta, non-Zionist *haredim* do not condemn the State of Israel *a priori*. Instead, they judge it on an ad hoc basis. Interestingly, in evaluating the Jewish state, they employ exactly the same criteria that they use to judge Jewish organizations in the Diaspora, i.e., their contribution to the furtherance of traditional Judaism. In the words of one *haredi* leader,

> There is no independent absolute value in the Torah except for the Holy one, blessed be He, and His service. . . . The value of the *yishuv* [the pre-state community] framework and its institutions is measured only by the extent to which they bring the people of the Lord closer to the Torah, the commandments, and the faith.[19]

Consequently, the non-Zionist *haredim* criticize only those aspects of Israeli society that are detrimental to traditional Judaism. That is all that matters as far as they are concerned.

Having pointed out the major differences between the two *haredi* worldviews, it is important to draw attention to a major similarity between them. Even though the Edah Haredit and Neturei Karta deny the legitimacy of any kind of Jewish state, they, like the non-Zionist *haredim*, do criticize the secular nature of the existing state. Anti-Zionists and non-Zionists alike are at pains to point out the deleterious effects of the present policies. According to both schools of thought, abandonment of the Torah is the underlying cause of all the country's problems. "Secularization," to quote one *haredi* newspaper, "is the root of all evil."[20]

Haredi spokesmen use different forms of rhetoric to drive this message home. Of particular importance, however, is the frequent resort to what Joel Best[21] has referred to as range claims, i.e., the contention that a problem permeates all sectors of the population. The function of such claims is to refute the argument that social ills are limited to those of lower socio-economic status or Oriental origin. Consequently, these claims must be accompanied by an explanation of the occurrence of social ills in wealthy and Western Jewish families.

According to the *haredi* way of thinking, all social problems result from spiritual rather than material deprivation.[22] And, they argue, all those who have rejected the yoke of the Torah live in a spiritual vacuum. Thus, it comes as no surprise to the *haredim* that social problems prevail amongst all sectors of the secular population. In fact, they are amazed that the situation is not worse.

To summarize—*haredim* criticize the State of Israel on three grounds. The Edah Haredit and Neturei Karta attack it for being a revolt against the Kingdom of Heaven. Moreover, they, together with other groups of *haredim*, criticize the state both for its harmful effects on traditional Judaism and for being responsible for all the country's social problems. Thus, while the anti-Zionists oppose the Jewish state on moralistic grounds, i.e., because of its inherent deficiencies and irrespective of its effects, non-Zionist *haredim* only criticize the state in causalistic terms. As far as they are concerned, it is the horrible consequences which the state engenders that undermine its legitimacy.

The arguments of anti- and non-Zionist *haredim* are similar in one important respect. They provide the rationale for both the *haredi* withdrawal from Israeli society and the attempt to dominate it. This is clearly evident in three areas of activity—education, parliamentary legislation, and extra-parliamentary protest.

Education

Immediately after the establishment of the State of Israel, the educational system was divided into different trends. Each political camp ran its own schools. However, in 1953, the State Education Law transferred administrative and pedagogical control to the government. From the very beginning, however, the *haredi* community opted out of this framework. Both Agudat Yisrael[23] and the Edah Haredit were allowed to set up their own educational systems. While they differed with regard to the exact nature of their independence from the government, they had, and for that matter still do have, one important characteristic in common. Both systems have complete autonomy over the appointment of teachers and the development of curricula.

The policy of withdrawal is reflected in the content as well as the form of education. Thus, the major aim of *haredi* schooling for boys is to provide a deep knowledge of traditional Jewish sources, especially the Talmud. This study is regarded as being a *mitzvah* (divine commandment) in its own right, as well as the most efficient way of ensuring that the younger generation will continue to adhere to the entire body of traditional commandments.

With regard to secular subjects, *haredim* not only consider them to be of no inherent value, they also view them as having a deleterious effect on Torah observance. Consequently, only those subjects without which it is impossible to make a living are taught in *haredi* schools. And, it should be added, even these subjects are restricted to the lower reaches of the educational system. Once boys begin to attend a *yeshiva* (talmudic academy) at age fourteen, all their time is devoted solely to the study of Torah. Everything else is taboo.

The *haredim* do not consider Torah study to be a religious obligation for women. Consequently, female education has always been much more restricted than that of the males. However, the situation has changed dramatically in the last sixty years, especially since the establishment of the State of Israel. Alongside the old Orthodox educational institutions for women, new ones have been have been set up that provide a broader education in both religious and secular subjects. This is, of course, a major break with tradition, made necessary by a highly significant trend—the growing number of married men studying full time. Insofar as learning in the *yeshiva* after marriage has now become the norm in the *haredi* community, an increasing number of women have had to become the major bread-winner of the family. Thus, even as the *haredi* men have withdrawn further from involvement in the surrounding society, *haredi* women have been forced to increasingly accommodate themselves to it.

Haredi education for both boys and girls is much more intensive than that provided by the state system. At the same time, serious attention is paid to the way in which *haredi* youth spend their leisure time. Popular leisure pursuits are either entirely forbidden (e.g., the *haredi* ban on television and other mass media) or altered so as to meet the needs of the Orthodox community. Thus, *haredi* children are permitted to read stories about the righteous, build models of the Holy Temple, and collect picture cards of illustrious rabbis. And, perhaps most interestingly, they are allowed to play new versions of old board games. Mitzvah Monopoly, for example, is essentially the same as the original Parker Brothers real estate trading game. There is, however, one important difference—participants have to amass good deeds rather than financial assets.

But *haredi* education does not only try to foster withdrawal from the surrounding society; it also attempts to change it. Since the Six Day War of 1967, the *haredi* community has been engaged in a wide variety of outreach activities specifically designed to attract young people who live beyond the dictates of Orthodox Judaism. They were initially directed at American Jewish students who were involved in the youth culture of the sixties. Since then, however, they have been extended, first to Israeli middle-class youth, and subsequently to disadvantaged youngsters of Sephardic background. Even the Israeli Prison Service has opened a *yeshiva* for those inmates interested in mending their ways.

The transition from the secular to the religious world almost always involves a total metamorphosis of values and behavior. Previous studies[24] have indicated that *baalei teshuvah* (previously unobservant Jews who have embraced a *haredi* lifestyle) tend to be more punctilious in their religious observance than those who have always been orthodox. It is suggested, however, that the tendency towards extremism is of a more general nature. *Baalei teshuvah* adopt a particularly rigorous stance regarding secular Israeli society. As a result of this personal experience, they are often the staunchest supporters of both withdrawal from the surrounding society as well as the attempt to dominate it.

Having passed from one world to another, the *baalei teshuvah* are particularly adamant about the impossibility of living in both at the same time and seek to embrace the new world in its entirety. However, even after doing so, *baalei teshuvah* remain continuously aware of the fragile nature of their new lifestyle and, therefore, of the perennial danger of returning to their old habits. Because of this fear, they are determined to eliminate every potential distraction and temptation by effecting a complete withdrawal. Nothing whatsoever can be left to chance.

Paradoxically, however, *baalei teshuvah* also see themselves as a bridge between the two worlds. Thus, not only are they in an ideal position to persuade the *haredi* community of the need for outreach activities, they also consider themselves best equipped to carry them out. Having experienced both worlds and the difficulties involved in moving from one to the other, *baalei teshuvah* feel that they are the most appropriate models for others considering a similar path. Having conquered their own evil inclination, they are now in a position to conquer secular society as a whole.

Many *baalei teshuvah* do, in fact, take an active part in outreach activities. In public meetings for potential repentants, they recount their happy tales.[25] Recollecting the miseries of a secular lifestyle, they describe their struggle to escape it and the joys of living in accordance with the Torah. While the close personal contact with secular youth engendered by these activities seems to pose a threat to the *baalei teshuvah*, exactly the opposite is the case. Witnessing to their newfound faith before non-believers tends to reinforce their own religious identity.[26] Indeed many *baalei teshuvah* actually engage in outreach activities more to convince themselves of the rightness of their views than to persuade others to follow in their footsteps.[27]

A similar situation exists at the communal level. *Haredi* publications are replete with stories about *baalei teshuvah* and their own happy tales. Particularly popular in this respect are the life-histories of reformed juvenile delinquents and even adult offenders who have gone straight and become Orthodox Jews. These "miracle stories" are not only considered to be a particularly effective way of persuading secular Israelis to follow in their footsteps; they are also regarded as a means of strengthening the resolve of the ultra-Orthodox. The fact that non-observant Jews who repudiate their secular lifestyle and accept the yoke of the Torah experience joy and fulfillment is seen as an additional reason for withdrawal from the surrounding society.

This is not to suggest, of course, that *haredim* feel no tension between the two approaches of withdrawal and attack in relation to the *baalei teshuvah*. While confident that the *teshuvah* movement is living proof of the collapse of secular values and a portent of the ultimate victory of Orthodoxy, the *haredim* are anxious about its immediate effects.[28] They, like the repentants themselves, are concerned about the continuing influence of the previous lifestyle. Hence, for example, *haredi* parents are reluctant to allow their children to marry *baalei teshuvah*. In this and other situations, successful conquest may, it is feared, jeopardize the integrity of the traditional *haredi* lifestyle.

Parliamentary Legislation

The *haredi* desire to separate themselves from the surrounding society is perhaps most clearly seen in their tendency to live in close proximity to one another, apart from the secular populace. Despite the continuous growth of the *haredi* community, it is still highly segregated from the rest of the population. Clearly, however, the separation of the *haredim* from the secular community is not merely physical; they also constitute two distinct cultural enclaves. All members of the *haredi* community live in accordance with the dictates of Orthodox Judaism or, to use a Talmudic term, within the "four cubits of Jewish law."

Although behavioral norms within the *haredi* community are determined by rabbinical interpretations of *halakhah* (Jewish religious law), the boundaries of Jewish law are not as immutable as they might appear to be. Faced with a halakhic problem, even *haredi* rabbis have a certain amount of flexibility. They are free to make stricter or more lenient decisions.

These rabbinical interpretations of *halakhah* determine behavioral norms within the *haredi* community. The tendency at the present time, however, is towards more stringent interpretations of the law. And this interpretive process is a cumulative one. Rival *haredi* leaders seem to be involved in an ongoing competition to see who demands the strictest adherence to the law. In each case, their decision is not offered as a preferred alternative; it is presented, instead, as the only authentic rendering of the Jewish tradition.[29]

This is not to suggest, though, that state legislation has no influence on religious observance. As Menachem Elon, a member of the Supreme Court and an expert on Jewish law, has pointed out,[30] state legislation fulfills two important functions in this regard—it both ensures the provision of religious services to those who require them and enforces certain religious norms among the entire population—or, in terms of this particular study, withdrawal and conquest, respectively. According to many observers, the field of legislation, like that of education, is currently characterized by a trend towards the strategy of domination.[31] However, a brief review of *haredi* legislative efforts since the establishment of the state suggests that the situation is somewhat more complicated than they would have us believe.

Agudat Yisrael (a religious party committed to a state ruled by traditional religious norms and principles) joined the first Israeli coalition government as part of the United Religious Front. Its declared aim was to prevent the introduction of anti-religious legislation or what Rabbi Yitzhak Meir Levin, the Minister of Social Welfare, referred to as "laws that will injure our innermost being, will make our situation tragic and unbearable."[32] Nevertheless, the major religious legislation was oriented more towards conquest than withdrawal. The "status quo" agreement which formalized the relationship between the government and the religious communities that had existed before the establishment of the state ensured continued financial support for religious educational institutions. More significantly, however, this agreement also decreed Saturday as the official rest day, severely limited public transportation on the Sabbath, insisted on the observance of the dietary laws in public institutions, and invested the rabbinical courts with complete control over laws of personal status, which concern birth, marriage, divorce, and death.

Agudat Yisrael left the coalition government in 1952 because of a disagreement over the question of army service for women, and it remained in opposition for 25 years. It did not even join the National Unity Government that was set up immediately before the Six Day War in 1967. However, this gives a somewhat misleading picture of the situation. There was, in fact, an informal understanding between Agudat Yisrael and the ruling Labor party. The former adopted a low profile in exchange for financial support for its independent school system. Thus, the major *haredi* party at that time retreated from its avowed aim of transforming Israeli society in order to further the policy of withdrawal.

Since the Likud's rise to power in 1977 until the last Knesset elections in June 1992, Agudat Yisrael was a member of the coalition government. While numerically its own parliamentary representation declined, this was offset by the rise of two new *haredi* parties—Shas and Degel Hatorah. Together these three parties held the balance of power between the two major political blocs—Labor and Likud. Notwithstanding the disagreements between them, these parties used this pivotal position to further the interests of the *haredi* community as a whole.

The *haredi* parties have been most active and, for that matter, most successful in obtaining public funding for their institutions. Every year, they make their support of the budget dependent on increased financial support for a whole gamut of *haredi* educational and social organizations. In the perennial debate about the significance of this additional funding, the *haredim* argue that it constitutes but a first step in the battle to achieve equality for their institutions. Their opponents, on the other hand, insist that the *haredi* community already receives an inordinate amount of the country's limited resources. Both sides would agree, however, that secular society is funding more and more organizations fostering withdrawal from it, and that *haredi* institutions are flourishing as never before.

The policy of withdrawal has also been furthered by other legislative means. Since the Likud party came to power, for example, religious women no longer have to appear before a review committee in order to gain exemption from military service. All that is now required is a notarized statement of religious commitment. There is little doubt, however, that the *haredi* parties have mainly used the legislative process as a means for controlling and gaining hegemony within the wider society. Since re-entering the coalition in 1977, they have managed, for instance, to pass laws prohibiting abortions on grounds of social distress, curtailing El Al flights on the Sabbath, and restricting the conditions under which autopsies can be carried out. At the present time, *haredi* politicians are, among other things, trying to ban pornography in public places and further restrict the breeding of pigs. Thus, the *haredi* attempt to dominate Israeli society continues unabated.

This represents a major change in policy from that of the period during which the *haredi* parties were in opposition. However, it is by no means a new phenomenon. As has already been pointed out, the religious legislation that was passed immediately after the establishment of the state was also designed to both defend the cultural boundaries of *haredi* society and dominate those who lived beyond them. These goals do not seem to have changed. Then, as now, religious legislation was more concerned with conquest than withdrawal.

This strategy of conquest through legislation is, of course, very different from the one described in the previous section on education. While the *teshuva* movement, for example, is based on a process of persuasion, *haredi* legislative activity constitutes an attempt to coerce the entire Jewish population of Israel to change certain aspects of its behavior regardless of whether or not they wish to do so. Compliance, not commitment, is what they are seeking. Nevertheless, education and legislation do have one important characteristic in common. In both cases, changing others helps *haredim* to remain the same.

Law not only changes behavior; it also designates public norms.[33] In fact, it fulfills the latter function even when unenforced. The mere fact that a particular law is on the statute books constitutes a public affirmation of certain social ideas and norms. And this, of course, is of great significance for a cognitive minority such as the *haredi* Jews. The fact that their commitment to *halakhah* is affirmed by secular laws makes it easier for them to bear the yoke of the Torah. Once again, therefore, attempts to dominate the surrounding society reinforce efforts to withdraw from it.

Extra-Parliamentary Protest

The *haredi* parties do not only operate within the parliamentary system. Ever since the establishment of the state, they have used extra-parliamentary means to further their interests. Thus, demonstrations have been organized in support of both withdrawal (e.g., against military service for women and male *yeshiva* students) and domination (e.g., over the public observance of the Sabbath). Both kinds of demonstrations can engender violence. Not surprisingly though, this violence is much more likely to be fomented by the anti-Zionist groups. As Lehman-Wilzig and Goldberg have pointed out,[34] the tendency for religious protest to be more violent than other forms of protest (38.4 percent as compared to 9.4 percent) can be attributed, above all, to the fact that almost half the demonstrations are organized by the Edah Haredit and Neturei Karta.

The violence of these groups has by no means been limited to public protest; they have also engaged in direct attacks against property and persons. This kind of intimidation, like the other forms of *haredi* action, is used to support both withdrawal from and conquest of the surrounding society. However, in the case of attacks on property and persons, the situation is different in one important aspect. Endeavoring to further the policy of withdrawal, they are moved to take action against *haredi* and secular Jews alike.

In each of the major concentrations of *haredi* populations, there is a "morality squad," whose major task is to take punitive action against those who deviate from communal norms. They are particularly concerned with the *shabavnikim* (youngsters who are still formally enrolled in a *yeshiva* in order to avoid military service, but who have, in fact, ceased their *yeshiva* learning entirely). However, these squads also take action against more respectable members of the community. Anybody who has a television set in his/her house, for instance, may become the target of these young zealots.

Similar violent actions are taken against secular Jews living in *haredi* areas.[35] Any breach of the *halakhah* can provide the rationale for violent action against their property or person. However, this is particularly likely to occur in response to violations of the Sabbath or the wearing of immodest dress.

Such actions highlight the lack of differentiation between the public and private realms within the *haredi* community. Transgression of the law even within one's own home (e.g., having a party on the Sabbath) can lead to a violent response. And the presence of secular Jews— either as residents or tradesmen—in a *haredi* enclave is often regarded as sufficient cause for violence. According to this way of thinking, the mere existence of alternative lifestyles constitutes a threat to the *haredi* way of life. Thus, pockets of such lifestyles either have to be eradicated or, at least, moved to a different part of town.

This is not to suggest that *haredi* violence is limited to the religious areas of the city. One example is the continuing struggle against pornography that began in the 1970s with the burning of sex shops in Jerusalem and Tel Aviv. Since then, the definition of pornography has been substantially widened and similar treatment is now accorded to bus shelters in the capital. Almost any advertisement that includes a woman is regarded as worthy of destruction.

It is, of course, beyond the confines of this discussion to present a detailed analysis of the way in which the perpetrators of these violent acts justify them, either in their own eyes or those of others. Mention should be made, though, of the frequent legitimating references to traditional sacred texts. The literature of the Edah Haredit and Neturei Karta is replete with biblical and Talmudic references concerning the duty both to reprimand other Jews and to assume responsibility for their wrongdoing. A frequently used example is that of the biblical zealot, Pinhas the Priest.[36] His killing of Zimri, a chief in the Simonite family, and his Midianite mistress in front of Moses and the entire congregation of the children of Israel is regarded as the clearest justification of their resort to force. Now as then, the argument goes, it is sometimes necessary to be zealous and take the law into one's own hands.

Violence is regarded by its *haredi* perpetrators as the best and, in certain circumstances, the only way of achieving their ends. However, even if they fail, their efforts are not thought to be in vain. Violent protest, it is believed, is always a *kiddush hashem* (a sanctification of God's name). Whether or not it has any immediate effects is, therefore, totally irrelevant.

Not surprisingly, violent demonstrators portray themselves as the only members of the community who are truly Orthodox and God-fearing. Their actions are documented in a series of books on the "campaigns of *haredi* Judaism."[37] Each volume recounts the story of a particular struggle (e.g., against the archaeological excavations in the City of David). Without exception, the narratives take the form of a morality play. The courage and personal sacrifice of the protesters is contrasted with the cruelty and hatred of the Israeli police. In short, the story is one of the forces of good fighting against the forces of evil.

This view of the situation is shared by many others in the *haredi* community. Almost all of these sympathizers, or passive zealots, as Menachem Friedman calls them, agree with the protesters' ends.[38] Even those among them who reject the use of violence admire the courage and personal sacrifice of those concerned. Not surprisingly, therefore, whenever zealots are taken into custody or put on trial, leaders of the different *haredi* groups try to put pressure on the powers that be, each in their own way. While the Edah Haredit and the Neturei Karta take to the streets, the *haredi* political parties ply the corridors of power.

The anti-Zionist groups often use such episodes as evidence of the *haredi* parties' lack of influence and, therefore, the folly of cooperating with the secular authorities. But this controversy within the *haredi* community, however basic it may be, must not be allowed to hide the unifying aspects of religious zealotry. Not only is there a broad range of support for those who engage in this kind of action, there is also widespread opposition to the response of the secular authorities. Consequently, even though only a small minority of *haredim* are involved in acts of extra-parliamentary protest, such actions serve to widen the gap between the *haredi* community and the surrounding society. Once again, activities aimed at domination paradoxically help further the policy of withdrawal.

Conclusions

Haredi Judaism is not simply a continuation of traditional religious patterns; it is rather the product of the clash between them and the modern secular world. In the State of Israel, this confrontation occurs in three major areas of activity—education, parliamentary legislation, and extra-parliamentary protest. In each of these spheres, *haredim* adopt two strategies—withdrawal from the surrounding society and the attempt to dominate it. As our discussion has shown, these modes of action are not in conflict with one another. In fact, exactly the opposite is the case. *Haredi* attempts to change Israeli society actually help the community to remain the same. Paradoxically, *haredi* efforts to conquer the world reinforce their endeavors to withdraw from it.

Notwithstanding the complementary nature of the two *haredi* strategies, they are based on very different images of those who have abandoned the "yoke of the Torah."[39] Advocates of separation speak of two distinct communities—Jews and Israelis. In many instances, they even go one step further and refer to secular Israelis as *goyim* (gentiles) or anti-Semites.

In contrast, the strategy of domination is based, in many instances at least, on an underlying assumption that *haredi* and secular Jews are part of the same community. This is particularly evident in the case of the *teshuvah* movement. Differences in the level of religious observance are regarded as unimportant. Emphasis is placed, instead, on the essential similarity among Jews—that they all have a special "spark of God" within them. This spark, it is argued, both unites all Jews and distinguishes them from the other nations of the world.

Despite these contrasting images of secular Jews, advocates of both *haredi* strategies are agreed as to who is ultimately responsible for the process of secularization. They both tend to divide secular Jews into two distinct groups—the corrupters and the corrupted.[40] According to this way of thinking, the Zionist movement has always been intent on destroying traditional Judaism. Throughout its history, and particularly during periods of mass migration (e.g., from North Africa and the Middle East in the 1950s, and from Russia and Ethiopia at the present time), secular leaders have done their utmost to "apostatize" religiously observant Jews. Consequently, those who have abandoned the "yoke of the Torah" are not held accountable for their misdeeds. Responsibility is attributed instead to those who have led them astray.

Thus, while *haredim* differ as to the exact nature of the corrupted, they are in complete agreement as to the identity of those who have corrupted them. And it is this view of the Israeli political establishment as the ultimate cause of the secularization process that provides the rationale for both the *haredi* withdrawal from society and the attempt to dominate it. Advocates of both approaches see themselves as countering the forces of corruption—as "sons of the light of Torah" engaged in a holy war against the "sons of secular darkness."[41]

NOTES

1. Peter L. Berger, *The Sacred Canopy: Elements of a Sociological Theory of Religion* (New York: Anchor Books, 1969), 107.
2. Ibid., 107–8.
3. Peter L. Berger, *A Rumour of Angels: Modern Society and the Rediscovery of the Supernatural* (Harmondsworth: Penguin Books, 1971), 18–19.
4. Peter L. Berger, *Facing up to Modernity: Excursions in Society, Politics and Religion* (New York: Basic Books, 1977), 175–77.
5. Eric J. Sharpe, *Understanding Religion* (London: Duckworth, 1983), 116–23.
6. Ibid., 120.
7. Jacob Katz, "Orthodoxy in Historical Perspective," *Studies in Contemporary Jewry* 2 (1986): 4–52.
8. This designation is based on a verse from *Isaiah* 66:5: "Hear the word of the Lord, you that tremble (*haredim*) at His word."
9. See, for instance, Joseph Shilhav and Menachem Friedman, *Growth and*

Segregation—The Ultra-Orthodox Community of Jerusalem (Hebrew) (Jerusalem: Jerusalem Institute for Israel Studies, 1985).

10. See, for instance, Israel Z. Rubin, *Satmar: An Island in the City* (Chicago: Quadrangle Books, 1972).

11. This school of thought finds its clearest expression in Janet Aviad's work on repentant Jews. For further details, see her "From Protest to Return: Contemporary Teshuvah," *Jerusalem Quarterly* 16 (Summer 1980): 71–82, and *Return to Judaism: Religious Renewal in Israel* (Chicago: University of Chicago Press, 1983).

12. Charles S. Liebman, "Extremism as a Religious Norm," *Journal for Scientific Study of Religion* 22 (1983): 77.

13. For a more detailed analysis of this topic, see Aviezer Ravitsky, "Exile in the Holy Land: The Dilemma of Haredi Jewry," *Studies in Contemporary Jewry* 5 (1989): 89–125, and Menachem Friedman, "The State of Israel as a Theological Dilemma," in Baruch Kimmerling, ed., *The Israeli State and Society: Boundaries and Frontiers* (Albany: State University of New York Press, 1989), 165–215.

14. Amnon Levy, *The Ultra-Orthodox* (Hebrew) (Jerusalem: Keter Books, 1989), 31–39.

15. Ibid., 39.

16. A community that incorporates within it those *haredi* Jews who do not recognize the State of Israel as a legitimate political entity.

17. The name, which is Aramaic for "guardians of the city," derives from a passage in the Jerusalem Talmud stating that religious scholars, rather than armed watchmen, are the defenders of the city.

18. Psalms 127:1.

19. Quoted in Ravitsky, "Exile in the Holy Land," 95.

20. *Shearim*, 15 December 1972.

21. Joel Best, "Rhetoric in Claims Making: Constructing the Missing Children Problem," *Social Problems* 34 (April 1987): 108.

22. For a more detailed analysis of this perspective, see Gerald Cromer, "Secularization is the Root of All Evil: The Response of Ultra-Orthodox Judaism to Social Deviance," *Proceedings of the Ninth World Congress of Jewish Studies*, vol. 3 (Jerusalem: World Union of Jewish Studies, 1986), 397–404.

23. Union or Association of Israel. A political party founded in 1948 to promote the observance of *halakhah* in public life.

24. See, for instance, Aviad, *Return to Judaism*, 106–26.

25. For further details, see Gerald Cromer, "Sad Tales and Happy Tales: The Politicization of Delinquents' Life Histories," *Political Communication and Persuasion* 5 (Fall 1988): 179–90.

26. William Shaffir, "Witnessing as Identity Consolidation: The Case of the Lubavitcher Chassidism," in Hans Mol, ed., *Identity and Religion: International Cross-Cultural Approaches* (Beverly Hills: Sage Publications, 1978), 39–57.

27. Gerald Cromer, "Repentant Delinquents: A Religious Approach to Rehabilitation," *Jewish Journal of Sociology* 23 (December 1981): 115.

28. On this point, see Aviad, *Return to Judaism*, 149–52.

29. See Menachem Friedman in this volume (chaps. 9 and 12). This process is also analyzed in Menachem Friedman, "Life Tradition and Book Tradition in the Development of Ultra-Orthodox Judaism," in Harvey E. Goldberg, ed., *Judaism Viewed from Within and Without* (Albany: State University of New York Press, 1987), 235–55.

30. Menachem Elon, *Religious Legislation in the Israel Legal System* (Hebrew) (Tel Aviv: Kibbutz Hadati, 5728 [1967]), 5.

31. See, for instance, Gary S. Schiff, "Beyond the Begin Revolution: Recent Developments in Israel's Religious Parties," in Gregory S. Mahler, ed., *Israel after Begin* (Albany: State University of New York Press, 1990), 284–88.

32. Quoted in Ravitsky, "Exile in the Holy Land," 106.

33. This argument is based on Joseph Gusfield, "Moral Passage: The Symbolic Process in Public Designations of Deviance," *Social Problems* 15 (Fall 1967): 176–78.

34. Sam Lehman-Wilzig and Giora Goldberg, "Religious Protest and Police Reaction in a Theo-Democracy: Israel, 1950–1979," *Journal of Church and State* 25 (Autumn 1983): 494–500.

35. For a detailed analysis of this phenomenon, see Avraham Farber, *Patterns of Haredi Victimization of Non-Haredi Residents as Part of the Struggle for Domination in Northwest Jerusalem* (Hebrew) (Master's thesis, Hebrew University, 1987).

36. See Numbers 25:1–15.

37. See, for instance, Zvi Meshi Zohar and Yehuda Meshi Zohar, *The Rebellion on the Temple Mount: A Diary of the Campaign* (Hebrew) (Jerusalem: Institute of Haredi Judaism, 5745 [1984]). According to a number of observers, these books are also used in fundraising missions abroad.

38. See Menachem Friedman in this volume, 155.

39. On this point, see Amnon Levy, "The Haredi Press and Secular Israeli Society," in Charles S. Liebman, ed., *Religious and Secular: Conflict and Accommodation between Jews in Israel* (Hebrew) (Jerusalem: Keter Books, 1990), 36–39.

40. For further details and another application of this model, see Jock Young, "The Myth of Drugtakers in the Mass Media," in Stanley Cohen and Jock Young, eds., *The Manufacture of News: Deviance, Social Problems and the Mass Media* (Beverly Hills: Sage Publications, 1981), 326–34.

41. Quoted in Levy, "Haredi Press," 37.

Part III

Religious Fundamentalism and Judaism:
Selected Issues

Chapter 11

Fundamentalism:
A Jewish Traditional Perspective

Aaron Kirschenbaum

In the American press, the treatment of fundamentalism generally tends to be confrontational and emotional. Additionally, it often implies that fundamentalism poses a threat to civil liberties. Of late, the term *fundamentalism* has emerged as a label of derogation in relation to Jewish Ultra-Orthodoxy. This rather new development was occasioned by two causes:

First, in the 1988 Israeli elections, the Ultra-Orthodox parties had surprising success (relative to previous performance). Inasmuch as coalition politics in Israel often enhance a small party's political clout far beyond that which would be warranted by its numbers, the Israeli public panicked at the possibility that its life would be controlled by clerical fiat.

Second, the 1988 election returns in Israel engendered fear and apprehension with the American Jewish public as well. The pivotal position in which the religious parties (Orthodox and Ultra-Orthodox) were placed raised the threat that the Israeli Law of Return would be amended to the effect that non-Orthodox converts to Judaism would not be registered as Jews by Israeli officialdom.

We were thus treated to a demagogic branding of Jewish Orthodoxy and Ultra-Orthodoxy as fundamentalist, with all the confrontational and emotional stirrings which the term conjures up: militantism, fanaticism, and "Khomeinism."

I wish to argue that, in the case of Judaism, any discussion of fundamentalism must first be preceded by a discussion of the differences and similarities between Orthodox and Ultra-Orthodox Jews. For the purposes of our discussion, how are we to understand the term *fundamentalism?* Surely not as the term is currently being used by students of the Middle East. As Elie Rekhess indicated (see chapter 6 of this volume), with regard to Islamic countries it is used to character- ize movements that strive for the return—of the individual, society, and the state—to Koranic fundamentals. However, although the Catholic Church strives for the return—of the individual, society, and the state—to Christian fundamentals, we do not hear of Catholic funda- mentalism.

On the contrary, historians of American religion apply the term exclusively to Protestant sects. These sects believe in the full literal inspiration of the Bible, in its complete, unerring, and infallible authority in dictating the meaning of life, and in the mandate to convert every person on earth to belief in and allegiance to Sacred Scripture. Nevertheless, this is still an insufficient basis by means of which to differentiate them from the Catholic Church.

In general, American fundamentalists are known for believing in the imminent bodily reappearance of Jesus on earth (millenarianism); combining religious revivalism with political activism in order to further a moral absolutism; and their wish to Christianize the nation by filling the government with "Bible-believing" Christians, by gaining ascend- ancy over the national media ("the electronic church"), and by the teaching of fundamentalist beliefs alongside science in the public schools.

I, however, prefer to focus on the theological underpinnings of American Protestant fundamentalism, namely, the adherence to the *literal* letter of the Sacred Word, without regard to its spirit and independent of a living interpretive tradition. This stance of literalism vis-à-vis Sacred Scripture differentiates Protestant fundamentalism from Catholicism as well as Orthodox Judaism.

The Faces of Jewish Orthodoxy in Israel and in America

What do we mean by Orthodox Judaism, and in what ways does it differ from Ultra-Orthodoxy? Rather than attempt to describe the sociologi- cal, organizational, or doctrinal aspects of (Ultra-) Orthodoxy, we shall resort to broad impressionistic outlines in an effort to achieve clarity and offer a general overview.

Orthodox Jews (known in Hebrew as *Dati'im*) are characterized by their adherence to traditional beliefs and religious practice. The traditional beliefs received their classical formulation in the Thirteen Principles formulated by the thirteenth-century Jewish philosopher, Moses Maimonides. Religious practice, called *Halakhah*, includes the entire body of ritual practices, religious standards, civil and criminal codes, and moral and ethical teachings. This body of Halakhah is based upon Sacred Scripture (the Old Testament) as interpreted by the Oral Tradition (the Talmud) and elucidated and applied by the great medieval rabbinic authorities.

Ultra-Orthodox Jews (referred to in Hebrew as *Haredim*) are characterized by their great punctiliousness in matters of faith and practice and by the severe limitations that they place on secular learning. In contrast to Orthodox Jews, Ultra-Orthodox Jews reject Western culture and delegitimize the secular State of Israel. Moreover, they tend to relegate women to the social role ordained by medieval tradition.

Although the lines separating the *Dati'im* from the *Haredim* are somewhat blurred, as a generalization one may say that Orthodox Jews, in contrast to Ultra-Orthodox Jews, maintain an acceptance (albeit a cautious and restricted one) of secular studies, are willing to cooperate with secular Jews (including the performance of military service in the Israeli Defense Forces), and generally tend to attribute a religious significance to the State of Israel.

The Ultra-Orthodox, the *Haredim*, have definitely rejected modernism including modern mores, modern literature, and modern education. Among the Ultra-Orthodox, there is a great mistrust of most of the cultural aspects of modernity. Whenever one attempts to argue the benefits of modern culture, the oft-heard response is, "Germany, the most cultural Western country of the twentieth century—look what they became." At the same time, the Ultra-Orthodox have not rejected the technical benefits of modernization. For example, they always want the best doctors.

Because all Israeli political parties are allowed free time on television, the Ultra-Orthodox are in a ticklish position. On the one hand, they know that their entire clientele does not watch television. On the other hand, they are unwilling to forego this opportunity. Therefore, they go through the motions of approaching the non-religious segment of the population through the mass media.

Orthodox Judaism is characterized by the effort to effect a synthesis with modern culture. Among the Orthodox (*Dati'im*) there were three major movements that sought to bridge the gap between Judaism and modernity: the *Torah im Derekh Erez* school of Samson Raphael Hirsch in Germany; the school of thought founded by Rabbi Abraham Isaac ha-Cohen Kook, the first Chief Rabbi of Israel; and the "Synthesis" (of Judaism and Modernity) movement launched by the Yeshiva University of New York. After the Holocaust, however, these three major modern attempts to bridge the gap were increasingly repudiated by the masses of Orthodox as well as Ultra-Orthodox Jewry.

Within the Orthodox camp, right-wing ultra-nationalists resemble the Ultra-Orthodox in rejecting modern literature as lewd and destructive; the movies, the media, and the press as immoral; and much in the social sciences as undermining faith.

Ultra-Orthodox Jewry in America and in Israel is generally divided into two main groupings, *Hasidim* and *Mitnagdim*. *Hasidim* are easily recognizable by their traditional black garb, their beards, and their curly side locks. Each hasidic sect is centered about a charismatic pietistic leader, called a *Rebbe*. Hasidism has been usually characterized, with some truth, as a folk movement dedicated to the service of God "through love and joy."

Mitnagdim, originally opponents of *Hasidim*, are traditional Jews who maintain an aristocracy of Torah learning. Based in institutions of higher religious studies, known as *yeshivot*, *Mitnagdim* are loyal to the leadership of non-Hasidic scholarly rabbinical authorities. It should be pointed out, however, that during the past two or three decades, the differences between *Hasidim* and *Mitnagdim* have tended to diminish, and "intermarriages" are not uncommon.

In Israeli Ultra-Orthodoxy, there has arisen a third constituent group, of an ethnic nature, made up of *Sephardim* (i.e., Jews who originate from North Africa, the Balkans, Syria, Lebanon, and Egypt) and Oriental Jews (i.e., those emanating from Iraq, Persia, and Yemen). These groups are, with exceptions, on a lower socio-economic level. Strongly traditional, the most potent factor in their emergence organizationally as a political party (Shas) is their ethnic affinities.

Shas's constituency leans toward hawkism. This hawkishness, which manifests itself in a strong antipathy to Arabs, results primarily from the shabby treatment the *Sephardim* suffered in the Arab countries from which most of them fled. Moreover, if I may be permitted a stereotype, they are not politically moderate—in anything. In contrast to its lay constituency, Shas's leadership follows the dovish ideology of Rabbi Schach, the head of the Ultra-Orthodox Yeshiva world, whom they accept as their leader.

The Ashkenazic (Jews of north European and western origins) Ultra-Orthodox in Israel, whether of hasidic persuasion or yeshiva-based, are split on the issue of hawkism. The yeshivas generally, under the aegis of Rabbi Schach, are dovish. As for the *Hasidim*, some of them are dovish, some are hawkish.

In the United States, the main body of Orthodox Jews is sometimes referred to as Modern Orthodoxy ("Modern", i.e., American as opposed to Eastern European) or Centrist Orthodoxy ("Centrist" as opposed to right-wing, i.e., Ultra-Orthodox Judaism). The intellectual content and rationale of Modern or Centrist Orthodoxy in America are formulated and propagated by Yeshiva University and its associated organizations.

In Israel, Orthodoxy's main organization is the National Religious Party, historically known as Mizrachi. Its intellectual underpinnings emanate from the Religious Kibbutz Movement, the Zionist *yeshivot*, and a number of religious academicians.

Special mention must be made of Gush Emunim, a grass-roots movement in Israel, which is right-wing Orthodox in creedal belief and religious observance, and fiercely nationalistic in its aim of creating the Greater Israel by settling throughout the West Bank. From its inception, Gush Emunim has been an Ashkenazic group, with very few *Sephardim* actively involved in their settlement activities on the West Bank.

At the same time, among the Orthodox there have emerged two dovish groups, Oz veShalom and Meimad, which are vehemently opposed to Gush Emunim. Oz veShalom is the religious segment of the Peace Now movement. Its intellectual activity, however, is limited to the question of peace with the Arabs.

Meimad is an Orthodox party which broke with the National Religious Party as a result of the latter's flirtation with Gush Emunim. It, too, is made up of Jewish intellectuals and is both somewhat more observant than Oz veShalom and less pacifistic. It is a sad reflection on Orthodoxy in Israel that Meimad could not get even one seat in the 1988 elections to the Knesset.

One issue on which the Orthodox and Ultra-Orthodox in Israel seem to agree is that of religious pluralism. If by pluralism we mean the doctrine that every group has a legitimate right to its own religious beliefs and practices, *Halakhah* is the very antithesis to pluralism. Traditional Judaism, including both Orthodoxy and Ultra-Orthodoxy, insists that it possesses the one "Truth" and, for Jews, the one "Way of Life." (Although differences in the interpretation of that "Truth" and that "Way of Life" certainly exist in [Ultra-] Orthodoxy, they are relatively minor vis-à-vis the heterodoxy of those "outside the Camp.") In the case of non-Jews, however, *Halakhah* is essentially pluralistic (bearing in mind the Noahide Code, those laws recorded in the Talmud as binding upon non-Jews).

Thus, in theory, the Orthodox have the same attitudes as the Ultra-Orthodox in the matter of pluralism. Moreover, the Orthodox themselves are going through a turn toward the right and, though still less punctilious in observance, they are becoming as unpluralistic as their Ultra-Orthodox brethren. Thus, whereas in the 1950s there was an attempt by the left-wing Orthodox of Israel to reach a rapprochement with the American-based Conservative movement, nobody in the Orthodox camp would dream of that today.

Literalism in Orthodox Judaism

As already mentioned, a major characteristic of fundamentalism as it is usually understood is adherence to the letter of the Sacred Word with little regard to its spirit. This literalistic approach to the sacred texts of one's religion is decidedly alien to the mainstream of historical, classical Judaism. Literalism was never a dominant feature in the Talmudic interpretation of Sacred Scripture or in the rabbinic interpretation of the Talmud.

To take one example, the statement "an eye for an eye" (Exodus 21:24; Leviticus 24:20) is never taken literally in the Talmud. According to Talmudic law, the *lex talionis* is neither *lex* nor *talio*. It is an expression meant to convey the fact that one who wounds another is obligated to pay compensation for five effects of the injury (damages, pain, medical treatment, enforced idleness, and humiliation). According to the authoritative interpretation of Maimonides, the spirit of the law is to the effect that one who puts out the eye of his fellow is *morally* deserving of having his eye put out.

Another example of the Talmud's anti-literalist attitude relates to the biblical passage calling for the "stoning" of the blasphemer (Leviticus 24:13–16) or, for that matter, of anyone sentenced to die. According to the Talmud, no blasphemer was ever stoned. As a final example, the fierce "Thou shalt cut off her hand" (Deuteronomy 25:12) was taken to mean that the prevention of an intended murder is preferable to taking the life of the intended murderer.

These and other similar examples clearly indicate that the Old Testament "God of Vengeance" is nothing more than the product of a non-Jewish literalist reading of the Bible.

Space does not permit me to elaborate on the similar non-literalist interpretation of the Talmud itself by medieval rabbinic interpreters. However, the interested reader is referred to my two-volume study on the phenomena of formalism and flexibility—and the subtle dialectic between them—in post-Talmudic literature entitled *Equity in Jewish Law*.

This non-literalist orientation persists even to this day. The pervasiveness of non-literalism in Orthodox Judaism is perhaps best explained by the dominant role played by the living Oral Tradition and by its bearers, the rabbis of each generation. (Similarly the dominant role played by the ongoing Church tradition and its bearers, the popes, explains the non-literalist orientation of Catholicism and its non-fundamentalist posture.)

Jewish Fundamentalism Today

Jewish Orthodoxy is in the ascendancy today both in Israel and in America. This contrasts with the first fifty years of the twentieth century, which was a period of disarray for traditional Judaism. During that period masses of Jews of Eastern Europe (Russia, Poland, Galicia, Hungary, Czechoslovakia), exposed for the first time to Western European modernism, underwent a dramatic transformation. The progressive disintegration of the traditional faith was accompanied and abetted by assimilation to contemporary movements. Moreover, emigration to the West (to Germany, France, England, and the United States) led to the increasing integration of Jews into the various Western societies. Finally, the Zionist movement, advocating a revolutionary solution to "the Jewish problem," influenced large numbers of Jews to deviate from the traditional position which patiently awaited a messianic solution to the Jewish problem.

After World War II, a remarkable transformation occurred in Orthodox Jewish life, first in the United States and, subsequently, in Israel. A new generation, no longer attracted to the values of the Western world and overwhelmed by the Holocaust, began returning to the tradition of their fathers. Their children, in turn, defect from that tradition in *decreasing* numbers. In addition, there has been an impressive growth in Torah education and in Torah scholarship, together with the mushrooming of both religious and educational institutions.

Thus, the dramatic success of the Ultra-Orthodox political parties in the 1988 Israeli elections should not be viewed as a resurgence of fundamentalism nor was it occasioned by the rise of "Khomeinism" among twentieth-century Jews. Rather, its causes are not difficult to discern: (1) a natural increase which proceeds in geometric progression because of the halakhic proscription on birth control; (2) a newly acquired self-confidence which has brought about a greater societal awareness, more political involvement, and a heightened militancy; (3) the awakening of ethnic pride among the Sephardic and Oriental Jews of Israel and its translation into ethnic power by the Shas Party; and (4) a *ba'al teshuvah* movement of "born-again" Jews, although numerically moderate, which has dramatized the ascendancy of (Ultra-) Orthodoxy.

Having appropriately situated fundamentalism in relation to Orthodox Judaism, we, nevertheless, wish to draw attention to two subgroups of (Ultra-) Orthodoxy that bear the closest resemblance to what could be called "Jewish fundamentalism": Habad and Gush Emunim.

Habad is a hasidic sect which is active both in America and in Israel. Although well within the parameters of mainstream Judaism, Habad tends toward a literalist interpretation of the verses of the Bible, the passages of the Talmud, and especially of those sections of kabbalistic literature that are of a messianic nature. In addition, Habad resembles American fundamentalism insofar as its messianic thrust has led to concerted efforts to reach the masses. Moreover, Habad outdoes all other Jewish groups in its utilization of the media. In contrast to all other groups of (Ultra-) Orthodox Jews, it is actively engaged in begetting "born-again" Jews.

I have already made reference to the right-wing Orthodox ultra-nationalist group known as Gush Emunim. It too possesses certain characteristics that are usually associated with fundamentalism. First of all, Gush Emunim tends toward a literalist reading of messianic passages in the traditional literature as well as of those passages in the Bible which delineate the ancient—hence, the desirable—borders of the Holy Land. However, although it also engages in outreach projects, its use of the media is low-key. Nevertheless, the program it pursues for active settlement of the West Bank and the marshalling of Israeli political partisan support to accomplish this is carried out in a manner which would justify the epithet "fundamentalistic."

But, although Habad and Gush Emunim are fundamentalistic in character, this does not justify applying the term to Orthodox and Ultra-Orthodox Jewry as a whole—neither in Israel nor in America.

NOTES

The original draft of this chapter was first presented at a May 1989 conference, "Fundamentalism as a Political Force in the Middle East," sponsored by the Berman Center for Jewish Studies and held at Lehigh University.

Chapter 12

The Market Model and Religious Radicalism

Menachem Friedman

Recently the term *fundamentalism* has become increasingly current as a characterization and description of religious groups that seek to present an alternative to the secular-liberal state of the West. In this context, the various fundamentalist groups are defined as a threat to the Western way of life. Fundamentalism as a social phenomenon is not perceived as the characteristic of one particular religion, but as a universal. It may be discerned, according to this view, in Western as well as in Islamic society, in Judaism, and in Middle Eastern religions, in Europe and America, as well as in Africa and the Far East.

The attempt to define the phenomenon so that it then encompasses all those groups and sects as fundamentalist encounters many difficulties. The phenomenon is so variegated that it is difficult, if not impossible, to find a common denominator to serve as the basis of an adequate operative definition. Nonetheless, the secular-liberal society of the West is unquestionably being threatened by radical religious-political movements. Whether Christian, Muslim, Jewish, or other, each group, in its own way and its own language, contends that it is capable of finding the cure for the sickness of Western society; each one, moreover, represents itself as a comprehensive alternative to modern secular society. Central to all the groups called fundamentalist is the element of protest against the West, modernity, and, in particular, modern means of communication (television).

To be sure, radical-fundamentalist groups are concerned with more than protest. They may be broadly characterized by the belief that they, and they alone, have the key to understanding history and, consequently, the capability of foreseeing the future. Present reality, as they understand it, is "ruptured," despoiled, and accursed in all respects (both manifest and concealed). The fundamentalist feels capable of both explaining the existing situation and positing the measures necessary to correct and reform the world. The basis for such contentions varies from one group to another and from one religion to another. Whereas some base their claim to truth on charismatic prophets, others rely on the proper understanding of sacred scriptures.

What Judaism, Islam, and Christianity have in common is their basis in revealed scripture—Torah, Qur'an, and New Testament. But the scriptures that inform the faith of the fundamentalist are ordinarily not understood literally; instead, they are subjected to a rich and complex hermeneutic. Thus, over the generations an extensive interpretive literature has developed, which seeks not only to provide the precise, correct interpretation of the traditional text, but also to endow it with contemporary significance. For, to those religions, God's utterances are not limited in time and place: the divine words expressed in sacred scripture form the exclusive source for understanding past, present, and future. Thus, a correct understanding of scripture makes both the present reality and the future as comprehensible as the distant past. The legitimate ("true") expositors of scripture, therefore, not only explicate the literal sense of the text, but also explain the realities of their own era in terms of scriptural concepts.

And yet, fundamentalism is not only a political protest movement threatening the modern social-political order. By virtue of its self-confident claim to a direct connection to scriptural truth, as expressed in its "correct" interpretation, fundamentalism, in one manner or another, also threatens the very traditional religion that it has presumably undertaken to preserve. Moreover, many fundamentalist groups, eschewing political protest, direct their principal concern to internal religious life. Thus, religious fundamentalism targets not only "apostates" or foreign nonbelievers, but establishment religion as well.

Many forms of fundamentalism, protesting against establishment religion, offer a purer, more valid religiosity that is less cognizant of existing reality and encompasses a fuller religious life, one that entails economic and social sacrifices. Such manifestations of strict, religious behavior are recognizable in almost all religions. Within the context of Jewish Orthodoxy, these phenomena, first discerned in the late fifties, have been dubbed "religious radicalism." Generally speaking, the strict religious behavior expresses itself in the adopting of norms known in halakhic language as *humrah* (stringency).

The aim of this chapter is to describe and analyze the phenomenon of Jewish religious radicalism against the historic background of halakhic decision making and its social effects. In addition, I shall focus on the internal dynamics of halakhic decision making in relation to the development of modern, secular society. Employing the "market model" developed by Peter Berger to explain the condition of religions in the modern world, I wish to argue that religious radicalism, in the sense explained above, can develop only in a modern society that permits free choice in the sphere of religion. Paradoxically, religious radicalism as a social phenomenon can develop only in a society that enables, as a viable alternative, the choice of a secular way of life utterly unconnected to religion.

I

Since the 1950s, elitist groups have emerged within the *haredi* (ultra-Orthodox) community who, owing to their inclination toward *humrah* as an expression of a distinctive Jewish religiosity, are perceived as being uncompromising with reality. These groups rapidly became points of reference for *haredi* society as a whole and, to a certain extent, for religious, non-*haredi* society as well. In the mid-sixties, Rabbi Simha Elberg had already comprehended this development in *haredi* society, as becomes clear from his following observations on the community of B'nai Brak, a suburb of Tel Aviv:

> I would define B'nai Brak in two words: World of the *humrot* [stringencies]! The B'nai Brak idea amounts to, and embodies, an extensive revolution in the entire alignment of religious life. B'nai Brak seeks stringencies, not leniencies. The rest of the world, even the religious world, generally looks for dispensations and the mitigation of religious obligation. In all areas of religious life, one finds expressions of the *kokha d'Hetera* [power of dispensation]. Not so in B'nai Brak. There, a Yeshiva student, under the spiritual influence of the Hazon Ish [Rabbi Abraham Yeshayahu Karlitz], seeks within the *Shulhan Arukh* [an authoritative code of Jewish law] the most restrictive, stringent, and punctilious view. Eschewing the phrase "There are those who call for lenient interpretation . . . ," he only seeks and trusts in the formula, "There are those who are *mahmirim* [the strict ones]." Thus, B'nai Brak embodies a world unto itself, the world of the most exalted Torah ideal. Before such an undiluted ideal everyone is compelled to bow his head and submit.[1]

It is difficult to overestimate the importance of these remarks and of the assertions they contain. B'nai Brak was founded in 1924 by a group of *Hasidim* from Poland. Its early years were marked by the abandonment of a traditional religious way of life, even though a religious atmosphere was maintained. After the State of Israel came into being, there occurred a steadily increasing influx of *Haredim* from other cities, along with new immigrants, while, simultaneously, secular Jews were leaving. But the factor which most determined the character of the city was the founding of the *haredi yeshivot* (Talmudic academies) that drew young scholars from Israel and abroad.

Within a short time B'nai Brak became the "City of Torah"—the religious and cultural center of the developing *haredi* community. One of the personalities exerting a decisive influence on the formation of the *haredi* religious style was Rabbi Abraham Yeshayahu Karlitz (1878–1953), better known as Hazon Ish (derived from the name of the halakhic works he had composed). Under his influence *yeshiva* students continued their studies after marriage in *kollelim* (academies of Talmudic study for married students), a phenomenon that utterly changed the character of the *haredi* community from the sixties onward.

Elberg, whom I cited above, was the first to fathom the revolution in religion brought about by these young men dubbed *avrechim* (a name for married *yeshiva* students). Religious radicalism—the adoption of *humrot* as the norms—was no longer merely an individual phenomenon of men of stature, but a social phenomenon manifested in a group defined both by its age (the young *avrechim*) and by its social status, i.e., as disciples of the Hazon Ish. This group expressed an apparently uncommon inclination: the conscious search for *humrot*, within the framework of halakhic decision making (*Shulhan Arukh*). This elite soon became an authority for the Orthodox community as a whole and a representative of what Elberg calls "the exalted Torah ideal," which is the outstanding expression of religious radicalism.

There is no doubt that today the "World of the *humrot*" described so vividly by Elberg is the prevailing phenomenon within the *haredi* community, and is spreading to other, non-*haredi* religious groups as well. The phenomenon is now viewed within religious circles as the clearest expression of what is called religious radicalism. My contention is that the development of the *humrot* phenomenon since the fifties is hardly an accident. It must be seen against the background of the displacement of traditional, religious Jewry from its accustomed landscape in Eastern Europe to the modern, open society in the West, where each citizen is free to express his or her own religious preference. The new social reality that accelerated the process of today's secularization somewhat paradoxically also facilitated the growth of the tendency toward *humrah*. In this new social reality, the traditional mechanisms that had confined such strict tendencies in the past lost their significance as well as their efficacy.

II

Humrah (stringency) and *kullah* (lenience) are two central concepts that represent the dynamic basis of halakhic decision making on the one hand, and the particular forms that individual decisions take on the other. These concepts express a permanent tension in religious life between the desire to fulfill all of the demands of the *halakhah* in the minutest detail so as to avoid thereby any suspicion of transgression, and the reality of daily life, which necessitates compromise and accommodation to changing economic, social, and political conditions. The history of *halakhah* is replete with signs of this tension, which from time to time acquire a personal dimension in the conflict between those halakhic authorities who tended to render decisions stringently, *mahmirim* (the strict ones), and those who are inclined to render them leniently, *mekillim* (the lenient ones). Nonetheless, as important, and even decisive, as the role of the personal inclination of the individual authority may have been in stringent or lenient halakhic decisions, it is, I would argue, the social dimension that in the final analysis determines the "limits" of *humrah* or *kullah*.

The inclination of the religiously sensitive[2] to be stringent with themselves, lest by not doing so they would fail to fulfill their full obligation (to their own way of life), is a natural one. Equally natural is the converse tendency to be as lenient as possible in the fulfillment of religious duties and to observe only the absolute minimum. The question to be discussed here, then, is not why some halakhic authorities incline to *humrah* and others to *kullah*, but to what extent society accedes to propensities toward *humrah* in decision making, and why.

In order to exemplify the dialectic between the inclination to *humrah* and the societal framework, I shall employ the example cited by Y. Ahituv in his article *"Teshuvah* [recommitment to religious life] and Religious Radicalism: A Study of the Two Phenomena from the Public and Private Perspective."[3] The essential story is as follows:

Safed in the sixteenth century was characterized by an atmosphere of religious revival deriving from the disruption of Jewish life in the wake of the Expulsion from Spain.[4] The revival expressed itself in manifestations of religious piety and the inclination to adopt *humrot*. One example of the latter refers to the practice of exempting produce grown by a Gentile from offerings and tithes.

The Torah stipulates (Numbers 15:17–21 and Deuteronomy 14:22–29) the obligation to set aside from produce grown in the Land of Israel offerings and tithes for the priests and Levites. Halakhic authorities disagreed over whether or not a Jew buying such produce from a non-Jewish farmer was obligated to set aside these offerings and tithes. Most authorities had accepted the view of Maimonides,[5] which exempted from this obligation the produce of a Gentile if it had been sold to a Jew after the threshing and winnowing were completed. But others disputed Maimonides' view.[6] Maimonides' verdict may be considered as an example of *kullah*, since it perforce reduces the cost of produce in the Land of Israel, where nearly all the farmers were non-Jews. Against the background of the sixteenth-century religious revival, some religiously sensitive Jews sought to be stringent with themselves by abstaining from eating all untithed produce of a Gentile. These did not contend that whoever ate the untithed produce of a Gentile was a transgressor; they merely demanded stringency for themselves, preferring the view of Rabbi Yizhak ben Asher HaLevi (one of the Tosafists [commentators of the Talmud]), who dissented from Maimonides in this matter.

One would have expected the halakhic authorities to have encouraged this manifestation of piety, as the *mahmirim* were only seeking to fulfill all the obligations recorded in halakhic literature (what harm lay in that?). However, the reaction of the leading halakhic authorities was uncompromisingly negative. In their view, deviation from the accepted halakhic norm toward greater *humrah* was a potential menace to society as a whole.

The *mahmirim* were not only strict with themselves, but they were inducing others to behave similarly. Eventually, matters reached the point that certain *mahmirim* formed a group which refrained from eating bread and fruit until a tithe had been set aside. Such a situation created a three-fold danger as far as the traditional Jewish community was concerned: (1) Even if the *mahmirim* did not make such claims overtly, they in effect relegated all others to a lesser social and religious status by presenting themselves as a strict elite. In this way, they threatened the standing of the religious leadership, which did not accept their view. (2) A traditional society is founded not only on scriptures, but also on a living tradition passed down from father to son, generation after generation. Thus, every innovation in the direction of *humrah* becomes a slight to previous generations, insofar as it suggests that their degree of religious affirmation was less than that of the present generation, the *mahmirim*. This poses a difficult challenge to a traditional society. (3) The existence of a group that refrained from sharing food with other Jews threatened the solidarity of the Jewish community, based as it was, in part, on the "common meal" that imposed distinctive norms (*kosher*) of eating among Jews and proscribed eating together with non-Jews.

We can form a picture of the social and religious conflict in Safed at that time from the remarks of one of the leading halakhic authorities, Rabbi Joseph Karo,[7] author of the *Shulhan Arukh*, the most important halakhic code in traditional Judaism. To Karo, the behavior of the *mahmirim* was "a slight to the honor of our ancestors," and a deviation from the biblical prohibition, "You shall not gash yourselves" (which the Talmud interpreted "You shall not form yourselves into separate groups"), a phrase which, according to the traditional hermeneutic, forbids Jews from forming a faction based on *humrah* and pietism.[8]   Matters finally reached the point where leading halakhic authorities excommunicated anyone who set aside produce grown by a non-Jew in the Land of Israel for tithing.

Further documentation for this episode reveals another dimension of the social significance of *humrah*. Rabbi Bezalel Ashkenazi was one of the most important of the small number of sages of the Land of Israel in the generation following the Expulsion from Spain. He relates that when he set out from Jerusalem on a matter concerning its Jewish inhabitants, there was a young man in the convoy who was a yeshiva student. When the company stopped to rest, Rabbi Bezalel unpacked his provisions and invited the young student to sup with him. The young man declined to share the Rabbi's bread on the grounds that he did not eat from untithed produce.[9]   Thus, in the incident related by Rabbi Bezalel, the conflict between *mahmirim* and traditional rabbis reached the level of personal offense. Even without explicitly intending to do so, the *mahmir* young man relegated his elder, the rabbi, to an inferior status. Rabbi Bezalel's story, doubtless written a considerable time after the event, still vividly depicts the sense of threat, anger, and offense he felt.

The spread of *humrah* within the framework of a traditional community, then, was hardly a simple process. As we have seen, the religious establishment had at its disposal the apparatus to contend with such processes, a matter that we shall discuss further. Nevertheless, it would be erroneous to think that the traditional Jewish community was always successful at curbing tendencies toward *humrah* and radicalism. As we stated earlier, the inclination toward *humrah* is a fundamental part of traditional religiosity, based as it is on the *halakhah*. Hence, there is a perpetual (dialectic) tension between the natural inclination to be strict and the communal need to confine and to isolate this tendency.

In my analysis of *humrah* I do not intend to deal with the phenomenon per se, but with its communal aspect; namely, the consolidation of elitist religious groups on the basis of stringent halakhic decisions and their consequent transformation into reference groups for Jewish society as a whole.

III

To further explain the social and religious problems deriving from a stringent rendering of *halakhah*, I would like to quote from the collection of *responsa* "Shevut Ya'akov" (The Response of Jacob), by Rabbi Jacob Reischer, one of the greatest halakhic arbitrators among Ashkenazic Jews in the early eighteenth century (d. 1733). Reischer served as rabbi in such important congregations as Prague, Ansbach, Worms, and Mainz. The collection of *responsa* "Shevut Ya'akov" insured his fame as a halakhic authority even beyond the territory of Ashkenazic Jewry. That Jewry, as reflected in the *responsa*, was still traditional since its established mode of life, based as it was on the *halakhah* and the customs crystallized and shaped within the Jewish community, bound both the individual and the group.

The text of the question posed to Rabbi Reischer is as follows:

> QUESTION: Recently some rabbis have come along and innovatively decreed in their communities that eating meat delivered there from *medinah* [a regional village-community] is tantamount to eating non-kosher meat. Further, they proscribe even the vessels in which such meat has been cooked. Have they acted properly and do they have a basis for their decision? I have not yet observed any senior rabbis instituting such a decree.

In order to understand the question, we must distinguish two types of Jewish community in Europe, in general, and in eighteenth-century Germany, in particular. Most Jews, including the intellectual and capitalistic elite, dwelt in communities that formed part of urban populations. But many other Jews lived in small rural settlements. Some of these settlements contained several Jewish families, while others contained only one. In Germany these rural Jews were organized in regional communities called, in the singular, *medinah*.

In the cities the rabbis of the community supervised religious functions. One of their most important duties was to supervise the process of *shehitah* (ritual slaughtering) as well as the *shohatim* (the authorized ritual slaughterers). Without rabbinical authorization, the *shohet* was not allowed to slaughter cattle or poultry for the community. The rabbi also rendered a decision whenever doubts arose as to whether the meat produced by the *shehitah* was kosher.

While the Jewish communities of the *medinah* were solicitous about their basic religious needs, their rabbinical supervision was limited and relatively poor in comparison to that of the large urban communities. The Jews of the *medinah* had a particular need for *melamdim* (tutors of elementary Jewish studies) for their children and *shohatim* in the immediate vicinity. The availability of a *shohet* in the settlements was of considerable economic importance: the rural Jews maintained livestock—cows and chickens—that not only provided for household needs, but generated a portion of the family income as well. Occasionally it was urgent for a chicken or cow to be slaughtered before it died and could be declared unfit for consumption as *trefah* (non-kosher) or a carcass. The residents of the *medinah* endeavored to sell the meat of this slaughtered animal to their Jewish neighbors as well as to the Jewish residents of the nearby city. By doing so, they minimized the economic harm that could result from the death of livestock.

Now we may readily suppose that the choice *shohatim* and *melamdim* did not reach those small, remote settlements. In general, *melamdim* were also *shohatim* and also performed other quasi-rabbinic functions. Frequently the rural *shohatim* had to rely on their own judgment when doubt arose as to whether the meat was kosher or not and they were unable to consult an eminent rabbinic authority. The declaration of meat as non-kosher had far-reaching economic consequences for the rural Jew who owned the livestock. Accordingly, the *shohet*, who was utterly dependent on his rural Jewish employer for a livelihood, had sufficient reason to render a lenient decision by *kullah*, occasionally deviating from the accepted halakhic standards to do so. The absence of a local rabbinic authority to scrutinize or criticize his decision made it easier for this *shohet* to exercise such leniency by declaring the meat kosher.

This, then, is the background of the halakhic decision of those rabbis who proscribed meat brought (after ritual slaughter) from the rural settlements (*medinah*) to the large community. The rabbis went so far as to rule that even the vessels in which such meat had been cooked were to be presumed non-kosher and therefore required rabbinic certification of fitness. The question and the *responsum* make clear that the meat brought from the settlements was not non-kosher per se. However, because the rabbis suspected that under the conditions mentioned above there was a possibility that some of the meat might be non-kosher, the prohibition was applied broadly to all meat "brought from the *medinah*." Moreover, the prohibition was not incumbent on the Jews of the settlements in which the livestock had been slaughtered. Thus, the meat was considered non-kosher only for the Jews of those communities in which the above-mentioned rabbis lived, whereas it was kosher for the inhabitants of the *medinah*, where it had originated.

To be sure, the position that those rabbis took derived from their sincere anxiety about the *kashrut* (kosher fitness) of the meat that the members of their communities were to eat, from the great responsibility incumbent upon them from their status, and from their conscience regarding religious issues. For all that, however, they were apparently unaware of the comprehensive social import of their ruling. The establishment of two norms and two standards in the traditional Jewish way of life was not based upon individually achieved status, but upon a formal distinction in residence, i.e., that which was permitted as kosher for the rural Jews was prohibited to those living in the large adjacent community. Thus, meat considered non-kosher for parents living in the urban community was considered kosher for the son living, as it happened, in the village across the river.

Rabbi Jacob Reischer, as a distinguished halakhic authority, discerned clearly the social and psychological significance of the approach of the stringent rabbis. He foresaw correctly what grave consequences would follow for the Jews, not on the circumscribed religious and halakhic plane, but on the social plane. This was his point of departure for his protest.

Reischer's negative position was already anticipated in the very formulation of the question, when he wrote, "Recently some innovative rabbis have come along . . . ." The negative connotation of the expression requires closer examination. As noted above, a traditional society is not enamored of innovators, even innovators inclined to *humrah*. According to Reischer, a decision based on *humrah* represents a conscious departure from generations of practice. Even if the new decision is well grounded in *halakhah*—and perhaps for that very reason—it has the potential of undermining the foundations of a traditional society. Every innovation based on *humrah* not observed by saintly ancestors of past generations necessarily undermines their status both as saintly leaders, and as authoritative sources for the present generation. Hence the clause "Recently some innovative rabbis have come along" may be viewed as essentially a delegitimating formula.

Reischer also suggested the latent social significance of prohibiting meat slaughtered in the settlements, that is, the creation of two distinct statuses, one considered superior to the other. Those considered inferior would then certainly have a basis for animosity, a notion here understood as a combination of hostility and resentment produced when certain groups become suspect owing to the level of their observance of religious duties. The prevention of such animosity is an essential and legitimate basis for halakhic argument, especially when it is clear that the suspect group manifestly has no ideological reason for the deviant behavior ascribed to it. As Reischer contended, the residents of the village settlements were certainly observant Jews above any suspicion that they would knowingly cause their customers to eat non-kosher meat. A general ban officially laying blame on the residents of the *medinah* had the potential of arousing animosity and of undermining Jewish solidarity, perhaps even the unity of the Jewish people. Preventing animosity is a religious obligation that transcends even the suspicion of eating non-kosher meat. Further, Rabbi Reischer contended that even if the *shohet* knows that the meat of the animal he has slaughtered is not kosher, but he does not make it known, those who eat the meat are not guilty of wrongdoing. Accordingly, mere suspicion is insufficient grounds for declaring the vessels in which the imported meat was cooked non-kosher.

Reischer summed up his *responsum* with a plea on behalf of the unity of the Jewish people and for the mutual bond maintained by Jews in their dealings with one another: "It is fitting that all the Jewish people be unified in the matter of eating and drinking so as not to cause in their own midst a rift like that which separates them from the others [the Gentiles]." For Jews, the common table at which they eat is the expression *par excellence* both of their separation from the non-Jewish world about them, and of their intrinsic unity. Undermining this fundamental principle inevitably impairs the shared identity of the traditional Jewish community as a whole.

IV

As noted above, deviation toward *humrah* is a natural and understandable impulse in a community of elevated religious sensitivity; indeed, there is support for the practice in the halakhic literature of all eras. Notwithstanding, a traditional society was obliged, *qua* its traditionality, to stop or to restrain such deviation as much as possible. Thus, as we have argued, change in the direction of *humrah* undermines the foundations of tradition no less than change in the direction of *kullah*. Halakhic literature and historical sources offer us abundant instances that confirm these assumptions. The well-known polemic against *Hasidism* at the end of the eighteenth century will serve as a prime example.

One of the earliest documents bearing on the disputes between the *Hasidim*, the disciples of Rabbi Yisrael Ba'al Shem Tov (the *Besht*), and the *Mitnagdim* (opponents) is the letter of Rabbi Abraham Katzenelbogen to Rabbi Levi Yitzhak of Berditchev (1784). Among other matters it concerns the adoption of the liturgical formulation (*nusah*) of the Ari,[10] known as the Sephardic formulation by the *Hasidim*, in place of the Ashkenazic formulation. Rabbi Katzenelbogen raises the following objection: "What fault was there to find with our fathers?"[11] This was one of the strongest arguments against the *Hasidim*, who had presumed to change so fundamental a part of the tradition as the prayer formulary.

But such an argument makes sense only within a traditional society, for only there does an ancestral custom remain in full force. Thus, every deviation from such custom toward *humrah* necessarily implies that either the customs of the ancestors were not halakhically valid or that the ancestors themselves fall short of the present generation. Such a possibility, however, could undermine the very foundations of a traditional society. To state the matter as a principle: whoever changes ancestral custom in the direction of *humrah* necessarily discredits the saintly ancestors and thus "finds fault with our fathers."

Perhaps the clearest and most significant expression of this issue is found among the remarks of Rabbi Menahem Hame'iri (1249–1306), who sought to defend the tradition of the Provence community against the disciples of Nahmanides (Rabbi Moshe ben Nachman), who had challenged that tradition on the basis of the written *halakhah*:

> Whoever seeks to challenge tradition should consider carefully that he has not disregarded our ancient ancestors and the early sages—how

much greater was their wisdom than ours—whose customs bespoke
their own rationale.   Better that he ascribe the matter to the
insufficiency of his own knowledge rather than to any insufficiency of
our ancestors or of the early sages.   For the power of their understanding extends ever upwards; it is longer than a goodly land and
wider than the sea. . . .[12]

A further example of the polemic between the *Hasidim* and the
Mitnagdim reveals both the complexity of the issue and the action taken
by the traditional community as it confronted manifestations of *humrah*
and hasidic activities.   The Brody community of Galicia sought, upon
threat of excommunication (20 Nissan 5532 [1772]), to enjoin the
Hasidim from praying according to the Sephardic formulation of the Ari
(R. Yizhak Luria) that they had adopted.   But within the Brody
community itself there was a small band of Kabbalists who had been
praying according to the Lurianic formulary for a long time.   The
excommunication at Brody, then, marks a clear distinction between the
first *Hasidim*, i.e., those Kabbalists permitted to pray according to the
Lurianic formulary, and the latter *Hasidim*, followers of the Ba'al Shem
Tov, who were prohibited by excommunication to pray thereby.[13]

This is an excellent example of the solution that the traditional
community found for the problem posed by the need to preserve
tradition on the one hand, and by the propensity of some to hasidic
behavior and *humrah* on the other, the latter being, after all, the
expression of personal religious need.   Those whom the Brody
community allowed to use the special prayer formulary were not
merely outstanding scholars, but also Kabbalists. They were individuals
unique in their customs and distinct from all others in their level of
individual pious behavior. Without endangering the foundations of its
own existence, the traditional community confronted this dilemma by
isolating the *mahmirim* and those who were piously inclined.   The
mahmirim, that is, those whose behavior does not correspond to that of
the saintly ancestors, are elevated to a level so high and so demanding
in all domains of behavior, that they cannot serve as examples for the
simple Jews, that is, for the great majority of the community. From a
sociological perspective, the social sanction against the stringent is
structurally similar to that applied to religious deviants, notwithstanding
the essential difference between the direct, immediate treatment meted
out to delinquent deviants and that accorded those who seek to be
stringent with themselves.

The traditional Jewish community contends with the *humrah* phenomenon from yet another perspective. The existence of the community as a compulsory framework necessitates a plain definition of the permissible and the prohibited, of the appropriate and the inappropriate. Accordingly, the community must consider the capacity of the majority of its members to deal successfully with halakhic demands as they are interpreted by those empowered to do so. The halakhic authorities were thus obliged to render decisions not only according to personal inclination, but must also take into account the capacity of the entire body, or at least the great majority, to live on the basis of *mahmir* halakhic decisions, whether in matters of civil procedure, matrimony, prohibitions, or permissions. It follows plainly that the community cannot allow particular groups of its members to establish stringent norms; at the most, it might agree that isolated individuals known for their abstemious lifestyle adopt norms of *humrah*, but only if in so doing they not undermine majority custom.

Further, the traditional community could not allow social schism on a religious-halakhic basis, for such a thing would threaten the integrity of the community as a religious body. If the *mahmirim* are not perceived as a spiritual elite, they proceed to delegitimize those whose behavior is otherwise, even if they did not consciously intend to do so at the outset. This social aspect particularly stands out in the remarks of Rabbi Jacob Reischer cited above.

V

As we have shown, the traditional society, where all are obligated to follow *halakhah*, has formed structures to impede the establishment of *humrah*-based innovations. Paradoxically, the modern processes of disintegration and erosion which made possible for the first time a Jewish identity not based upon halakhic obligation also made possible the establishment of norms of *humrah* within the communal and voluntary structures that supplanted the traditional society.

This thesis is based on ideas developed by Peter Berger, particularly in his article, "A Market Model for the Analysis of Ecumenicity."[14] Berger's point of departure is the impact of secularization on the status and position of religious institutions. The principal effect of such processes has been the freeing of social institutions from the need for religious legitimations. On the social and political level, the process of secularization has found expression in the establishment of the voluntary religious community.   In modern Western society, the individual is under no obligation to be a member of any religious community whatsoever, as religion is seen as the citizen's private concern.   Moreover, he himself can choose whatever religious association—or "church"[15]—if any, he wishes to affiliate with, and he can independently determine his degree of obligation to it.   More generally, religion and its institutions have lost the monopolistic position they once had as the sole definers and determiners of the primary value system in society and as the enforcers of the individual's obligation to religion and church.   In modern secular society, the individual citizen's freedom to define and determine his relationship with his church is not a one-time opportunity; it exists, in principle, at all times.

In Berger's view, the degree of the citizen's obligation to his church has, of necessity, economic significance.   First of all, in an open society the church as an organization is maintained by the contributions of believers.   Hence, religious institutions have a vital economic interest, not merely a spiritual concern, in affiliating as many believers as possible, especially those with means.

As remarked above, an open society has a large number of churches, none of which enjoys monopolistic status.   Such a situation, wherein various churches coexist and compete within a modern, open society, may, following Berger, be defined as a "market situation." This is a universal, comprehensive concept that serves to illuminate various aspects of the situation in a new and original light.

Berger has dealt extensively with the implications of a market situation for determining the qualities of religious leadership.   For example, a market situation requires religious leaders who excel in selling the religion and the church.   Leaders who attract youth, who know how to win over people of means or of political influence, generally become more important and powerful than those whose authority is grounded in learning or intellectual capacity.   In this context it is also possible to discern the increased power of secular (nonclerical) leaders in the church hierarchy.

A market situation is fundamentally a competitive situation; in our context the religions and the churches compete with one another to gain the believer's faith, heart, and money.   The more open and free the market, the greater the variety of faiths and churches, as well as the various currents within the same church, available to the consumer. Yet, as in a modern secular society in general, the notion of a free market in religion does not connote an absence of limits and rules.   In fact, one can demonstrate objective limits, as well as limits imposed by the various churches themselves in the context of their market activity. For example, Jewish religious bodies generally refrain from actively proselytizing non-Jews. On the other hand, varied approaches to such activity are evident within the Jewish market. Nevertheless, and notwithstanding their specific declared positions on drafting new members, each religious group, even each synagogue, must be concerned with being abandoned by its members. Hence, the possibility that the free individual may abandon his church has a decisive influence on the church itself.

VI

Like other religious communities, the Orthodox Jewish community has been obliged to accommodate itself to the new status of religion within modern, secular society. On the organizational level this new status becomes apparent in the fundamental change that has occurred in the structure of the community: from a traditional community delimited by geographical boundaries, to one defined by voluntary boundaries. For example, the obligation of a Jew living in Prague to the Jewish religion and the traditional community had been determined by the simple circumstance that he lived within the limits of the Jewish ghetto of Prague. In our era, however, the obligation of a Jew living in New York to one of the thousands of Jewish congregations scattered about that metropolis depends principally on his willingness to take on the obligations of membership in a congregation.

The development of the Orthodox Jewish community into a voluntary community, that is, a congregation, a body that includes only those who voluntarily affiliate with it, exemplifies clearly the sense of a market situation, even within a community that delimits itself as *a priori* beholden to *halakhah*. It is within the Orthodox community that we can most readily discern the influence of the market situation on the status of rabbis as religious leaders. Here, too, the structure of their relationship to the lay leadership of the congregation, the *gabbais* (head manager of a synagogue) and the president, becomes clear.

For the purposes of my analysis, I shall use by way of example the Orthodox community of the United States, an ideal typical community characterized by a market situation of free competition. The many sources we have for the life of this community in the present century indicate clearly the weakening of the rabbi's position within the congregation, his utter dependence on the lay leadership, and the

importance of his ability to enthrall his congregants with his performance and his sermons; or alternately, his practice of not raising overly
sensitive subjects bearing on his congregants' religious observance, such
as might impair his status and authority.[16]   In view of the eroding
status of religion and tradition, the economic difficulties of Sabbath
observance, and the active work of the competitors—Conservative and
Reform Jews—leaders of Orthodox Jewish congregations needed rabbis
who differed from their traditional, Eastern European forebears.
Instead of being scholarly, they should be charismatic and should turn
a blind eye toward lapses from *halakhah* when the vital economic and
communal interests of the congregation were at stake. This situation,
which is reflected universally, is part of the passage from a traditional
to a voluntary community, even in Eastern Europe. There, however,
the transition was more gradual and slower, and so less harsh than in
the United States.

The transition to the structure of a voluntary community manifested itself as well in the consolidation and establishment of numerous
varieties and alternatives in the Orthodox way of life. It is customary
to think that the processes of secularization and modernization
generally enabled individuals and groups to deviate from the traditional
halakhic way of life, and to establish alternative styles of Jewish identity,
whether religious (as with the varieties of Reform Judaism), or national
(as with secular nationalism). Yet, the disintegration of the traditional
Jewish community as the framework of a way of life incumbent on all
of its members was also manifested in the appearance of various
nuances in the Orthodox way of life; viz., social structures bound in
principle to the *halakhah* as the basic norm, but translating such duty
into different forms.

VII

Berger's market model has been used to explain how religious groups
adapt to modernity in all its aspects. According to market model
concepts, the struggle between Orthodox and non-Orthodox communities in the marketplace of religious beliefs and ideologies of the
modern, open society becomes the background for the deviation from
tradition and the propensity toward *kullah* alternatives found in halakhic
literature. Accordingly, deviation from tradition signals adaptation to
market conditions, that is, taking into account the tastes of potential
customers. The history of Orthodoxy in Western Europe and in the

United States clearly reflects such processes, which originate in the need to compete with alternative religious models. The use of the market model allows us to see adaptations and concessions by religious groups as an economic mechanism that, on the one hand, serves to arrest the desertion of synagogues (the voluntary community) and, on the other, serves to attract new members, particularly those of means and those of the younger generation.

However, the market model also allows us to understand the growth of an antithetical development within Orthodox communities: viz., extreme reaction and religious radicalism. My contention is that, in addition to adaptation to modernity, rampant reaction and radicalism alike also develop and burgeon in the fertile ground of a modern, secular society. Accordingly, more than reflecting continuity with traditional Judaism, religious radicalism and the propensity to *humrah* in *halakhah* are social phenomena that reflect the structural changes of modern, secular society.

It is customary to divide Orthodox communities into two principal types: (a) the modern religious type, and (b) the traditional religious type. The point of departure for such a distinction is the degree of the adjustment to modern culture. In general, one may say that the modern religious person remains bound by *halakhah* as traditionally interpreted but, at the same time, sees himself as part of modern society with respect to its culture and values. The traditional religious type, however, sees himself bound not only by *halakhah*, but by a tradition, particularly that which was crystallized in Eastern Europe.

Of course, in reality, matters are much more complicated: just as modern religious behavior is split into many different varieties, so too traditional religious behavior has been characterized from the beginning by its variegation. This variegation derives, first of all, from the attitude toward tradition, a matter which is, by its very nature, particular and local. It also results from the adaptation of traditional Orthodox Judaism to modernity in many areas, in one form or another; for example, in dress and language, and even in education. The degree of adaptation to and compromise with modern life is therefore a basic criterion for distinguishing among the various Orthodox groups and communities in modern, open society.

Among the Orthodox groups, moreover, there is a continuum: on the "right" side we may place the reactionary groups that seek to preserve as much of the traditional religious way of life as possible; on the "left," the communities which, notwithstanding their professed obligation to *halakhah*, take an active role in modern society and produce the artifacts of its culture. Both of these extremes live their religious styles in voluntary associations within the market situation, which is a basic feature of modern Western society. The continual interaction among tradition, *halakhah*, and modernity within diverse Orthodox communities points to a dialectic tension that is one of the principal characteristics of the Orthodox way of life.

From this perspective there are many, both within and beyond the pale of Orthodoxy, who read the societal map of Orthodox Judaism as hierarchically structured: i.e., the more a group or community stands to the right, the more religious, authentic, and Orthodox it is perceived to be. Conversely, the more a group is based to the left, the more compromising, the less Orthodox, and therefore the less religious it is perceived to be.

The conception of a hierarchically structured society, whether or not it accurately reflects the reality, has been, and continues to be, very acceptable to the traditional religious groups that today are called *haredi*. As a matter of fact, the conception has become a central component of their self-image; those who manifest modern religious behavior function, in their view, as a negative reference group. Furthermore, the consolidation of the *haredi* style has, from the beginning, entailed the delegitimation of modern religious behavior as adaptive, compromising, and in search of *kullot*. Indeed, within the *haredi* worldview, the terms *kallim* (easy ones) and *pashranim* (compromisers) are used to characterize the religious Zionist (Mizrachi) movement, which is perceived as the representative *par excellence* of modern religious behavior.[17]

Yet paradoxically, the hierarchical structure mentioned above characterizes *haredi* religiosity no less than modern religiosity. Insofar as *Haredim* have consistently defined their religiosity as a religiosity of fine detail, that is, of uncompromising obligation to the minutiae of *halakhah*, *haredi* religiosity partakes of a hierarchical structure determined by fineness of detail and obligation to religious tradition. For as we have indicated, a certain degree of accommodation to, and compromise with, modernity characterizes nearly all groups that define themselves as Orthodox, including the *Haredim*.

The existence of such a hierarchical structure clearly reveals once again that the Jewish community, as a social and religious framework, is delimited not by geographic boundaries, but by voluntary choice. Neither the number of Orthodox communities and the number of other communities nor the movement from one community to another is limited by law. In this situation, then, the market model makes possible a more complex explanation of the inner dynamic that changes the character of those groups claiming authenticity and continuity with traditional society. This inner dynamic becomes manifest in the instituting of new norms of *humrah* and religious radicalism.

VIII

The voluntary community, even the Orthodox one, is a selective community. Just as it is unable to force its rules on those unwilling to affiliate with it, so it need not accept all who wish to affiliate with it. Accordingly, the voluntary community can establish distinctive directives binding its members alone, but not all those who define themselves as Orthodox in nearby communities within the same geographic limits. When there are alternative Orthodox communities within the same geographic limits of the large modern city, *mahmir* communities may then seemingly be freed from all-embracing responsibility to those unable, or unwilling, to uphold the norms customary in those communities.

The market situation necessitates an elective process whereby people join or leave churches as they freely wish. Consequently, those prepared to abide by all *mahmir* halakhic decisions are free, as it were, of those who are not suited to do so. Accordingly, in a community so ordered, it is possible to establish *mahmir*, even extreme, approaches to *halakhah* more easily and efficiently than in traditional society, which never operated on an elective basis. The greater the varieties of religious identity, whether Reform or Orthodox, the greater social and religious significance attaches to the aforementioned selection. So, too, groups inclined to accept *mahmir* halakhic decisions and to be fastidious in religious observance will take shape more simply and easily.

As noted, the change of boundaries in the Jewish community, that is, its redefinition as a voluntary and not a geographic framework, inevitably changes its frame of reference and, consequently, its framework of religious responsibility. Within the traditional community the religious leadership had to reckon with a rather diverse membership and to consider whether the majority were capable of abiding by its decrees. But within the modern voluntaristic order, which is, as constituted, homogeneous compared to the traditional community, the scope of considerations is limited by the boundaries of the community.

The halakhic authority tends to adapt his decisions to a broad framework ranging from *humrah* to *kullah*, and in accord with the needs of the community requiring his decision making. It follows that the halakhic authority of a voluntary community accommodates his decision making to the religious level of the community members alone. Other Jews, even if they are from the same locale (i.e., within the same city or within the same neighborhood), are not relevant to his consideration. This means that in a community composed of those inclined to be particularly strict, the halakhic authority will decide in the direction of *humrah*, and conversely. The principles of the market situation, which make possible voluntary communal organization according to *mahmir* halakhic norms of strictness and scrupulous enhancement, allow rabbis to make halakhic decisions in a differential manner in accord with the nature of the homogeneous community they encounter.

To summarize, in the structure of a market situation, most of the arguments set forth by Rabbi Reischer against meat slaughtered in rural areas as described in Section III above lose their significance. Only within the framework of the traditional community defined by clear geographic boundaries, a community encompassing and imposing its halakhic authority without exception upon all who live within its urban limits, would it have been possible to declare that whoever has his *shehitah* banned is a transgressor. In that context, the ban on the rural *shehitah* in the *medinah* thereby acquires a delegitimating force, as if those who violate it are no longer Jews in the communal sense. However, in the case of a voluntary society, such a prohibition, which, incidentally, is very widespread today, may be viewed as a *humrah* that lacks the delegitimating force to remove those who transgress the prohibition from the community of "observers of *torah* and *mizvot*" (religious obligations).

IX

It might have been possible to discern tendencies toward *humrah* in religious communities even as traditional society was disintegrating.[18] But the dominant process in Jewish society has been in the opposite direction, with Jewish life in Eastern and Western Europe until the post–World War II period characterized by the erosion of religious tradition.   Consequently, attention was drawn to the process of deviation from the tradition in the form of inclination toward *kullah*, a process which resulted from the impact of the market situation on the traditional communal framework.

Furthermore, until World War II, the relationship to tradition within Jewish society was still intertwined with the direct relationship to the traditional community and to the extended family as a multi-generational and multi-branched order. Thus, a change in the direction of *humrah* was occasionally taken as a challenge to the ancestors and to extended-family tradition that was still functioning in large parts of the Jewish settlements in Eastern Europe. After the Holocaust, when the traditional community had been essentially wiped out, the remnants were removed to the West—to the United States, Western Europe, and Israel—and reorganized there within the framework of the voluntary community. As a result, within this pluralistic market, impediments that prevented the establishment of *humrah* norms as distinguishing marks of particular groups disappeared.[19]

Paradoxically, the very erosion of the traditional halakhic way of life allowed the next generation, raised within the Western voluntaristic community, to choose the path of *humrah*. Ironically, this younger generation often perceived their parents' traditional lifestyle as a deviation from their own romantic image of an "authentic traditional lifestyle rooted in an idealized past," an image symbolized by *humrah*.

Naturally, economic relief and the development of a "community of scholars" after World War II also contributed to the establishment of an extremist, *mahmir* tendency within the Orthodox community.[20] Nonetheless, the market situation, which made possible the organization of the voluntary community, provided the conditions which made possible the emergence of this tendency.

TRANSLATED BY HOWARD MARBLESTONE

NOTES

1. See S. Elberg, "The Heavenly and the Earthly Jerusalem," *Diglenu* (organ of the Agudat Yisrael Youth Movement) (Kislev-Teveth, 5725 [1965]). The substance of his remarks had been published one year earlier in his article, "B'nai Brakism," *Happardes* (organ of the Union of Orthodox Rabbis in the United States and Canada) 48, 3 (Kislev 5724 [1964]). Both articles are in Hebrew.
2. The Hebrew term, *ba'ali nephesh*, derives from Proverbs 23:2. See

Babylonian Talmud, Pesahim 40:1: "a *ba'al nephesh* is a *Hasid*, a fearer of Heaven, who is solicitous for his soul." The term has had wide currency among *poskim* (halakhic authorities and renderers of rabbinic decisions) in recent generations to characterize those of religious sensitivity inclined to personal *humrah*. The expression connotes admiration and positive assessment of the phenomenon. See, for example, "Laws of Shabbat," section 246, 5 in the *Mishnah Berurah* (six-volume commentary on the first part of the *Shulhan Arukh*, the authoritative sixteenth-century code of Jewish law composed by Joseph Karo) by Rabbi Israel Meir HaKohen (1838–1932), also known as the Hafetz Hayyim: "every *ba'al nephesh* will sense by himself."

3. In the journal *Amudim* (organ of the Religious Kibbutz Movement) (Heshvan 5748 [1988]), 43–49, in Hebrew.

4. On this atmosphere, see H. H. Ben Sasson, *Studies in Medieval Jewish History* (Tel Aviv: 1958), 286–89, in Hebrew.

5. See Maimonides, *Mishneh Torah*, Hilkhot Terumah, chap. 1, halakhah 11.

6. Rabbi Yizhak Ben Asher HaLevi, known by the acronymic title RIBA, one of the chief Tosafists (exegetical annotators of the Talmud) of German (Ashkenazic) Jewry in the twelfth century. See *Keseph Mishneh* by Rabbi Joseph Karo, author of the *Shulhan Arukh*, on Maimonides, Hilkhot Terumah, chap. 1, halakhah 11.

7. See Karo, *Keseph Mishneh*.

8. "You must not gash yourselves" (Deuteronomy 14:1), which according to another sense of the root may mean, "You must not break apart into factions." See Babylonian Talmud, Yebamot 13:2.

9. See section 1 of the *Responsa* of Rabbi Bezalel (ben Abraham) Ashkenazi (Venice: 1595).

10. "The divine rabbi," Yizhak Ashkenazi Luria (1534–1572), one of the greatest and most significant Kabbalists, who exerted a dramatic influence on Judaism.

11. See M. Wilensky, *Hasidim and Mitnagdim: On the History of the Polemic, 5532–5575 (1772–1815)*, vol. 1 (Jerusalem, 5730 [1970]), 123, in Hebrew.

12. Rabbi Menahem Hamme'iri, *Shield of Our Fathers*, Hebrew edition of Y. M. List (London: 1909), 10.

13. See Wilensky, *Hasidism and Mitnagdim*, 44–49, especially 47. See as well M. Dubnov, *History of Hasidism*, vol. 1 (Tel Aviv: 1930), 118–26, in Hebrew.

14. The article was published in *Social Research* 30 (Spring 1963): 77–93. See also Peter Berger, *The Sacred Canopy: Elements of a Sociological Theory of Religion* (Garden City: 1969).

15. The term "church" here and below refers to a religious structure and its organization, not to any particular religion.

16. A well-known joke reflects this reality: In his first sermon at an American Orthodox synagogue during the forties, the rabbi spoke about the calamity of violating the Sabbath. The *gabbais* became anxious and told him that, in their congregation, he must not speak on so sensitive a subject.

Accordingly, on the following Sabbath he spoke about rules of family (sexual) purity. Again the *gabbais* became nervous and let him know that in America one doesn't talk about such subjects. The rabbi accepted their advice and on the next Sabbath spoke on the state of *kashrut* (dietary prohibitions). Again the *gabbais* were alarmed and warned him not to speak on that matter since it was making the big wigs (literally: propri- etors, especially those whose money supports the congregation) uncom- fortable. The rabbi was astonished and asked, "What should I speak about, then?" The *gabbais* answered, "Speak about *Yiddishkeit* (Jewishness)!"

17. Many examples of this attitude can be found in the brochure "Anthology of Torah Knowledge," M. Scheinfeld, ed., which is appended to the booklet "Anticipating the Messiah," by A. Wasserman (Tel Aviv: 5722 [1962]), 79–93, both works in Hebrew.

18. This is the meaning of the transition from traditional community to Orthodoxy. See Y. Katz, "Orthodoxy from an Historical Perspective," *Kivvunim* 33 (Fall 5747 [1988]): 89–100, in Hebrew. See also M. Samet, "Orthodoxy," *Kivvunim* 63 (Summer 5747 [1988]): 99–114, in Hebrew.

19. On this aspect of religious radicalism see my article, "Life Tradition and Book Tradition in the Development of Ultra Orthodox Judaism," in H. E. Goldberg, ed., *Judaism Viewed from Within and from Without*, Anthropological Studies (Albany: 1986).

20. On this subject see my articles, "The Changing Role of the Community Rabbinate," *Jerusalem Quarterly* (Fall 1982): 79–99; and "Haredim Confront the Modern City," in P. Medding, ed., *Studies in Contemporary Jewry*, vol. 2 (Bloomington: 1986), 74–96.

Chapter 13

Fundamentalism and Political Development: The Case of Agudat Yisrael

Alan L. Mittleman

The term *fundamentalism* was originally a proper noun denominating a conservative, evangelical religious movement in American Protestantism. The name was taken from the title of a series of twelve booklets, *The Fundamentals: Testimony to the Truth,* published between 1910 and 1915. In recent years, both scholars and the media have broadened the use of the term to refer to religious and political phenomena in a variety of cultural contexts.

Virtually all scholars bemoan this expanded use of fundamentalism, for it has caused a great deal of confusion. Can religions other than Protestantism produce fundamentalist phenomena? If so, what are they like? What exactly do we mean by fundamentalism? On what level of generality must we use the term for it to apply to say Buddhist, Hindu, or Muslim movements? What features of fundamentalism do we wish to emphasize when we move across cultures? Does fundamentalism have an inner structure or logic which any given case in any given religion must exemplify, or is fundamentalism more of a family resemblance term? Methodological questions such as these preoccupy scholars.

Understandably, confusion also prevails in the Jewish context. Some purists insist, for example, that the distinctly determinative feature of fundamentalism in Protestantism, biblical inerrancy, is simply not found in Judaism. Insofar as Judaism stresses commentary, interpretation, and rabbinic tradition, Judaism fails categorically to be fundamentalist.[1] Such an approach, however, suffers from a bit of over-literalism itself. Unless we want to be philosophical nominalists of the crassest sort, insisting that similarity of name need never indicate similarity of property, we must admit that there are strong resemblances between phenomena in Judaism and in other contemporary world religions to which the label fundamentalism gives expression. I shall now review the theories of several scholars who assume that fundamentalism is an appropriate and illuminating concept to apply to Judaism. Having done so, I will propose my own model, which will not so much contradict as complement those of others. I shall then offer a case study to show how my model works.

Theories of Jewish Fundamentalism

The analysts of Jewish fundamentalism differ on at least two major issues. For some, such as James Davison Hunter, Hava Lazarus-Yafeh, Israel Idalovichi, and Charles S. Liebman, fundamentalism and modernity are significantly related phenomena. For others, such as Ian Lustick, fundamentalism is de-coupled from modernity and thought to be a recurrent theme in Jewish history. The relationship of fundamentalism to modernity is also a major theme in the general literature.[2] More specific to the Jewish discussion is the disagreement about whether ultra-Orthodox Jews (the so-called *haredim*) are properly included in the category or whether it should only or primarily apply to religio-political activists such as Gush Emunim. Hunter and Lustick, for example, would exclude the *haredim*; Lazarus-Yafeh, Idalovichi, and Liebman include them.

James Davison Hunter has proposed a global theory of fundamentalism, which accounts for, among other cases, Jewish fundamentalism. In Hunter's view, "fundamentalism is Orthodoxy in confrontation with modernity."[3] Fundamentalism represents the path taken by traditional believers who neither opt out of the modern world (with its rationality, pluralism, public-private dualism, and secularity) nor accommodate themselves to it. Rather, fundamentalists confront modernity in order to subjugate it. "All fundamentalist sects share the deep and worrisome sense that history has gone awry. What 'went wrong' with history is modernity in its various guises. The 'calling' of the fundamentalist, therefore, is to make history right again."[4]

In tandem with the dominant motive of "making history right again" (as a leitmotif of social action), Hunter explores other characteristics of contemporary fundamentalist movements such as organized anger, nationalism, and scripturalism. Hunter sees Gush Emunim as a paradigmatic fundamentalist movement. The sectarian hasidism of the Satmar, on the other hand, is not fundamentalist because it opts out of modernity rather than confront it.

Hunter's view has the advantage of being truly comparative, applying a single explanatory principle to a broad range of cases. Its disadvantage is that it does not convincingly distinguish between traditional religion and fundamentalism. One could argue that even the most traditional Jewish groups have been shaped by, rather than simply withdrawn from, modernity.[5] (I shall argue this below with the example of Agudat Yisrael.)

More generally, one could argue from the perspective of the phenomenology of religion, that religious action per se represents a return to primordial patterns. Religious men and women want to live *in illo tempore*, in sacred time. Religions organize time, space, and society in such a way as to recreate the purity and vitality of the cosmic origins.[6] Thus, given such a general theory of religion, the fundamentalist motif of making history right is an entirely typical, pan-historical phenomenon. While I would not want to discard the insight that fundamentalists want to make history right again, I would want to know much more about those factors which differentiate fundamentalism from traditional Judaism, given the non-static nature of the latter.

Hava Lazarus-Yafeh, similarly, sees fundamentalism as "a global wave of negative reaction to modernity and Western values, brought about by a variety of factors of varying importance in the different contexts of [Judaism, Islam, and Christianity]."[7] She cites ten characteristics of fundamentalism in the three monotheistic religions, including self-definition as a counter-society, rejection of democracy as a political form, virulent criticism of institutionalized religion, ambivalent relationship to science and technology, and scriptural literalism or its equivalent, apocalypticism.

Lazarus-Yafeh acknowledges that all of these phenomena have pre-modern manifestations. Yet, while one can point to millenarian messianism or anti-rationalism in the Jewish past, the fact that fundamentalism is a mass phenomenon, embedded in the cultural dilemmas of mass societies, signals its unique tie to modernity. Furthermore, insofar as the focus of much fundamentalist anger is the unique cultural construct of "the modern West," fundamentalism is a highly particular phenomenon.

Focusing more on morphological elements than explanation, Lazarus-Yafeh does not offer a theory of fundamentalism's origins. She suggests, rather tentatively, that the causes of fundamentalism are to be found in alienation from modern societies, spurred by the decline of those secular worldviews such as liberalism and socialism which once legitimated them. Why modern societies should be more disappointing to their members than pre-modern ones is left unexplored. Clearly, a more developed characterization of what went wrong with modernity is necessary for this theory to be convincing.

Israel Idalovichi characterizes fundamentalism as a

> general religious or national intolerance. This intolerance is based on a determinate, theoretically established belief system, which represents, at the same time, a program for a community of believers. These latter believe themselves to be in sole possession of the truth and feel an obligation to compel outsiders to embrace their truth and the blessedness which flows from it.[8]

Idalovichi identifies four types of contemporary Jewish fundamentalism each with some sort of roots in the Jewish past:

1. Ultra-Orthodoxy represents a rigid crystallization of late medieval Judaism. It arose in defensive reaction to upheavals in Jewish life, from Shabbtai Zvi through the Enlightenment and Emancipation. Fundamentalism of this sort represents an unnatural cessation of the inherent flexibility, creativity, and non-dogmatic intellectuality of the tradition.[9]

2. Mystical messianism, the driving force behind Gush Emunim, is the opposite of ultra-Orthodoxy. It represents the millenarian activism which Judaism, after the Shabbatian debacle, suppressed. Unlike the ultra-Orthodox, this group believes in utopian-political action as a form of messianic theurgy. Sacralization of Zionist imperatives will hasten the end of days.

3. Extreme nationalist chauvinism, associated with the Kach party, is grounded in very simplistic scripturalism and expresses itself in virtually totalitarian conceptions of social policy. The historical antecedent of this movement is the Maccabean struggle against the Hellenizers.

4. Secular Zionist appropriation of the Bible, without regard to its rabbinic development, made scripture into a legitimation for statism. This civil religious misappropriation in which state and people are transcendent objects also functions as fundamentalism for Idalovichi. This form has the shallowest roots in Jewish history.

What all of these forms have in common is their attempt to dam up the flow of tradition and freeze it for defensive purposes. Fundamentalism is the expression of traditionalists' anxiety rendered acute by the unparalleled challenges of modernity.[10] Its aim is the re-sacralization of experience and society.

There is undoubtedly truth in Idalovichi's account. What seems to be lacking are criteria which could distinguish between "ordinary" intensive religiosity and fundamentalism. While it is true that tradition is flexible, it also has its boundaries and minimal consensus. Is any expression of strong insistence on a non-negotiable truth or practice then ipso facto fundamentalism? Idalovichi seems to have committed himself to this overly inclusive definition. Like Hunter's, his account requires sharper distinctions between traditionalism and fundamentalism.

Charles Liebman's account of fundamentalism, or extremism as he prefers to call it, attempts to provide just such distinctions, and to specify what, in Jewish modernity, occasions fundamentalist reaction. In his usage, Jewish fundamentalism/extremism refers to movements which want religion "to comprise the sole content of culture, the foundation of human association, the blueprint for goals."[11] In the sense that all of Orthodoxy aspires to this, Orthodoxy per se is fundamentalist. Nevertheless, in order to account for the tremendous diversity within Orthodoxy, Liebman moderates his claim considerably. He thus limits fundamentalism to two strands within Orthodoxy, both of which are concerned with the radical re-sacralization of the world. Modern or accommodationist Orthodoxy, on the other hand, accepts a fundamental dichotomy between religion and world and is willing to live on amiable terms with secularity.

Orthodoxy per se is a modern phenomenon. It is a response to "disenchantment" and is to be distinguished from prior Jewish traditionalism. Orthodoxy is a self-conscious commitment to a way of life over/against a modern *Lebenswelt* which disconfirms it at every turn. This discontinuity between Orthodoxy and the world distinguishes Orthodoxy from unselfconscious traditionalism. In the traditional society, there was a mutually supportive relationship between religion and way of life. Conditions of scarcity, for example, made the practice of reciting blessings over food and grace after meals, both of which emphasize God's providential role in providing food, credible. Under modern conditions of abundance and rationalization of food production, these beliefs seem farfetched.

In modern society, therefore, Orthodoxy has had to create a *Lebenswelt* where daily reality confirms religion. The first strand, "rejectionist" Orthodoxy, withdraws from modern society to create a world apart. The second strand, "affirmationist/transformationist"

Orthodoxy, validates certain elements of modernity and thereby seeks to dominate and reclaim society.

For the rejectionists, the counter-reality is the *yeshiva*, a pure and sacred space, governed by the rhythms of sacred time. The *yeshiva* becomes the center of the world; all else is peripheral. Rejectionist Orthodoxy does not feel the need to deal with other Jews outside of its sanctum and can indulge the extremist impulses of the tradition. (Here is the point at which Liebman ties fundamentalism to the general phenomenology of Judaism. Extremism is normative in the sense that the tradition praises religious virtuosity.) The virtuous tendency toward the strict interpretation of law is maximized insofar as it now binds only those who are zealously committed to it. Isolation from other Jews and rejection of non-indigenous Jewish ideas and values expands unchecked.

In this sense, the *haredim* qua fundamentalists/extremists are a relatively modern phenomenon. Only the disintegration of the traditional Jewish community, the *kehilla*, made it possible for rejectionists to disavow all responsibility to more moderate elements.[12] Thus, according to Liebman, modernity creates the conditions for Jewish fundamentalism both by its disenchanting character (a general feature) and its demolition of the integrated Jewish community (a particular feature).

The other strand, "affirmationist/transformationist" Orthodoxy, wants to control society such that it confirms religion. However, such a program is only conceivable in Israel, where Gush Emunim is the textbook example of this sort of fundamentalism.[13]

Liebman presents the difference between rejectionists and transformationist/affirmationists as basically a matter of prudence. While one group believes that the time is right for a takeover, the other, based upon a different calculation, advocates a policy of withdrawal and waiting. Yet the decision to become involved with politics, that is, not merely to take an interest in the political sphere but to strongly thematize it as a focus of sacred action, cannot simply be a matter of prudential calculation. It is too central to the self-definition and inner logic of the movements involved to be a variable. Thus, while I agree with much of Liebman's analysis, much greater attention needs to be paid to the political dimension of the phenomenon. Ian Lustick does precisely that.

Ian Lustick, like Idalovichi and Liebman, roots fundamentalism in tendencies inherent in the phenomenonology of Judaism and in historical Jewish movements. Unlike the others, however, he completely decouples fundamentalism and modernity. For Lustick, the

Maccabees, Zealots, Shabbateans, and other messianists are all fundamentalists. A belief system is fundamentalist "insofar as its adherents regard its tenets as uncompromisable and direct transcendental imperatives to political action oriented toward the rapid and comprehensive reconstruction of society."[14] The strong focus on political action in this definition leads Lustick to exclude quietistic groups such as the *haredim*, at least insofar as they are quietistic. In Lustick's view, traditional, rabbinic Judaism was "rigorously observant, but politically cautious." The category of fundamentalism is therefore reserved for the incautious, non-pragmatic practitioners of theo-politics.

This definition has the advantage of focusing attention on the political dimension of fundamentalism. Its disadvantage is that identifying all Jewish expressions of radical, transcendence-driven political action with fundamentalism does not allow us to specify what is distinctive about modern fundamentalism. Indeed, insofar as the *haredim* sometimes enter into political action on the basis of transcendent imperatives, they would have to be classified as fundamentalists—a result Lustick wants to avoid. Lustick's definition is essentialistic both with respect to history and with respect to action. It assumes that there is nothing categorically distinctive about modernity. Thus, although the particular social/political constellation of facts in which fundamentalism finds itself may vary, the underlying logic and dynamic are the same.

Such a stipulation of structural constants in Judaism and Jewish history requires a more vigorous argument than Lustick provides. Some sustained attention to the unique character of modernity is a prerequisite, I think, to any adequate theory of fundamentalism. As a result of this inattention, Lustick's definition seems highly stipulative.

The Perspective of Political Development

On the basis of the preceding discussion, it seems correct to say that fundamentalism is an adaptation of traditional Judaism to the pressures of modernity. Yet, when we consider this adaptation solely on the level of worldview, we find that the conceptual boundary between tradition in general and fundamentalism in particular is quite vague. The fundamentalist construction of the stock of tradition will always seem more or less authentic and a more or less credible version of tradition.

The distinguishing features of fundamentalism come more clearly into view when we consider its social characteristics. What distinguishes it from prior expressions of tradition are its social base, its way of legitimating social action, the social structural relationships out of which it develops, and its political focus. Yet insofar as a tradition—Jewish, no less than Catholic, Muslim, or Hindu—has an ongoing political dimension, we must be very careful in spelling out what is meant by "political focus."

Unlike Lustick, who sees fundamentalism simply as Judaism's most intensive political mode regardless of historical epoch, I view fundamentalism as the *modern* form of transcendence-driven politics. Thus, fundamentalism is both political and modern. That is to say, fundamentalism is the religious answer to a modern political problem, namely, the problem of the secularization of the polity, which is a consequence of the political development of traditional societies. "Political development" refers to the process "of differentiation, by which integralist sacral societies governed by religio-political systems are being transformed into pluralist de-sacralized societies directed by greatly expanded secular polities."[15] The secularization of the polity, beginning in the West in the late middle ages and occurring more recently in the third world, is the feature of modernity most relevant to an understanding of fundamentalism.

The secularization of the polity has assumed a variety of forms. In the United States, secularization took place initially through separation of the institutional structures of religion and government.[16] Subsequently, the political culture became secularized through increasing secularization of society. In the former USSR, secularization occurred through the violent domination of religion by an aggressively expanding polity. In the relatively new nations of the third world such as Indonesia and India, secularization has occurred through transvaluation of religious values into national ones, correlated with the construction of new forms of national identity to replace prior, religion-based loyalties.

In every case, predominantly secular ideologies come to displace religious ones as legitimating bases for the polity. Although religious legitimation may endure in an attenuated fashion as civil religion, its role is ancillary. The grounds of legitimation are largely rational as are the criteria on which the polity is evaluated (e.g., efficiency).

With the demise of pre-modern religio-political arrangements and the rise of modern mass politics, particularly in the new nations, the role of religious groups vis-à-vis the polity has changed. Proximity to the center of power can no longer be taken for granted and religious groups must reorganize themselves to become effective agents under changed political conditions. First, religious reform, generally in the direction of modernism, must occur. Both religious figures (e.g., Iqbal in Pakistan) and political leaders (Kemal at first in Turkey or Gandhi in India) sought to make traditional religion suitable for the new reality of the nation-state by thematizing those aspects of the stock of tradition most compatible with it. Often governments enforced modernist reforms, as happened, for example, in Egypt under Nasser. Second, insofar as modern politics (unlike pre-modern politics) is a mass phenomenon, political development entails laicization. Organization of the laity into modern, religio-political parties or associations (such as the Christian Democratic movement, the Muslim Brotherhood, India's Rashtriya Swayamsevak Sangh, Latin American base communities, etc.) are evidence of the new situation in which religious groups find themselves. While previously a close relationship between religious elites and the center of power sufficed, in a secularized polity influence means influence among the masses.[17] New formations with a mass base can be more effective political forces than traditional elites, particularly in those societies where the elites did not possess a high level of corporate identity and complexity (e.g., Islam, Judaism, or Hinduism in contrast to Catholicism). In elite-oriented religions (Catholicism, Buddhism), new elite structures have been created (bishops' conferences, monks' associations) in order to strengthen political influence.

Against this background of intrareligious and religio-political structural change, we are now in a position to appreciate the distinctive qualities of fundamentalism. The social base for fundamentalism is found in the new reality of lay religio-political organizations. Fundamentalist groups like the Muslim Brotherhood are distinguished from the general organizational pattern (which include such emphatically non-fundamentalist phenomena as Christian Democratic parties) by their radicalism. In contrast to those espousing reformist-modernist adaptations to the secularizing polity, fundamentalist groups represent anti-secularizing forces which, for operational reasons, have accommodated themselves to the dominant secular structure. The key point is that fundamentalist movements, unlike traditional sacral institutions, are uniquely modern organizations of deliberately articulated corporate complexity, autonomy (hence the rejection of state-supported orthodoxies), and identificational distinctiveness such that they can act effectively among the masses.

Ideologically, fundamentalism represents an attempt to reclaim religion as the main legitimating basis for the polity. Thus, it is a counter-reaction to the secularizing polity's reliance on ideology, popular sovereignty, and efficiency. It is also a reaction to the secularization of group identity, most often represented by nationalism. Fundamentalism reasserts the salience of the (often exclusive) religious content of culture and nationhood. It does so, however, out of a partially or wholly secularized context in which it must play by a set of rules not of its own choosing. This set of structural relationships, only available in modernity, distinguishes fundamentalism from traditional religio-political activity.

Agudat Yisrael and Jewish Political Development

The basic pattern of secularization of the polity, creation of lay (or at any rate, mass) religio-political structures, and simultaneous participation in and rejection of modern religio-political structural arrangements is exemplified in the Agudat Yisrael movement. Following a brief history of the movement, I shall focus on its ideology and constitutional self-definition.

Agudat Yisrael, an international political movement of ultra-Orthodox Jews, was founded in 1912 in Katowice, in the former German province of Silesia. Its founders were both highly modernized German Jews and Eastern traditionalists just embarking upon a confrontation with modernity. Despite their common belief in the revealed and sacred character of Jewish law and their commitment to live according to its dictates, these founders shared little in common. They occupied different positions with respect to modernity in general and to the political development of both their Jewish and their host societies. As such, their attitudes toward their common project differed dramatically. Insofar as the German Jews were reacting to an advanced secularized political culture, their response was fundamentalist in terms of my model. The Eastern traditionalists, on the other hand, entering into a process of political development for the first time, adopted a reformist stance vis-à-vis the undifferentiated sacral society of their past. Agudah thus represents an interesting test case for our concept of fundamentalism. Insofar as within one movement we have groups at different points along the process of political development, we can compare their conceptions of political organization and action in terms of our conception of fundamentalism.

For Eastern Jews, Agudat Yisrael was formed in the context of a modernizing, differentiating society. Differentiation of the traditional religio-political order represented by the *kehilla* had already begun in the eighteenth century.   New forms of religious society such as Hasidism and the great Lithuanian Yeshivot had come into being. By the late nineteenth century, secular movements such as Zionism and socialism had emerged.   Thus, Agudah in the East represents an attempt to reorganize the ensemble of traditional forces into an effective political actor in the context of a modernizing, secularizing nation state (Poland) as well as in the increasingly pluralistic, voluntaristic context of Jewish society.

The felt need for a new form of organization is indicative of the inability of traditional means of political activity, such as *shtadlanut* (ad hoc Jewish intervention with the political elite), to respond to the challenges of the modern state. It further indicates the inadequacy of traditional religious authority to counter the inroads of secularizing Jewish movements such as Zionism and socialism. Deeply distrustful of politicization as a sign of new cultural developments, which were "forbidden by the Torah," the heads of Lithuanian Yeshivot and Hasidic dynasties nonetheless validated the Agudah movement as a purely defensive stratagem. Their challenge was to exploit political development and activity for legitimate purposes while containing their subversive, secularizing potential.

For the German Jews in Agudat Yisrael, political development did not represent modernization so much as a reaction against several generations of expansive secularization. Thoroughly modern, they sought religious salvation through politics. Thus, Agudah was conceived as a way of employing a distinctly modern, rational instrument—a political party—in order to achieve an anti-modern end: theocracy. While the Eastern traditionalists allowed for political development as a means for keeping modernity at bay, the German Jews thought to sanctify politics in order to bring about the consummation of history. The Easterners, precisely while differentiating and rationalizing politics, tried to hold to a modest, pragmatic attitude toward political activity. The Westerners, on the other hand, invested the political realm with cosmic symbolic weight and purpose. While these divergent attitudes were equally balanced in the beginning, the Eastern view prevailed as the century progressed. Agudah was thus at best only partially fundamentalist at its origins.

Historical Background

For the Eastern traditionalists, a long tradition of political quietism, in part a response to Jewish millenarian activism, made the very idea of far-reaching (as opposed to adventitious) political activism suspect. Since the loss of political independence in antiquity, the rabbis believed that they were powerless to effect radical changes in their condition of exile.[18] Dependent upon the gentile powers, they awaited the ultimate divine redemption, which alone would alter their circumstance. Political activity, excluding the internal ordering of the Jewish community, consisted of strategic interventions with the gentile powers in order to maintain or, if possible, to improve the status quo. Without denying the sagacity of pre-modern Jewish politics, this conception of political activity was strictly practical.[19] Political activity was a holding action designed to buy time while the messiah tarried. An unwelcome thing, politics was forced upon the Jews.

This pre-modern attitude continued to prevail among the Orthodox leadership in the East into the early twentieth century. The idea that history is dynamic (an essential prerequisite for fundamentalism), that Jews can alter their destiny in a fundamental way through political action remained, for the vast majority of the rabbinic leadership, foreign and subversive. Even more subversive, however, was the ever-growing pluralism of the communities represented by the intrusion of secular forces such as Zionism and socialism. The founding of a religious Zionist movement (Mizrachi) in 1901 underscored the proximity and urgency of the threat.

Some rabbinic leaders felt that Zionism and socialism had to be countered with their own weapons, namely organized political action conducted by a supra-local body at a level of organizational competence and complexity commensurate with that of the secular opposition. The strengthening of Orthodox institutions and values, as well as the representation of Orthodox interests in the political sphere, required the development of political structures out of the traditional religio-social background. Political action, they believed, had to become rational. Thus, the impetus to modern political development arrived in the East.

Yet although cognizant of the threat of encroaching modernity, other rabbinic leaders viewed "politicization as a betrayal of the religious tradition that Orthodox politicians would be defending."[20] They contended that to become political meant to abandon the absolutist stance of the tradition. An Orthodox political party would have to engage in bargaining, compromise, and parliamentary cooperation. How could Orthodox Jews, whose only reason for being was an absolute, unconditionally true Torah, project themselves, in the name of that Torah, into a parliamentary political culture? These "pure" traditionalists sensed the inherent, secularizing dynamic of political development. The "reformist" counter-argument was that the political representation of Orthodox interests was not discontinuous with an important strand of the tradition, *shtadlanut*, that is, statesman-like representation of the community's interest to the powers that be.[21] For this latter group, primarily the Gerer Hasidim and heads of Lithuanian Yeshivot, *shtadlanut* served to legitimate the new political structure as well as to serve as a norm for political action.

The event that spurred the creation of Agudah was the departure, in 1911, of some religious Zionists from the Tenth Zionist Congress. The religious Zionist movement, which had been rejected by the vast majority of traditionalists in Eastern Europe as an unacceptable syncretism, had an uneasy relationship with the Zionist movement as a whole. As long as Zionism focused on the practical activity of colonization, a few Orthodox leaders were willing to go along. In 1911, however, the Zionist Congress decided to sponsor cultural and educational work along the lines of the predominant nationalist and secularist ideology. In response, some Mizrachi delegates walked out. This group soon made common cause with the anti-Zionist traditionalists who were developing the groundwork for Agudat Yisrael.

Although organized in 1912, Agudat Yisrael did not become fully functional until after the First World War. By the 1920s, Agudat Yisrael had become the second strongest political party among Jews in Poland, representing major cities like Warsaw and Lodz in the Sejm. Its politics were minimalist. Agudah professed Polish patriotism, assumed the goodwill of the gentile majority, and sought to improve Jewish rights within the existing political framework. That the Polish branch of Agudah conceived of modern parliamentary politics as an extension of medieval *shtadlanut* was often noted by its Zionist, socialist, and nationalist opponents.[22] Agudist party organizations also existed in Hungary, Czechoslovakia, and Lithuania. It was most successful in Poland, owing to the support of a large Hasidic group, the dynasty of Gur. The Eastern Agudah thus typifies what we have characterized as the first stage of religious accommodation to political development: the formation of new, lay-oriented groups with a reformist or innovative strategy, able to navigate the waters of a secularizing polity.

While traditionalists in the East were willing to participate in a political movement, it was Western Orthodoxy that had the knowhow and resources to create one. Western Orthodox Jews, citizens of industrial nation-states, were thoroughly modernized. A large number of Jewish groups had formed in the nineteenth century to represent the

Jewish interests to the polity, particularly in Germany. Thus, the German Jews had already gone through the experience of communal disintegration and realignment that the Eastern European Jews were now encountering for the first time.

The German Jewish community was deeply divided. Orthodoxy, already a minority, was divided against itself. Most of German Orthodoxy cooperated with non-Orthodox Jews. The majority of Orthodox rabbis and synagogues participated in common communal structures (*Einheitsgemeinden*) which provided for separate services to accommodate Orthodox needs. Some Orthodox, however, believed the dominant Liberal Judaism to be a heresy of such magnitude that even the tacit acknowledgment which participation in common structures signified was unacceptable. Under the leadership of Samson Raphael Hirsch (1808–1888), these Jews won the right (in 1876) to secede from the general Jewish community and form their own separatist structures (*Austrittsgemeinden*). These separatist groups eventually formed a loose organization (*Freie Vereinigung für die Interessen des Orthodoxen Judentums*) which, by 1905, elevated non-cooperation with both religious liberals and Orthodox pluralists to a defining condition of Orthodoxy.

The ideologues of separatism, principally disciples of Hirsch, viewed separatist communities as restorations of the old theocratic polity of Judaism and hence the sole valid form of Jewish community. Of course, such communities were not mere restorations, but deliberately designed counter-realities which negated the now secularized institutions of Jewish community. Within German Orthodoxy, political organization acquired a soteriological dimension.

While the manner of worship and conduct of life within Frankfurt's or Berlin's separatist community did not differ from that of the Orthodox in unified communities, the mere existence of independent entities seemed to fulfill a crucial principle of the Torah. The Torah was viewed as a political instrument: a constitution. Its divine Giver was the head of state. The sole sovereignty of God was acknowledged, on the individual level, by a life of fidelity to the commandments. But how, in the absence of Davidic monarch, holy land, and Sanhedrin, could divine sovereignty be expressed on the communal level?

The answer of the Orthodox separatists took a negative form: by absolute non-recognition of the communal structures of those who deviate from the Torah. While they might be individually acknowledged as sinning brethren and therefore merit dialogue and care, their communities must be seen as institutionalized rebellion against divine law. The separatist communities, as—by their own lights—renewers of Divine/Torah sovereignty, repudiated modern principles of political organization such as democratic pluralism.   To live in a society governed by Torah required the rejection of other governing principles. Clearly, separatist Orthodoxy had a distinctly political conception of Jewish communal life.   This strong thematization of the political dimension is a necessary condition for fundamentalism.

Separatist Orthodoxy was unsuccessful in establishing a positive content for a Torah society, except in its theoretical literature. That fundamentalist aspiration would have to wait for the more promising conditions of a Jewish state. Nonetheless, the separatists rationalized the theocratic ideal on a larger scale. The idea of Agudat Yisrael was developed by the separatist group from 1905 on. More than simply a geometrical expansion of separatist Orthodoxy's political activism, Agudat Yisrael might be seen as an attempt to provide a positive content to the urge to live in a Torah-governed society, at least for its German participants. While the Eastern Jewish interest in a political movement was defensive, mildly modernist, and pragmatic, the German interest was utopian, restorative, and in some respects messianic.

The German experience, unlike the Eastern one, was driven by an abiding sense of spiritual malaise. Having successfully assimilated into the German middle classes, Orthodox Jews retained traditional observance but sacrificed a traditional outlook. Their insistence on pure, separatist communities was an attempt to recreate what was imagined to be a traditional communal structure. Yet, insofar as its principle was wholly negative, it showed how attenuated the traditional way of life had become. While mindful of "*talis* and *tefillin*" (that is, commitment to traditional observance), Orthodox minds were shaped by Goethe and Schiller no less than everyone else's. They brooded about the fact that, in contrast to "Torah's demand for totality" (*Totalitätsanspruch der Torah*), their Jewishness defined, at best, limited dimensions of their lives rather than the whole of life (*Lebenstotalität*).[23]

Political activity is a response, for German Orthodoxy, to what Weber called the "disenchantment of the world."[24]   The life of the Orthodox, no less than that of the Liberal or secular German Jew, had long lost the dimension of miracle and mystery. A modernist theological transvaluation prevailed as Orthodoxy embraced a post-Kantian theology wherein life according to the commandments was understood as a means of moral training (*Bildung*). By the nineteenth century, Judaism had become, for Orthodox and Liberal Jew alike, a religion within the limits of reason alone. Ethics replaced the old tradition of mysticism as the fundamental mythic legitimation of the religious life.

One response to disenchantment was to invest a rational/technical (i.e., disenchanted) medium such as politics with transcendent significance. Politics becomes a medium of sanctification, a form of theurgy. It not only alters historical states of affairs, it restructures cosmic order; that is, it transforms disorder into order. The cosmic disorder is evidenced by Israel's diaspora situation. Political activism establishes a symbolic center around which the scattered tribes of Israel may regroup. The mere existence of this symbolic center—that is, the cluster of committees which make up the Agudah—re-establishes the divine reign over Israel and, consequently, over history.

Convictions of this order pervade the writings of the Agudist ideologues of Frankfurt. For Jacob Rosenheim (1870–1965), the principal architect of Agudat Yisrael and its world president, the founding of the Agudah constituted an act of historical and cosmic moment. The name itself, in Rosenheim's view, is redolent with meaning. The Hebrew term *agudah*, deriving from the verbal root "to bind," means "band" or "association." Thus the name of the movement, the "band of Israel," implies both the actualized result of the process of binding and the process itself. A principal citation of the word *agudah*, noted by Rosenheim, occurs in one of the most solemn and messianic prayers of the Jewish New Year service. This prayer envisions a future epoch in which all creatures will become full of the "fear of the Lord," recognizing Him as Creator and Sovereign. They will become "one band" (*agudah ahat*) to do His will. Pending this complete cosmic transformation, Israel is the present locus of fear of the Lord and acknowledgment of His sovereignty. The name of the movement, therefore, signifies an incipient messianic dynamic. The binding together of Israel under the sovereignty of God anticipates and promotes the universal redemption.

In Jacob Rosenheim's view, Israel was once such a unity. The experience of modernization, however, shattered Western Jewry into various trends and diminished its ties with Eastern Jewry. The function of an Orthodox world organization is restorative. It must give concrete historical expression to the spiritual reality of *klal Israel*, the transcendent (as well as transcendental) unity of Israel. Conscious of the enormous historical import of the project, Rosenheim asserted that

> Agudat Yisrael is the first historical attempt, after the fall of the Jewish State, to regenerate the Jewish People—despite its diaspora in all lands—in the form of a living organism, so that its anarchic masses can

be ordered and assembled round God's Law as a unified and will-determining center.[25]

With the founding of Agudat Yisrael, the transcendent was seen as having become empirical once again. Israel has arisen from "historical anonymity" not in the form of one

> association among other associations . . . or a practical society limited to some individual tasks. Rather, what is envisioned as the ultimate aim is the revival of an archetypal Jewish possession: the traditional concept of the totality of Israel, filled and borne by Torah as its organizing soul. This is the reality we will realize in the midst of the world of culture and through the technical means which culture now gives us by our Agudat Yisrael.[26]

In religious terms, redemption has been partially, proleptically achieved by the act of restoring the sovereignty of God over Israel through the concrete polity which Agudah represents.

In Rosenheim's conception, the founding and shaping of Agudat Yisrael bore symbolic significance of both historical and cosmic proportions. Politics, a formerly peripheral activity, became central. Political action became a privileged way of realizing divine will. The actions of the reborn body of Israel in history reflect the destiny of the divine in the world. Thus, Agudah becomes the symbolic center of the Jewish lifeworld. Its internal organization, committees, meetings, decisions, and rituals "will mark [to use a phrase of Clifford Geertz's] the center as center and give what goes on there its aura of being not merely important but in some odd fashion connected with the way the world is built."[27]

The way the Agudah was built was to symbolize how God rules over Israel, given the puriform, diaspora reality of the Jews. The constitution of the movement is a peculiar amalgam of modern democratic institutions and ancient hierarchical structures. Any Jew who "recognizes the binding nature of the Torah for himself and the Jewish people" could join.[28] The primary structures were independent local associations that were unified on the national level in the various European states. Each national group had a governing board, selected democratically from the local associations and a rabbinical council also chosen from the membership. The national groups sent delegates to a convention (*Kenessiah Gedolah* or "great assembly") scheduled to meet every five years. The *Kenessiah Gedolah*, in turn, elected one hundred of its members into a Central Committee, which—in its various subcommittees—ran Agudat Yisrael until the next round of elections. Atop the whole structure was the Council of Torah Sages (*Moetzet G'dolei ha-Torah*). The practical function of the Council was to determine whether proposed political courses of action accorded with or violated the Torah. The Council thus had veto power over any policy the Central Committee might advocate. Symbolically, the Council linked Agudat Yisrael with the ancient Sanhedrin. Rosenheim was explicit about this: Agudat Yisrael, under the guidance of its sages, was to function for world Jewry as the Sanhedrin did for the ancient Jews of the land of Israel.

Yet for all of his sense of historical moment, Rosenheim eschewed a radical view of political action. Having achieved a model of order, a symbolic historical/cosmic center, he sought to sanctify the disenchanted in a piecemeal and tactical fashion. Increasingly influenced by the Eastern traditionalists, he conceived of the tasks of the Agudah in terms of minimalist, practical politics. His slogan, incorporated in the first paragraph of Agudah's constitution, was, "Agudat Yisrael strives to solve the present tasks of the Jewish People, constituted through Torah, in the spirit of the Torah." The problems to be solved, e.g., financial support and improvement of Jewish schools, improvement of the economic status of the Eastern masses, securing civil rights, combating anti-Semitic propaganda and laws (cf. paragraph 2 of the constitution), were not novel in kind but only in degree.

While Rosenheim's concept of Agudah is more symbolically charged than that of the Eastern traditionalists, his concept of what political action means is similar to theirs. It is not so much action as such which reorders and redeems, but the achievement of a political structure per se. In Rosenheim's theoretical writings, he argues that politics is an extension of ethics and that ethics establishes the purity of the individual soul. The messianic future is the completion of a perfected ethical process, wherein individuals in society achieve holiness together.

Rosenheim is unwilling to read a messianic dynamic into historical events. The mood of his work, while intensely practical and political in the conventional sense of the word, is one of ahistorical, somewhat ethical, somewhat mystical sanctification. Thus the tendency to neutralize fundamentalism, in the sense of uncompromising transcendence-driven politics, was implicit even on the German side of Agudah.

The younger elements of Agudah, however, advocated a more uncompromising radicalism. More romantic, more alienated from modernity than their elders, they suspected that beneath Rosenheim's metaphysical rhetoric, a conservative and bourgeois ethos was being legitimated. Feelings of inauthenticity and millenarian longing were particularly acute for those who came of age before the First World War. Shaped by the yearnings of the German youth movement and similar *fin de siècle* social forces, the mood of young German Orthodox Jews was one of spiritual restlessness and romantic hunger for true, total forms of Jewish community. Seeking a community grounded in a positive application of Torah, they criticized their parents' ideal of *Bildungsbürgerlichkeit* and *Ausstritt* as negative and partial. They sought a transvaluation of prevailing Orthodox values. The watchword of this generation, coined by its leading spokesman, Isaac Breuer (1883–1946), was "*Neuorientierung*": the need for a radical, "new orientation."

Unlike Rosenheim, Breuer believed that God was acting in a sudden, visible way in history. To him, the Balfour Declaration (1917) was an unmistakable sign and challenge, calling Israel as a whole, and Agudat Yisrael as a vanguard, to rise to its "metahistorical" destiny. One of Agudah's most charismatic and rigorous intellectuals, Breuer urged the movement to direct its attention to the development of a theocracy in Palestine. Discerning the footsteps of the messiah in the horror of the Great War, he concluded that European society—Jewish society included—was irremediably corrupt. The only hope, now opened up by Lord Balfour, was to end the Diaspora, prepare the way in the wilderness, and work for the messiah's coming. Breuer's unabashed messianism, first announced in his 1918 book, *Messiaspuren*, caused a great stir in Agudist and general Orthodox circles in Frankfurt.

Breuer strongly typifies what Jacob Talmon terms "political messianism." Impatient with Rosenheim's static, restorative conception of Agudah, Breuer was utopian- and future-oriented. The old world of diaspora accommodation, bourgeois mentality and values, alienated social life, and fragmentary religiosity must fall away in a new era of historical integration. Breuer believed that the goal of political action in history was to bring this about. Indeed, as a political messianist, he believed that this was not only possible but was already under way. His entire endeavor was directed, therefore, against the politics of *shtadlanut* in which, he believed, both East and West, to their mutual detriment, met. Not surprisingly, Breuer failed—while Rosenheim succeeded—to shape the Agudah movement around his ideas. Even Breuer, in the wake of the Holocaust, moderated his program and compromised with the Zionist leadership to spur the establishment of statehood.

With the demise of German Orthodoxy, Agudat Yisrael was dominated by the survivors of Eastern Jewry whose conception of political activism as *shtadlanut* shaped Agudah's future role as a party in Israel's parliamentary democracy. Having accommodated itself to a secular order, Agudah's fundamentalism (now fully neutralized) was taken over, in the course of Israel's political development, by newer, indigenous Israeli movements.

What emerges from this analysis is the salience of modern political structures for any definition of fundamentalism. The fundamentalist religio-political project is not an immediate reaction to the secularized, modern polity, but a delayed reaction. It requires an intermediary stage in which religious groups have already worked out their accommodation with the modernizing political order. These accommodations are found wanting by the fundamentalists and replaced by more radical survival strategies. Fundamentalism is thus a stage in the process of the political development of religious groups.

NOTES

1. Leon Wieseltier, "The Jewish Face of Fundamentalism," in Norman J. Cohen, ed., *The Fundamentalist Phenomenon* (Grand Rapids: Wm. B. Eerdmans Publishing Co., 1990), 194. The position that Wieseltier represents is explicitly rejected by Israel Idalovichi, "Der Jüdische Fundamentalismus in Israel," in *Fundamentalismus in der modernen Welt* (Frankfurt am Main: Suhrkamp Verlag, 1989), 101. On the other hand, Charles Liebman finds fundamentalism an inappropriate term for Judaism on account of Judaism's rich interpretive tradition. Protestantism is supposedly a tradition-poor religion and scriptural inerrancy as a rigid dogma can fill the vacuum. Liebman prefers "extremism" in the Jewish context, but does use "fundamentalism" advisedly. Cf. Charles Liebman, *Deceptive Images* (New Brunswick: Transaction Books, 1988). For an exploration of Idalovichi's and Liebman's views, see the text below.

2. Efforts to distinguish fundamentalism (as a distinctly modern phenomenon) from general Christian orthodoxy may be found in Norman J. Cohen, ed., *The Fundamentalist Phenomenon* (Grand Rapids: Wm. B. Eerdmans Publishing Co., 1990).

3. James Davison Hunter, "Fundamentalism in its Global Contours," in Cohen, *The Fundamentalist Phenomenon*, 57. See also James Davison Hunter in this volume (chap. 2).

4. Hunter, "Fundamentalism in its Global Contours," 59. See also Hunter in this volume (chap. 2).

5. Menachem Friedman has argued that *haredi* Judaism is a dynamic

confrontation rather than a static survival. Haredism is an innovative response to the breakdown of an integrated traditional society. It is characterized by an elitist identity and the conscious choice of a consistent, high level of stringency in observance nourished by "book tradition" in the absence of all embracing "life tradition." Cf. Menachem Friedman, "Life Tradition and Book Tradition in the Development of Ultraorthodox Judaism," in Harvey E. Goldberg, ed., *Judaism Viewed from Within and Without: Anthropological Studies* (Albany: SUNY Press, 1987). See also Menachem Friedman in this volume (chaps. 9 and 12).

6.   Mircea Eliade, *The Sacred and the Profane* (San Diego: Harcourt, Brace, Jovanovich, 1987).

7.   Hava Lazarus-Yafeh in this volume (chap. 3), 43.

8.   Idalovichi, "Der Jüdische Fundamentalismus in Israel," 107 (my own translation).

9.   Idalovichi's position is similar to that of Jaroslav Pelikan in his critique of fundamentalism vis-à-vis traditional Christian orthodoxy. Cf. Pelikan, "Fundamentalism and/or Orthodoxy," in Cohen, *The Fundamentalist Phenomenon*, 3ff. Given Menachem Friedman's persuasive work on the development of haredism, Idalovichi's notion of haredism as crystallization and stasis is unconvincing. See also Friedman in this volume (chaps. 9 and 12).

10.   "Since the industrial revolution, our society has increasingly fallen under the law of (technical rationality) and its governing form of intercourse with persons and things. Without doubt, the disappointment over scientific and social progress occasions the regression to fundamentalist ideologies." Idalovichi, "Der Jüdische Fundamentalismus in Israel," 119.

11.   Liebman, *Deceptive Images*, 45.

12.   Ibid., 36.

13.   "Impatience, perhaps frustration with the lack of success of the transformationist effort, coupled with the fervent belief in its practicality, leads its adherents deeper and deeper into the world of politics and power and to the sanctification of instrumentalities (for example the state and the army) which are, in practice, secular." Ibid., 52.

14.   Ian Lustick, *For the Land and the Lord* (New York: Council on Foreign Relations, 1988), 6. See also Ian Lustick in this volume (chap. 7).

15.   Donald Eugene Smith, *Religion and Political Development* (Boston: Little, Brown and Company, 1970), 1.

16.   Smith lists four modes of secularization: polity separation (in which the polity severs or does not initially create connections with religion), polity expansion (in which the polity takes over functions once conducted by religious institutions, thus establishing the full internal sovereignty of the state), polity transvaluation (at the level of political culture a shift takes place in the basis of legitimacy of the polity, loyalty is displaced from a religious to a political focus, and group identity is secularized), and polity

dominance (unlike separation, where ties are severed, here new ties are created to dominate and subjugate religion). Ibid., chap. 4.

17. Ibid., 125.

18. Jacob Katz, "Orthodoxy in Historical Perspective," in Peter Y. Medding, ed., *Studies in Contemporary Jewry* II (Bloomington: Indiana University Press, 1986), 9.

19. Ismar Schorsch has argued for the existence of a "conscious political tradition" among ancient, medieval, and modern Jews, dispelling what he takes to be the myth of pre-modern Jewish political passivity. I agree with his (and subsequently, David Biales') reading. Nonetheless, this thesis does not contradict my own judgment as to the relative weight of political activity in the traditional Jewish universe of values. Cf. Ismar Schorsch, *On the History of the Political Judgment of the Jew* (New York: Leo Baeck Institute, 1976).

20. Gershon C. Bacon, "The Politics of Tradition: Agudat Israel in Polish Politics, 1916–1939," in Medding, *Studies in Contemporary Jewry* II, 145.

21. Ibid., 151.

22. Ibid., 152.

23. Mordechai Breuer, *Jüdische Orthodoxie im Deutschen Reich* (Frankfurt/Main: Jüdische Verlag bei Athenaeum, 1986), 34.

24. Hans H. Gerth and C. Wright Mills, eds., *From Max Weber* (New York: Oxford University Press, 1978), 51.

25. Jacob Rosenheim, *Agudistische Schriften* (Frankfurt/Main: Verlag des Israelits und Hermon, 1929), 114.

26. Rosenheim, *Agudistische Schriften*, 6–7.

27. Clifford Geertz, *Local Knowledge* (New York: Basic Books, 1983), 124.

28. Rosenheim, *Agudistische Schriften*, 164.

About the Editor

LAURENCE J. SILBERSTEIN is Philip and Muriel Berman Professor of Jewish Studies in the Department of Religion Studies, Lehigh University, and Director of the Philip and Muriel Berman Center for Jewish Studies. He received his Ph.D. from Brandeis University and was the recipient of a Fellowship for Independent Research from the National Endowment for the Humanities. He is author of *Martin Buber's Social and Religious Thought: Alienation and the Quest for Meaning* and editor of *New Perspectives on Israeli History: The Early Years of the State*. His articles on modern Jewish thought have appeared in *Soundings, The Encyclopedia of Religion, Journal of the American Academy of Religion*, and *Journal of the Middle East Studies Association*. His current research involves the application of contemporary theories of discourse and ideology to the modern interpretation of Judaism and Jewish history.

About the Contributors

GERALD CROMER teaches in the Department of Criminology at Bar-Ilan University. He has published numerous articles on various aspects of political extremism in Israel and is currently engaged in research on religious zealotry among Israeli ultra-Orthodox Jews.

MENACHEM FRIEDMAN is Professor of the Sociology of Religion at the Department of Sociology at Bar-Ilan University and Senior Research Fellow at the Jerusalem Institute for Israel Studies. He recently published *Haredi (Ultra-Orthodox) Society: Sources, Trends and Processes* (Hebrew).

SUSAN HARDING, Professor of Anthropology at the University of California, Santa Cruz, is author of *Remaking Ibieca: Agrarian Reform under Franco* and co-editor of *Statemaking and Social Movements: Essays in Theory and History.* She is currently completing *Miraculous Discourse,* an ethnography of narrative politics in Jerry Falwell's community during the 1980s.

JAMES DAVISON HUNTER, Professor of Sociology and Religious Studies at the University of Virginia, has written widely on religion, moral discourse, and political and cultural change in American life. His books include *Evangelicalism: The Coming Generation, Articles of Faith: Articles of Peace,* and *Culture Wars: The Struggle to Define America.*

AARON KIRSCHENBAUM is Professor in the Department of Jewish Law at Tel Aviv University. His publications include *Halakhic Perspectives in Law: Formalism and Flexibility in Jewish Civil Law* and *Beyond Equity: Halakhic Aspirationism in Jewish Civil Law,* volumes 1 and 2 of *Equity in Jewish Law.*

HAVA LAZARUS-YAFEH is Professor of Islamic Civilization at the Hebrew University of Jerusalem. She is author of numerous articles and books in Hebrew on Islam; her recent publications in English include *Intertwined Worlds: Islam and Bible Criticism.*

IAN S. LUSTICK, a member of the Political Science Department of the University of Pennsylvania, holds the Richard L. Simon Term Chair in the Social Sciences. He is the author of the forthcoming volume *State-Building and Its Reversal: Thresholds of Expansion and Contraction for Britain, France, and Israel in Ireland, Algeria, and the West Bank and Gaza.*

ALAN L. MITTLEMAN is the Muhlenberg Scholar in Jewish Studies and Assistant Professor of Religion at Muhlenberg College. He has published widely in the field of Jewish political thought and is the author of *Between Kant and Kabbalah: An Introduction to Isaac Breuer's Philosophy of Judaism.*

JAMES PISCATORI teaches in the Department of International Politics at the University College of Wales. He is a contributor to such journals as the *Middle East Journal* and *International Affairs* and is the author of *Islam in a World of Nation-States* and editor of *Islam in the Political Process.*

ELIE REKHESS is Senior Research Fellow at the Moshe Dayan Center for Middle Eastern and African Studies and Lecturer in the Department of Middle Eastern and African History at Tel Aviv University. From 1988 to 1990, he served as the Philip and Muriel Berman Visiting Scholar at Lehigh University. He has written extensively on Israel's Arab populations and Palestinian politics. His forthcoming book *Between Communism and Arab Nationalism* discusses the political orientation of Arabs in Israel.

EHUD SPRINZAK teaches political science at the Hebrew University of Jerusalem. He is an authority on political extremism, violence, and terrorism. He recently published *The Ascendance of Israel's Radical Right.*

Index